PARAMEDIC
CERTIFICATION
EXAM

PARAMEDIC CERTIFICATION EXAM

Third Edition

LEARNINGEXPRESS®

NEW YORK

Library of Congress Cataloging-in-Publication Data:
Paramedic certification exam.—3rd ed.
     p. cm.
    Previous ed. had title: Paramedic licensing exam.
    ISBN 1-57685-544-9
  1. Emergency medicine—Examinations, questions, etc. 2. Emergency medical technicians—Licenses—
  United States I. LearningExpress (Organization) II. Title. Paramedic licensing exam.
RC86.9.P34 2006
616.02'5—dc22

                                            2005035269

Printed in the United States of America

9 8 7 6 5 4 3 2 1

Third Edition

ISBN 1-57685-544-9

Regarding the Information in This Book
We attempt to verify the information presented in our books prior to publication. It is always a good idea,
however, to double-check such important information as deadlines and application and testing procedures,
as such information can change from time to time.

For more information or to place an order, contact LearningExpress at:
  55 Broadway
  8th Floor
  New York, NY 10006

Or visit us at:
  www.learnatest.com

List of Contributors

Virginia Brennan, Ph.D. is a linguist and editor in Nashville, Tennessee.

Angel Clark Burba, MS, EMT-P is an Assistant Professor and Program Coordinator for Emergency Medical Technician–Paramedic Program at Howard Community College in Maryland. She serves on the Education Committee of the National Association of EMS Educators (NAEMSE).

Jan Gallagher, Ph.D. is an editor living and working in New Jersey.

Bill Garcia, EMT-P is a founding editor of *Rescue* magazine and serves in the U.S. Navy. He is based in Maryland.

Dawn S. Pakora, EMT-P is a part-time faculty member of EMS at the University of Maryland–Baltimore County and a full-time EMS provider. She has been in EMS for 23 years.

Elaine Silverstein is a writer and editor living and working in New Jersey.

Steven C. Wood is the EMS coordinator in charge of operations for the City of San Diego, Division of EMS. He has been in EMS for 18 years.

Contents

CHAPTER

1 ▶ About the EMT-Paramedic Exam

CHAPTER SUMMARY

This chapter tells you how to become certified as an Emergency Medical Technician-Paramedic (EMT-Paramedic). It outlines the certification requirements of the National Registry of Emergency Medical Technicians (NREMT) and tells you how to use this book to study for the written exam.

THE NATIONAL REGISTRY of Emergency Medical Technicians (NREMT) was established in 1970 in response to a suggestion by the U.S. Committee on Highway Safety. Today, the NREMT is an independent, nonprofit agency whose job is to certify that EMTs and paramedics have the knowledge and skills to do their jobs—to save lives and preserve health. By setting uniform national standards for training, testing, and continuing education, the NREMT helps ensure patient safety throughout the United States.

In all 50 states, the National Registry and state offices of Emergency Medical Services work together to establish certification requirements for EMTs and paramedics. All states test individuals seeking to become EMTs or paramedics. Some states make sole use of NREMT tests, while others offer state tests. (A list of specific certification requirements for all 50 states appears in Chapter 8.)

Important Address & Phone Number

National Registry of Emergency Medical Technicians, Inc.
Rocco V. Morando Building
P.O. Box 29233
Columbus, Ohio 43229
614-888-4484
www.nremt.com

The curriculum for paramedic education and testing comes from the Department of Transportation National Highway Traffic Safety Administration National Standard Curriculum (DOT/NHTSA NSC). It was reviewed and revised from 1996–1999. The curriculum was phased in as the basis for educational programs and testing. The NREMT tests and the state tests are all based on this curriculum. The practice tests in this book, and the review of the practical exam in Chapter 7, are also based on the curriculum. By preparing with this book, as a supplement to your paramedic education program, you will be ready to succeed on the paramedic certification exam.

▶ Minimum Requirements

To apply for national registration as an EMT-Paramedic with the NREMT, you must meet the following requirements:

- You must be at least 18 years old.
- You must hold current National Registry or state certification at the EMT-Basic level.
- You must have successfully completed a state-approved EMT-Paramedic program that reaches or goes beyond the behavioral objectives of the National Standard EMT-Paramedic Curriculum (NSC) within the last two years.
- If your state does not mandate national EMT-Paramedic training, you must submit documentation of current state paramedic certification.

- You must truthfully complete the felony statement on the application and, if necessary, submit documentation.
- You must submit current CPR credentials (from the American Red Cross or the American Heart Association). (See section provided on the NREMT Paramedic application.)
- You must submit proof of your competence in EMT-Basic level skills, signed by the director of your training program or the service director of training and operations. (See section provided on the NREMT Paramedic application.)

▶ How to Apply

When you have met or can meet all the requirements outlined above and are ready to take the exam, call or write to the National Registry, or visit them online, to get an application and find out where you can take the exam in your state. **Tip:** The National Registry website is worth a visit even if you already have the forms in hand. (See the sidebar for the National Registry's mailing address, phone number, and website address.)

The National Registry will tell you how to arrange to take the examination. In many cases, you will be referred to the state EMS office, but in others, you will be instructed to make individual arrangements to take the exam. Do not delay making contact with the National Registry, as it is the source of most of the information you will need to apply, test, and become certified.

Finally, you must submit to the National Registry an application stating that you have met all of the requirements, together with the application fee. The amount of the fee changes periodically; both the registration form and the National Registry website will tell you the current cost.

▶ The EMT-Paramedic Written Exam

The EMT-Paramedic written exam consists of 180 multiple-choice questions. You will have three hours to complete the exam. The questions are divided into six major content areas, each corresponding to components of the DOT/NHTSA National Standard Curriculum. The first table that follows lists the number of questions in each topic area on the National Registry Examination and provides a breakdown of the exams in this book for comparison.

To pass the exam, you must obtain a minimum score on each part of the exam, as well as an overall average score. Your exam results will indicate your actual score, the required minimum score for each part, and the overall passing score for that particular examination. If you fail to obtain the overall passing score, or if you fail any part of the exam, you will fail the entire exam. You should try and obtain a minimum score of 75 on each of the topic areas as well as an overall score of 75.

You are allowed three opportunities to pass the exam. If you fail on your third try, you must complete 48 hours of remedial training before you will be allowed to take the exam a fourth time. The remedial training must cover the content of the 1999 National Standard Curriculum to a specific minimum standard (see the "Remedial EMT-Paramedic Training" table).

BREAKDOWN OF QUESTIONS ON NREMT EXAM AND EXAMS IN THIS BOOK

Topic Area	Number of Questions				
	NREMT Range	Test 1	Test 2	Test 3	Test 4
1. Airway	27–33	30	27	29	33
2. Cardiology	30–36	34	33	32	33
3. Trauma	26–34	33	27	31	32
4. Medical	26–34	28	32	29	32
5. Obstetrics and Pediatrics	24–32	24	31	28	26
6. Operations	26–32	31	30	31	24
TOTAL	180	180	180	180	180

REMEDIAL EMT-PARAMEDIC TRAINING

Material Reviewed	Minimum Number of Hours
Preparatory	6
Airway Management and Ventilation	6
Medical	18
Trauma	10
Special Considerations	6
Operations	2
Total hours of educational review (minimum)	48

When you take a retest, you will be required to retest on all 180 questions.

Note: The National Registry will make suitable accommodations for candidates with documented learning disabilities. Call or write to request a copy of the Examination Accommodations Policy if you require such accommodations. Please note that accommodations must be requested and approved well in advance of any testing attempts.

▶ The EMT-Paramedic Practical Exam

After a lengthy period of review, revision, and pilot testing in the 1990s, the National Registry presented new practical exam instruments for EMT-Paramedics in October 2000. The revised Advanced Level Practical Exam is intended to assess the abilities of new EMT-Paramedics to do their job on the scene, out of a hospital setting. Skills are assessed by means of scenarios in which the candidate plays the part of the EMT-Paramedic called on for help.

The National Registry emphasizes that the practical exam is designed not as a teaching instrument but as a testing instrument; the candidate must go into the exam prepared to function as an EMT-Paramedic, not expecting to learn how to become one. The National Registry's practical tests assess skills in accordance with the 1994 EMT-Basic National Standard Curriculum and the behavioral and skill objectives of the 1999 EMT-Intermediate and EMT-Paramedic National Standard Curricula, as well as current American Heart Association guidelines for Advanced Cardiac Life Support (ACLS) and Basic Cardiac Life Support (BCLS).

EMT-Paramedic candidates taking the National Registry practical exam are tested on 12 skills when taking the full test:

1. Patient Assessment—Trauma
2. Ventilatory Management—Adult
3. Ventilatory Management—Dual Lumen Airway Device
4. Cardiac Management Skills—Dynamic Cardiology
5. Cardiac Management Skills—Static Cardiology
6. Oral Station—Case A
7. Oral Station—Case B
8. IV and Medication Skills—Intravenous Therapy
9. IV and Medication Skills—Intravenous Bolus Medications
10. Pediatric Ventilatory Management
11. Pediatric Intraosseous Infusion
12. Random Basic Skills—one of the following:
    Spinal Immobilization (Seated Patient);
    Spinal Immobilization (Supine Patient);
    Bleeding Control/Shock Management

See Chapter 7 of this book for details about how each of these skills is assessed on the practical exam.

The practical exam is scored Pass/Fail, with each skill scored separately. If you fail five or fewer skills when taking the whole test, you are entitled to retest up to two times on just those skills you failed. If you fail again on both retests (for even one skill), you will be required to take remedial training over all 12 of the skills and then to retest on all the skills on another date. In order to sign up to take the full practical exam again, you will have to provide documentation of remedial training, signed by the EMT-Paramedic Training Program Director or Physician Medical Director of training/operations for your program.

Candidates for EMT-Paramedic certification who have already passed the NREMT-Intermediate/99 practical exam within the preceding 12 months have a leg up: They can apply the results of the Intermediate exam to their first full attempt of the NREMT-Paramedic exam for these four skills:

1. IV Therapy
2. IV Bolus Medications
3. Pediatric Intraosseous Infusion
4. Random Basic Skills

If you take this route (applying the four passed Intermediate skills to your Paramedic practical test), the rules for Pass/Fail are similar to those just outlined. However, if you fail, and fail both retests, you must undergo remedial training in all 12 skills and then take the practical exam again, but this time on all 12 skills.

No matter what the approach, failing six or more skills means the candidate fails the entire practical exam. In that case, he or she must document remedial training on all 12 skills before retesting. The maximum number of times a candidate may take the full practical exam is three (a *full practical exam* being a test on all 12 skills with two opportunities for retesting on failed skills). If a candidate failed the full exam three times, he or she would have to complete a new state-approved EMT-Paramedic training program in order to test again.

▶ Using This Book to Prepare

In addition to information about the EMT-Paramedic practical exam (Chapter 7), this book contains four complete practice written tests, each containing 180 items similar to those on the National Registry EMT-Paramedic written exam. The table on page 3 shows the breakdown of content areas in each of the practice tests in this book.

The first step in using this book to prepare for the EMT-Paramedic written examination is to read Chapter 2, which presents the nine-step LearningExpress Test Preparation System. This chapter provides essential test-taking strategies that you can practice as you take the exams in this book.

Next, take one complete practice exam and score your answers using the answer key. Complete explanations of the answers are provided in the answer key—make use of them! You will not be permitted to use any electronic devices (PDA, calculator, etc.) while taking the actual exam, so don't use them on the practice tests, either.

Remember, the overall passing score for the written exam is 75%. If you notice that you are missing a lot of questions in one content area, you should concentrate future studying in that area, in addition to making a comprehensive review of the curriculum in preparation for the actual exam.

As you take each test in this book, pay particular attention to the material at the beginning of each chapter, as we have supplied specific strategies for how to focus with each test. After reading and studying this book, you'll be well on your way to obtaining certification as an EMT-Paramedic. Good luck as you advance in this rewarding and worthwhile career!

CHAPTER

2 ▶

The LearningExpress Test Preparation System

CHAPTER SUMMARY

Taking the EMT-Paramedic exam can be tough. It demands a lot of preparation if you want to achieve a top score, and your career in e mergency medical services depends on your passing the exam. The LearningExpress Test Preparation System, developed exclusively for LearningExpress by leading test experts, gives you the discipline and attitude you need to score high.

FIRST, THE BAD news: Taking the EMT-Paramedic exam is no picnic, and neither is getting ready for it. Your future career as a paramedic depends on your getting a passing score, but there are all sorts of pitfalls that can keep you from doing your best on this all-important exam. Here are some of the obstacles that can stand in the way of your success:

- Being unfamiliar with the format of the exam
- Being paralyzed by test anxiety
- Leaving your preparation to the last minute
- Not preparing at all!
- Not knowing vital test-taking skills: how to pace yourself through the exam, how to use the process of elimination, and when to guess
- Not being in tip-top mental and physical shape
- Arriving late at the test site, having to work on an empty stomach, or shivering through the exam because the room is cold

What's the common denominator in all these test-taking pitfalls? One word: *control.* Who's in control, you or the exam?

Now the good news: The LearningExpress Test Preparation System puts *you* in control. In just nine easy-to-follow steps, you will learn everything you need to know to make sure that *you* are in charge of your preparation and your performance on the exam. *Other* test takers may let the test get the better of them; *other* test takers may be unprepared or out of shape, but not

you. You will have taken all the steps you need to take to get a high score on the EMT-Paramedic exam.

Here's how the LearningExpress Test Preparation System works: Nine easy steps lead you through everything you need to know and do to get ready to master your exam. Each of the steps includes both reading about the step and one or more activity. It's important that you do the activities along with the reading, or you won't get the full benefit of the system. Each step tells you approximately how much time that step will take you to complete.

Step 1.	Get Information	50 minutes
Step 2.	Conquer Test Anxiety	20 minutes
Step 3.	Make a Plan	30 minutes
Step 4.	Learn to Manage Your Time	10 minutes
Step 5.	Learn to Use the Process of Elimination	20 minutes
Step 6.	Know When to Guess	20 minutes
Step 7.	Reach Your Peak Performance Zone	10 minutes
Step 8.	Get Your Act Together	10 minutes
Step 9.	Do It!	10 minutes
Total		3 hours

We estimate that working through the entire system will take you approximately three hours, though it's perfectly OK if you work more quickly or slowly than the time estimates assume. If you can take a whole afternoon or evening, you can work through the whole LearningExpress Test Preparation System in one sitting. Otherwise, you can break it up and do just one or two steps a day for the next several days. It's up to you—remember, *you're* in control.

▶ Step 1: Get Information

Time to complete: 50 minutes
Activities: Read Chapter 1, "The EMT-Paramedic Exam" and Chapter 8, "State Certification Requirements"
Knowledge is power. The first step in the LearningExpress Test Preparation System is finding out everything you can about the EMT-Paramedic exam. Once you have your information, the next steps in the LearningExpress Test Preparation System will show you what to do with it.

Part A: Straight Talk about the EMT-Paramedic Exam

Why do you have to take this exam, anyway? Simply put, because lives depend on your performance in the field. The EMT-Paramedic written exam is just one part of a whole series of evaluations you have to go through to show that you can be trusted with the health and safety of the people you serve. The written exam attempts to measure your knowledge of your trade. The practical skills exam attempts to measure your ability to apply what you know.

It's important for you to remember that your score on the EMT-Paramedic written exam does not determine how smart you are or even whether you will make a good paramedic. There are all kinds of things a written exam like this can't test: whether you are likely to show up late or call in sick a lot, whether you can keep your cool under the stress of trying to revive a victim of cardiac arrest, whether you can be trusted with confidential information about people's health. Those kinds of things are hard to evaluate, while whether you can fill in the right little circles on a bubble answer sheet is easy to evaluate.

This is not to say that filling in the right little circles is not important! The knowledge tested on the written exam is knowledge you will need to do your job. And your ability to enter the profession you've trained for depends on your passing this exam. And that's why you're here—using the LearningExpress Test Preparation System to achieve control over the exam.

Part B: What's on the Test

If you haven't already done so, stop here and read Chapter 1 of this book, which gives you an overview of EMT-Paramedic written exams in general and the National Registry of Emergency Medical Technicians (NR-EMT) exam in particular.

Many states use the NR-EMT exam, but others do not. Turn to Chapter 8 for a state-by-state overview of certification requirements. If you haven't already received the full rundown on certification procedures as part of your training program, you can contact the state EMS agency listed in Chapter 8 for details.

▶ Step 2: Conquer Test Anxiety

Time to complete: 20 minutes
Activity: Take the Test Stress Test

Having complete information about the exam is the first step in getting control of it. Next, you have to overcome one of the biggest obstacles to test success: anxiety. Test anxiety can not only impair your performance on the exam itself, but it can even keep you from preparing! In Step 2, you'll learn stress management techniques that will help you succeed on your exam. Learn these strategies now, and practice them as you work through the exams in this book, so they'll be second nature to you by exam day.

Combating Test Anxiety

The first thing you need to know is that a little test anxiety is a good thing. Everyone gets nervous before a big exam—and if that nervousness motivates you to prepare thoroughly, so much the better. It's said that Sir Laurence Olivier, one of the foremost British actors of this century, was ill before every performance. His stage fright didn't impair his performance; in fact, it probably gave him a little extra edge—just the kind of edge you need to do well, whether on a stage or in an examination room.

On page 11 is the Test Stress Test. Stop here and answer the questions on that page to find out whether your level of test anxiety is something you should worry about.

Stress Management before the Test

If you feel your level of anxiety getting the best of you in the weeks before the test, here is what you need to do to bring the level down again:

- **Get prepared.** There's nothing like knowing what to expect and being prepared for it to put you in control of test anxiety. That's why you're reading this book. Use it faithfully, and remind yourself that you're better prepared than most of the people taking the test.
- **Practice self-confidence.** A positive attitude is a great way to combat test anxiety. This is no time to be humble or shy. Stand in front of the mirror and say to your reflection, "I'm prepared. I'm full of self-confidence. I'm going to ace this test. I know I can do it." Say it into a tape recorder and play it back once a day. If you hear it often enough, you'll believe it.
- **Fight negative messages.** Every time someone starts telling you how hard the exam is or how it's almost impossible to get a high score, start telling them your self-confidence messages. If that someone is *you*, telling yourself *you don't do well on exams, you just can't do this*, don't listen. Turn on your tape recorder and listen to your self-confidence messages.
- **Visualize.** Imagine yourself reporting for duty on your first day as a paramedic. Think of yourself responding to calls, interacting with patients, preserving health, and saving lives. Visualizing success can help make it happen—and it reminds you of why you're doing all this work preparing for the exam.
- **Exercise.** Physical activity helps calm your body down and focus your mind. Besides, being in good physical shape can actually help you do well on the exam. Go for a run, lift weights, go swimming—and do it regularly.

Stress Management on Test Day

Several techniques can bring down your level of anxiety on test day. They'll work best if you practice them in the weeks before the test, so you know which ones work best for you.

- **Deep breathing.** Take a deep breath while you count to five. Hold it for a count of one, then let it out on a count of five. Repeat several times.
- **Move your body.** Try rolling your head in a circle. Rotate your shoulders. Shake your hands from the wrist. Many people find these movements very relaxing.
- **Visualize again.** Think of the place where you are most relaxed: lying on the beach in the sun, walking through the park, or whatever. Now close your eyes and imagine you're actually there. If you practice in advance, you'll find that you only need a few seconds of this exercise to experience a significant increase in your sense of well-being.

When anxiety threatens to overwhelm you in the middle of the exam, there are additional things you can do to manage the stress level:

- **Repeat your self-confidence messages.** You should have them memorized by now. Say them quietly to yourself, and believe them!
- **Visualize one more time.** This time, visualize yourself moving smoothly and quickly through the test, answering every question correctly, and finishing just before time is up. Like most visualization techniques, this one works best if you've practiced it ahead of time.
- **Find an easy question.** Skim over the test until you find an easy question, and answer it. Filling in even one circle gets you into the test-taking groove.
- **Take a mental break.** Everyone loses concentration once in a while during a long test. It's normal, so you shouldn't worry about it. Instead, accept what has happened. Say to yourself, "Hey, I lost it there for a minute. My brain is taking a break." Put down your pencil, close your eyes, and do some deep breathing for a few seconds. Then you're ready to go back to work.

Try these techniques ahead of time, and watch them work for you!

You need to worry about test anxiety only if it is extreme enough to impair your performance. The following questios will diagnose your level of test anxiety. In the blank before each statement, write the number that most accurately describes your experience.

0 = Never 1 = Once or twice 2 = Sometimes 3 = Often

___ I have gotten so nervous before an exam that I simply put down the books and didn't study for it.

___ I have experienced disabling physical symptoms, such as vomiting and severe headaches, because I was nervous about an exam.

___ I have simply not showed up for an exam because I was scared to take it.

___ I have experienced dizziness and disorientation while taking an exam.

___ I have had trouble filling in the little circles because my hands were shaking too hard.

___ I have failed an exam because I was too nervous to complete it.

___ Total: Add up the numbers in the blanks above.

Your Test Stress Score

Here are the steps you should take, depending on your score. If you scored:

- **Below 3,** your level of test anxiety is nothing to worry about; it's probably just enough to give you that little extra edge.
- **Between 3 and 6,** your test anxiety may be enough to impair your performance, and you should practice the stress management techniques listed in this section to try to bring your test anxiety down to manageable levels.
- **Above 6,** your level of test anxiety is a serious concern. In addition to practicing the stress management techniques listed in this section, you may want to seek additional, personal help. Call your local high school or community college and ask for the academic counselor. Tell the counselor that your level of test anxiety sometimes keeps you from being able to take the exam. The counselor may be willing to help you or may suggest someone else you should talk to.

▶ Step 3: Make a Plan

Time to complete: 30 minutes

Activity: Construct a study plan

Maybe the most important thing you can do to get control of yourself and your exam is to make a study plan. Too many people fail to prepare simply because they fail to plan. Spending hours on the day before the exam poring over sample test questions not only raises your level of test anxiety, but is also no substitute for careful preparation and practice over time.

Don't fall into the cram trap. Take control of your preparation time by mapping out a study schedule. On the following pages are two sample schedules, based on the amount of time you have before you take the EMT-Paramedic written exam. If you're the kind of person who needs deadlines and assignments to motivate you for a project, here they are. If you're the kind of person who doesn't like to follow other people's plans, you can use the suggested schedules here to construct your own.

Even more important than making a plan is making a commitment. You can't review everything you learned in your paramedic course in one night. You have to set aside some time every day for study and practice. Try for at least 20 minutes a day. Twenty minutes daily will do you much more good than two hours on Saturday.

Don't put off your studying until the day before the exam. Start now. A few minutes a day, with half an hour or more on weekends, can make a big difference in your score.

▶ Schedule A: The 30-Day Plan

If you have at least a month before you take the EMT-Paramedic exam, you have plenty of time to prepare—as long as you don't waste it! If you have less than a month, turn to Schedule B.

Time	Preparation
Days 1–4	Skim over the written materials from your training program, particularly noting 1) areas you expect to be emphasized on the exam and 2) areas you don't remember well. On Day 4, concentrate on those areas.
Day 5	Take the first practice exam in Chapter 3.
Day 6	Score the first practice exam. Use the outline of skills on the test given in Chapter 1 to determine your strongest and weakest areas. Identify two areas that you will concentrate on before you take the second practice exam.
Days 7–10	Study the two areas you identified as your weak points. Don't worry about the other areas.
Day 11	Take the second practice exam in Chapter 4.
Day 12	Score the second practice exam. Identify one area to concentrate on before you take the third practice exam.
Days 13–18	Study the one area you identified for review. In addition, review both practice exams you've taken so far, with special attention to the answer explanations.
Day 19	Take the third practice exam in Chapter 5.
Day 20	Once again, identify one area to review, based on your score on the third practice exam.
Days 20–21	Study the one area you identified for review.
Days 22–25	Take an overview of all your training materials, consolidating your strengths and improving your weaknesses.
Days 26–27	Review all the areas that have given you the most trouble in the three practice exams you've taken so far.
Day 28	Take the fourth practice exam in Chapter 6 and score it. Note how much you've improved!
Day 29	Review one or two weak areas.
Day before the exam	Relax. Do something unrelated to the exam and go to bed at a reasonable hour.

▶ Schedule B: The 10-Day Plan

If you have two weeks or less before you take the exam, you may have your work cut out for you. Use this 10-day schedule to help you make the most of your time.

Time	Preparation
Day 1	Take the first practice exam in Chapter 3 and score it using the answer key at the end. Turn to the list of subject areas on the exam in Chapter 1, and find out which areas need the most work, based on your exam score.
Day 2	Review one area that gave you trouble on the first practice exam.
Day 3	Review another area that gave you trouble on the first practice exam.
Day 4	Take the second practice exam in Chapter 4 and score it.
Day 5	If your score on the second practice exam doesn't show improvement on the two areas you studied, review them. If you did improve in those areas, choose a new weak area to study today.
Day 6	Take the third practice exam in Chapter 5 and score it.
Day 7	Choose your weakest area from the third practice exam to review.
Day 8	Review any areas that you have not yet reviewed in this schedule.
Day 9	Take the fourth practice exam in Chapter 6 and score it. Brush up on any areas that are still giving you trouble.
Day before the exam	Relax. Do something unrelated to the exam and go to bed at a reasonable hour.

▶ Step 4: Learn to Manage Your Time

Time to complete: 10 minutes to read, many hours of practice!

Activities: Practice these strategies as you take the sample tests in this book

Steps 4, 5, and 6 of the LearningExpress Test Preparation System put you in charge of your exam by showing you test-taking strategies that work. Practice these strategies as you take the sample tests in this book, and then you'll be ready to use them on test day.

First, you'll take control of your time on the exam. EMT-Paramedic exams have a three-hour time limit, which may give you more than enough time to complete all the questions—or may not. It's a terrible feeling to hear the examiner say, "Five minutes left," when you're only three-quarters of the way through the test. Here are some tips to keep that from happening to *you*.

- **Follow directions.** If the directions are given orally, listen to them. If they're written on the exam booklet, read them carefully. Ask questions *before* the exam begins if there's anything you don't understand. If you're allowed to write in your exam booklet, write down the beginning time and the ending time of the exam.
- **Pace yourself.** Glance at your watch every few minutes, and compare the time to how far you've gotten in the test. When one-quarter of the time has elapsed, you should be a quarter of the way through the test, and so on. If you're falling behind, pick up the pace a bit.
- **Keep moving.** Don't linger on one question. If you don't know the answer, skip the question and move on. Circle the number of the question in your test booklet in case you have time to come back to it later.

- **Keep track of your place on the answer sheet.** If you skip a question, make sure you skip on the answer sheet, too. Check yourself every five to ten questions to make sure the question number and the answer sheet number are still the same.
- **Don't rush.** Though you should keep moving, rushing won't help. Try to keep calm and work methodically and quickly.

▶ Step 5: Learn to Use the Process of Elimination

Time to complete: 20 minutes

Activity: Complete worksheet on Using the Process of Elimination

After time management, the next most important tool for taking control of your exam is using the process of elimination wisely. It's standard test-taking wisdom that you should always read all the answer choices before choosing your answer. This helps you find the right answer by eliminating wrong answer choices. And, sure enough, that standard wisdom applies to your exam, too.

Let's say you're facing a question that goes like this:

13. Which of the following lists of signs and symptoms indicates cardiac compromise?
   a. headache, dizziness, nausea, confusion
   b. dull chest pain, sudden sweating, difficulty breathing
   c. wheezing, labored breathing, chest pain
   d. difficulty breathing, high fever, rapid pulse

You should always use the process of elimination on a question like this, even if the right answer jumps out at you. Sometimes, the answer that jumps out isn't right after all. Let's assume, for the purpose of this exercise, that you're a little rusty on your signs and symptoms of cardiac compromise, so you need to use a little intuition to make up for what you don't remember. Proceed through the answer choices in order.

So you start with answer **a**. This one is pretty easy to eliminate; none of these signs and symptoms is consistent with cardiac compromise. Mark an **X** next to choice **a** so you never have to look at it again.

On to the next. "Dull chest pain" looks good, though if you're not up on your cardiac signs and symptoms, you might wonder if it should be "acute chest pain" instead. "Sudden sweating" and "difficulty breathing"? Check. And that's what you write next to answer **b**—a check mark, meaning, "Good answer, I might use this one."

Choice **c** is a possibility. Maybe you don't really expect wheezing in cardiac compromise, but you know "chest pain" is right, and let's say you're not sure whether "labored breathing" is a sign of cardiac difficulty. Put a question mark next to **c**, meaning, "Well, maybe."

Choice **d** strikes you about the same, with "difficulty breathing" being a good sign of cardiac compromise. But wait a minute. "High fever"? Not really. "Rapid pulse"? Well, maybe. This doesn't really sound like cardiac compromise, and you've already got a better answer picked out in choice **b**. If you're feeling sure of yourself, put an **X** next to this one. If you want to be careful, put a question mark.

Now your question looks like this:

13. Which of the following lists of signs and symptoms indicates cardiac compromise?
  X a. headache, dizziness, nausea, confusion
  ✔ b. dull chest pain, sudden sweating, difficulty breathing
  ? c. wheezing, labored breathing, chest pain
  ? d. difficulty breathing, high fever, rapid pulse

You've got just one check mark, for a good answer. If you're pressed for time, you should simply mark answer **b** on your answer sheet. If you've got the time to be extra careful, you could compare your check-mark answer to your question-mark answers to make sure that it's better.

It's good to have a system for marking good, bad, and maybe answers. We're recommending this one:

X = bad
✔ = good
? = maybe

If you don't like these marks, devise your own system. Just make sure you do it long before test day—while you're working through the practice exams in this book—so you won't have to worry about it during the test.

Even when you think you're absolutely clueless about a question, you can often use the process of elimination to get rid of one answer choice. If so, you're better prepared to make an educated guess, as you'll see in Step 6. More often, the process of elimination allows you to get down to only two possibly right answers. Then you're in a strong position to guess. And sometimes, even though you don't know the right answer, you find it simply by getting rid of the wrong ones, as you did in the previous example.

Try using your powers of elimination on the questions in the Using the Process of Elimination worksheet beginning on the next page. The questions aren't about paramedic work; they're just designed to show you how the process of elimination works. The answer explanations for this worksheet show one way you might use the process to arrive at the right answer.

The process of elimination is your tool for the next step, which is knowing when to guess.

Use the process of elimination to answer the following questions.

1. Ilsa is as old as Meghan will be in five years. The difference between Ed's age and Meghan's age is twice the difference between Ilsa's age and Meghan's age. Ed is 29. How old is Ilsa?
   a. 4
   b. 10
   c. 19
   d. 24

2. "All drivers of commercial vehicles must carry a valid commercial driver's license whenever operating a commercial vehicle." According to this sentence, which of the following people need NOT carry a commercial driver's license?
   a. a truck driver idling his engine while waiting to be directed to a loading dock
   b. a bus operator backing her bus out of the way of another bus in the bus lot
   c. a taxi driver driving his personal car to the grocery store
   d. a limousine driver taking the limousine to her home after dropping off her last passenger of the evening

3. Smoking tobacco has been linked to
   a. increased risk of stroke and heart attack.
   b. all forms of respiratory disease.
   c. increasing mortality rates over the past ten years.
   d. juvenile delinquency.

4. Which of the following words is spelled correctly?
   a. incorrigible
   b. outragous
   c. domestickated
   d. understandible

Answers

Here are the answers, as well as some suggestions as to how you might have used the process of elimination to find them.

1. d. You should have eliminated answer **a** off the bat. Ilsa can't be four years old if Meghan is going to be Ilsa's age in five years. The best way to eliminate other answer choices is to try plugging them in to the information given in the problem. For instance, for answer **b**, if Ilsa is 10, then Meghan must be 5. The difference in their ages is 5. The difference between Ed's age, 29, and Meghan's age, 5, is 24. Is 24 two times 5? No. Then answer **b** is wrong. You could eliminate answer **c** in the same way and be left with answer **d**.

2. c. Note the word not in the question, and go through the answers one by one. Is the truck driver in choice **a** "operating a commericial vehicle"? Yes, idling counts as "operating," so he needs to have a commercial driver's license. Likewise, the bus operator in answer **b** is operating a commercial vehicle; the question doesn't say the operator must be on the street. The limo driver in **d** is operating a commercial vehicle, even if it doesn't have a passenger in it. However, the cabbie in answer **c** is *not* operating a commercial vehicle, but his own private car.

3. a. You could eliminate answer **b** simply because of the presence of the word *all*. Such absolutes hardly ever appear in correct answer choices. Choice **c** looks attractive until you think a little about what you know—aren't *fewer* people smoking these days, rather than more? So how could smoking be responsible for a higher mortality rate? (If you didn't know that *mortality rate* means the rate at which people die, you might keep this choice as a possibility, but you'd still be able to eliminate two answers and have only two to choose from.) And choice **d** is plain silly, so you could eliminate that one, too. And you're left with the correct choice, **a**.

4. a. How you used the process of elimination here depends on which words you recognized as being spelled incorrectly. If you knew that the correct spellings were *outrageous*, *domesticated*, and *understandable*, then you were home free. Surely you knew that at least one of those words was wrong!

▶ Step 6: Know When to Guess

Time to complete: 20 minutes
Activity: Complete worksheet on Your Guessing Ability
Armed with the process of elimination, you're ready to take control of one of the big questions in test taking: Should I guess? The first and main answer is *yes*. Some exams have what's called a "guessing penalty," in which a fraction of your wrong answers is subtracted from your right answers—but the EMT-Paramedic exam does not work like that. The number of questions you answer correctly yields your raw score. So you have nothing to lose and everything to gain by guessing.

The more complicated answer to the question "Should I guess?" depends on you—your personality and your "guessing intuition." There are two things you need to know about yourself before you go into the exam:

- Are you a risk-taker?
- Are you a good guesser?

You'll have to decide about your risk-taking quotient on your own. To find out if you're a good guesser, complete the Your Guessing Ability worksheet that begins on page 18. Frankly, even if you're a play-it-safe person with lousy intuition, you're still safe in guessing every time. The best thing would be if you could overcome your anxieties and go ahead and mark an answer. But you may want to have a sense of how good your intuition is before you go into the exam.

The following are ten difficult questions. You're not supposed to know the answers. Rather, this is an assessment of your ability to guess when you don't have a clue. Read each question carefully, just as if you did expect to answer it. If you have any knowledge at all of the subject of the question, use that knowledge to help you eliminate wrong answer choices. Use this answer grid to fill in your answers to the questions.

Answer Grid

1.	ⓐ	ⓑ	ⓒ	ⓓ	5.	ⓐ	ⓑ	ⓒ	ⓓ	9.	ⓐ	ⓑ	ⓒ	ⓓ
2.	ⓐ	ⓑ	ⓒ	ⓓ	6.	ⓐ	ⓑ	ⓒ	ⓓ	10.	ⓐ	ⓑ	ⓒ	ⓓ
3.	ⓐ	ⓑ	ⓒ	ⓓ	7.	ⓐ	ⓑ	ⓒ	ⓓ					
4.	ⓐ	ⓑ	ⓒ	ⓓ	8.	ⓐ	ⓑ	ⓒ	ⓓ					

1. September 7 is Independence Day in
   a. India.
   b. Costa Rica.
   c. Brazil.
   d. Australia.

2. Which of the following is the formula for determining the momentum of an object?
   a. $p = mv$
   b. $F = ma$
   c. $P = IV$
   d. $E = mc^2$

3. Because of the expansion of the universe, the stars and other celestial bodies are all moving away from each other. This phenomenon is known as
   a. Newton's first law.
   b. the big bang.
   c. gravitational collapse.
   d. Hubble flow.

4. American author Gertrude Stein was born in
   a. 1713.
   b. 1830.
   c. 1874.
   d. 1901.

5. Which of the following is NOT one of the Five Classics attributed to Confucius?
   a. the *I Ching*
   b. the *Book of Holiness*
   c. the *Spring and Autumn Annals*
   d. the *Book of History*

6. The religious and philosophical doctrine that holds that the universe is constantly in a struggle between good and evil is known as
   a. Pelagianism.
   b. Manichaeanism.
   c. neo-Hegelianism.
   d. Epicureanism.

7. The third Chief Justice of the U.S. Supreme Court was
   a. John Blair.
   b. William Cushing.
   c. James Wilson.
   d. John Jay.

8. Which of the following is the poisonous portion of a daffodil?
   a. the bulb
   b. the leaves
   c. the stem
   d. the flowers

9. The winner of the Masters golf tournament in 1953 was
- **a.** Sam Snead.
- **b.** Cary Middlecoff.
- **c.** Arnold Palmer.
- **d.** Ben Hogan.

10. The state with the highest per capita personal income in 1980 was
- **a.** Alaska.
- **b.** Connecticut.
- **c.** New York.
- **d.** Texas.

▶ Answers

Check your answers against the correct answers below.

1. c.
2. a.
3. d.
4. c.
5. b.
6. b.
7. b.
8. a.
9. d.
10. a.

How Did You Do?

You may have simply gotten lucky and actually known the answer to one or two questions. In addition, your guessing was more successful if you were able to use the process of elimination on any of the questions. Maybe you didn't know who the third Chief Justice was (question 7), but you knew that John Jay was the first. In that case, you would have eliminated answer **d** and therefore improved your odds of guessing right from one in four to one in three.

According to probability, you should get $2\frac{1}{2}$ answers correct, so getting either two or three right would be average. If you got four or more right, you may be a really terrific guesser. If you got one or none right, you may be a really bad guesser.

Keep in mind, though, that this is only a small sample. You should continue to keep track of your guessing ability as you work through the sample questions in this book. Circle the numbers of questions you guess on as you make your guess; or, if you don't have time while you take the practice tests, go back afterward and try to remember which questions you guessed at. Remember, on a test with four answer choices, your chances of getting a right answer is one in four. So keep a separate "guessing" score for each exam. How many questions did you guess on? How many did you get right? If the number you got right is at least one-fourth of the number of questions you guessed on, you are at least an average guesser, maybe better—and you should always go ahead and guess on the real exam. If the number you got right is significantly lower than one-fourth of the number you guessed on, you would be safe in guessing anyway, but maybe you'd feel more comfortable if you guessed only selectively, when you can eliminate a wrong answer or at least have a good feeling about one of the answer choices.

► Step 7: Reach Your Peak Performance Zone

Time to complete: 10 minutes to read; weeks to complete

Activity: Complete the Physical Preparation Checklist

To get ready for a challenge like a big exam, you have to take control of your physical, as well as your mental, state. Exercise, proper diet, and rest will ensure that your body works with, rather than against, your mind on test day, as well as during your preparation.

Exercise

If you don't already have a regular exercise program going, the time during which you're preparing for an exam is actually an excellent time to start one. And if you're already keeping fit—or trying to get that way— don't let the pressure of preparing for an exam fool you into quitting now. Exercise helps reduce stress by pumping wonderful good-feeling hormones called *endorphins* into your system. It also increases the oxygen supply throughout your body, including your brain, so you'll be at peak performance on test day.

A half hour of vigorous activity—enough to raise a sweat—every day should be your aim. If you're really pressed for time, every other day is OK. Choose an activity you like and get out there and do it. Jogging with a friend always makes the time go faster, or take a radio.

But don't overdo it. You don't want to exhaust yourself. Moderation is the key.

Diet

First of all, cut out the junk. Go easy on caffeine and nicotine, and eliminate alcohol and any other drugs from your system at least two weeks before the exam.

What your body needs for peak performance is simply a balanced diet. Eat plenty of fruits and vegetables, along with protein and complex carbohydrates. Foods high in lecithin (an amino acid), such as fish and beans, are especially good "brain foods."

The night before the exam, you might "carbo-load" the way athletes do before a contest. Eat a big plate of spaghetti, rice and beans, or whatever your favorite carbohydrate is.

Rest

You probably know how much sleep you need every night to be at your best, even if you don't always get it. Make sure you do get that much sleep, though, for at least a week before the exam. Moderation is important here, too. Extra sleep will just make you groggy.

If you're not a morning person and your exam will be given in the morning, you should reset your internal clock so that your body doesn't think you're taking an exam at 3 A.M. You have to start this process well before the exam. Here's how it works: Get up half an hour earlier each morning, and then go to bed half an hour earlier that night. Don't try it the other way around; you'll just toss and turn if you go to bed early without having gotten up early. The next morning, get up another half an hour earlier, and so on. How long you will have to do this depends on how late you're used to getting up. Use the Physical Preparation Checklist on page 22 to make sure you're in tip-top form.

▶ Step 8: Get Your Act Together

Time to complete: 10 minutes to read; time to complete will vary
Activity: Complete Final Preparations worksheet

You're in control of your mind and body; you're in charge of test anxiety, your preparation, and your test-taking strategies. Now it's time to take charge of external factors, such as the testing site and the materials you need to take the exam.

Find out Where the Test is and Make a Trial Run

The testing agency or your EMS instructor will notify you when and where your exam is being held. Do you know how to get to the testing site? Do you know how long it will take to get there? If not, make a trial run, preferably on the same day of the week at the same time of day. Make note, on the Final Preparations worksheet on page 24, of the amount of time it will take you to get to the exam site. Plan on arriving 10–15 minutes early so you can get the lay of the land, use the bathroom, and calm down. Then figure out how early you will have to get up that morning, and make sure you get up that early every day for a week before the exam.

Gather Your Materials

The night before the exam, lay out the clothes you will wear and the materials you have to bring with you to the exam. Plan on dressing in layers; you won't have any control over the temperature of the examination room. Have a sweater or jacket you can take off if it's warm. Use the checklist on the Final Preparations worksheet on page 24 to help you pull together what you'll need.

Don't Skip Breakfast

Even if you don't usually eat breakfast, do so on exam morning. A cup of coffee doesn't count. Don't eat doughnuts or other sweet foods, either. A sugar high will leave you with a sugar low in the middle of the exam. A mix of protein and carbohydrates is best: Cereal with milk or eggs with toast will do your body a world of good.

Physical Preparation Checklist

For the week before the test, write down 1) what physical exercise you engaged in and for how long, and 2) what you ate for each meal. Remember, you're trying for at least half an hour of exercise every other day (preferably every day) and a balanced diet that's light on junk food.

Exam minus 7 days

Exercise: _____ for _____ minutes

Breakfast: _____

Lunch: _____

Dinner: _____

Snacks: _____

Exam minus 6 days

Exercise: _____ for _____ minutes

Breakfast: _____

Lunch: _____

Dinner: _____

Snacks: _____

Exam minus 5 days

Exercise: _____ for _____ minutes

Breakfast: _____

Lunch: _____

Dinner: _____

Snacks: _____

Exam minus 4 days

Exercise: _____ for _____ minutes

Breakfast: _____

Lunch: _____

Dinner: _____

Snacks: _____

Exam minus 3 days

Exercise: _____ for _____ minutes

Breakfast: _____

Lunch: _____

Dinner: _____

Snacks: _____

Exam minus 2 days

Exercise: _____ for _____ minutes

Breakfast: _____

Lunch: _____

Dinner: _____

Snacks: _____

Exam minus 1 day

Exercise: _____ for _____ minutes

Breakfast: _____

Lunch: _____

Dinner: _____

Snacks: _____

Step 9: Do It!

Time to complete: 10 minutes, plus test-taking time
Activity: Ace the EMT-Paramedic exam!
Fast-forward to exam day. You're ready. You made a study plan and followed through. You practiced your test-taking strategies while working through this book. You're in control of your physical, mental, and emotional state. You know when and where to show up and what to bring with you. In other words, you're better prepared than most of the other people taking the EMT-Paramedic exam. You're psyched.

Just one more thing. When you're done with the exam, you will have earned a reward. Plan a celebration. Call up your friends and plan a party, have a nice dinner for two, or go see a good movie—whatever your heart desires. Give yourself something to look forward to.

And then do it. Go into the exam, full of confidence, armed with test-taking strategies you've practiced till they're second nature. You're in control of yourself, your environment, and your performance on the exam. You're ready to succeed. So do it. Go in there and ace the exam. And look forward to your career as a paramedic!

Final Preparations

Getting to the Exam Site

Location of exam site: _____

Date: _____

Departure time: _____

Do I know how to get to the exam site?   Yes ___   No ___   (If no, make a trial run.)

Time it will take to get to exam site: _____

Things to Lay Out the Night Before

Clothes I will wear   ___

Sweater/jacket   ___

Watch   ___

Photo ID   ___

Four #2 pencils   ___

Other Things to Bring/Remember

_____   _____

_____   _____

_____   _____

_____   _____

CHAPTER

3 ▶ Paramedic Practice Exam 1

CHAPTER SUMMARY

This is the first of four practice exams in this book based on the National Registry EMT-Paramedic written exam. Use this test to find out how much you remember from your training program and where your strengths and weaknesses lie.

L IKE THE OTHER tests in this book, this test is based on the National Registry's written exam for Paramedics. See Chapter 1 for a complete description of this exam.

Take this first exam in as relaxed a manner as you can, without worrying about timing. You can time yourself on the other three exams. You should, however, make sure that you have enough time to take the entire exam in one sitting, at least two hours. Find a quiet place where you can work without being interrupted.

The answer sheet you should use is on the following page, and then comes the exam. The correct answers, each fully explained, come after the exam. When you have read and understood the answer explanations, turn to Chapter 1 for an explanation of how to score your exam.

Exam 1

1.	ⓐ	ⓑ	ⓒ	ⓓ	46.	ⓐ	ⓑ	ⓒ	ⓓ	91.	ⓐ	ⓑ	ⓒ	ⓓ
2.	ⓐ	ⓑ	ⓒ	ⓓ	47.	ⓐ	ⓑ	ⓒ	ⓓ	92.	ⓐ	ⓑ	ⓒ	ⓓ
3.	ⓐ	ⓑ	ⓒ	ⓓ	48.	ⓐ	ⓑ	ⓒ	ⓓ	93.	ⓐ	ⓑ	ⓒ	ⓓ
4.	ⓐ	ⓑ	ⓒ	ⓓ	49.	ⓐ	ⓑ	ⓒ	ⓓ	94.	ⓐ	ⓑ	ⓒ	ⓓ
5.	ⓐ	ⓑ	ⓒ	ⓓ	50.	ⓐ	ⓑ	ⓒ	ⓓ	95.	ⓐ	ⓑ	ⓒ	ⓓ
6.	ⓐ	ⓑ	ⓒ	ⓓ	51.	ⓐ	ⓑ	ⓒ	ⓓ	96.	ⓐ	ⓑ	ⓒ	ⓓ
7.	ⓐ	ⓑ	ⓒ	ⓓ	52.	ⓐ	ⓑ	ⓒ	ⓓ	97.	ⓐ	ⓑ	ⓒ	ⓓ
8.	ⓐ	ⓑ	ⓒ	ⓓ	53.	ⓐ	ⓑ	ⓒ	ⓓ	98.	ⓐ	ⓑ	ⓒ	ⓓ
9.	ⓐ	ⓑ	ⓒ	ⓓ	54.	ⓐ	ⓑ	ⓒ	ⓓ	99.	ⓐ	ⓑ	ⓒ	ⓓ
10.	ⓐ	ⓑ	ⓒ	ⓓ	55.	ⓐ	ⓑ	ⓒ	ⓓ	100.	ⓐ	ⓑ	ⓒ	ⓓ
11.	ⓐ	ⓑ	ⓒ	ⓓ	56.	ⓐ	ⓑ	ⓒ	ⓓ	101.	ⓐ	ⓑ	ⓒ	ⓓ
12.	ⓐ	ⓑ	ⓒ	ⓓ	57.	ⓐ	ⓑ	ⓒ	ⓓ	102.	ⓐ	ⓑ	ⓒ	ⓓ
13.	ⓐ	ⓑ	ⓒ	ⓓ	58.	ⓐ	ⓑ	ⓒ	ⓓ	103.	ⓐ	ⓑ	ⓒ	ⓓ
14.	ⓐ	ⓑ	ⓒ	ⓓ	59.	ⓐ	ⓑ	ⓒ	ⓓ	104.	ⓐ	ⓑ	ⓒ	ⓓ
15.	ⓐ	ⓑ	ⓒ	ⓓ	60.	ⓐ	ⓑ	ⓒ	ⓓ	105.	ⓐ	ⓑ	ⓒ	ⓓ
16.	ⓐ	ⓑ	ⓒ	ⓓ	61.	ⓐ	ⓑ	ⓒ	ⓓ	106.	ⓐ	ⓑ	ⓒ	ⓓ
17.	ⓐ	ⓑ	ⓒ	ⓓ	62.	ⓐ	ⓑ	ⓒ	ⓓ	107.	ⓐ	ⓑ	ⓒ	ⓓ
18.	ⓐ	ⓑ	ⓒ	ⓓ	63.	ⓐ	ⓑ	ⓒ	ⓓ	108.	ⓐ	ⓑ	ⓒ	ⓓ
19.	ⓐ	ⓑ	ⓒ	ⓓ	64.	ⓐ	ⓑ	ⓒ	ⓓ	109.	ⓐ	ⓑ	ⓒ	ⓓ
20.	ⓐ	ⓑ	ⓒ	ⓓ	65.	ⓐ	ⓑ	ⓒ	ⓓ	110.	ⓐ	ⓑ	ⓒ	ⓓ
21.	ⓐ	ⓑ	ⓒ	ⓓ	66.	ⓐ	ⓑ	ⓒ	ⓓ	111.	ⓐ	ⓑ	ⓒ	ⓓ
22.	ⓐ	ⓑ	ⓒ	ⓓ	67.	ⓐ	ⓑ	ⓒ	ⓓ	112.	ⓐ	ⓑ	ⓒ	ⓓ
23.	ⓐ	ⓑ	ⓒ	ⓓ	68.	ⓐ	ⓑ	ⓒ	ⓓ	113.	ⓐ	ⓑ	ⓒ	ⓓ
24.	ⓐ	ⓑ	ⓒ	ⓓ	69.	ⓐ	ⓑ	ⓒ	ⓓ	114.	ⓐ	ⓑ	ⓒ	ⓓ
25.	ⓐ	ⓑ	ⓒ	ⓓ	70.	ⓐ	ⓑ	ⓒ	ⓓ	115.	ⓐ	ⓑ	ⓒ	ⓓ
26.	ⓐ	ⓑ	ⓒ	ⓓ	71.	ⓐ	ⓑ	ⓒ	ⓓ	116.	ⓐ	ⓑ	ⓒ	ⓓ
27.	ⓐ	ⓑ	ⓒ	ⓓ	72.	ⓐ	ⓑ	ⓒ	ⓓ	117.	ⓐ	ⓑ	ⓒ	ⓓ
28.	ⓐ	ⓑ	ⓒ	ⓓ	73.	ⓐ	ⓑ	ⓒ	ⓓ	118.	ⓐ	ⓑ	ⓒ	ⓓ
29.	ⓐ	ⓑ	ⓒ	ⓓ	74.	ⓐ	ⓑ	ⓒ	ⓓ	119.	ⓐ	ⓑ	ⓒ	ⓓ
30.	ⓐ	ⓑ	ⓒ	ⓓ	75.	ⓐ	ⓑ	ⓒ	ⓓ	120.	ⓐ	ⓑ	ⓒ	ⓓ
31.	ⓐ	ⓑ	ⓒ	ⓓ	76.	ⓐ	ⓑ	ⓒ	ⓓ	121.	ⓐ	ⓑ	ⓒ	ⓓ
32.	ⓐ	ⓑ	ⓒ	ⓓ	77.	ⓐ	ⓑ	ⓒ	ⓓ	122.	ⓐ	ⓑ	ⓒ	ⓓ
33.	ⓐ	ⓑ	ⓒ	ⓓ	78.	ⓐ	ⓑ	ⓒ	ⓓ	123.	ⓐ	ⓑ	ⓒ	ⓓ
34.	ⓐ	ⓑ	ⓒ	ⓓ	79.	ⓐ	ⓑ	ⓒ	ⓓ	124.	ⓐ	ⓑ	ⓒ	ⓓ
35.	ⓐ	ⓑ	ⓒ	ⓓ	80.	ⓐ	ⓑ	ⓒ	ⓓ	125.	ⓐ	ⓑ	ⓒ	ⓓ
36.	ⓐ	ⓑ	ⓒ	ⓓ	81.	ⓐ	ⓑ	ⓒ	ⓓ	126.	ⓐ	ⓑ	ⓒ	ⓓ
37.	ⓐ	ⓑ	ⓒ	ⓓ	82.	ⓐ	ⓑ	ⓒ	ⓓ	127.	ⓐ	ⓑ	ⓒ	ⓓ
38.	ⓐ	ⓑ	ⓒ	ⓓ	83.	ⓐ	ⓑ	ⓒ	ⓓ	128.	ⓐ	ⓑ	ⓒ	ⓓ
39.	ⓐ	ⓑ	ⓒ	ⓓ	84.	ⓐ	ⓑ	ⓒ	ⓓ	129.	ⓐ	ⓑ	ⓒ	ⓓ
40.	ⓐ	ⓑ	ⓒ	ⓓ	85.	ⓐ	ⓑ	ⓒ	ⓓ	130.	ⓐ	ⓑ	ⓒ	ⓓ
41.	ⓐ	ⓑ	ⓒ	ⓓ	86.	ⓐ	ⓑ	ⓒ	ⓓ	131.	ⓐ	ⓑ	ⓒ	ⓓ
42.	ⓐ	ⓑ	ⓒ	ⓓ	87.	ⓐ	ⓑ	ⓒ	ⓓ	132.	ⓐ	ⓑ	ⓒ	ⓓ
43.	ⓐ	ⓑ	ⓒ	ⓓ	88.	ⓐ	ⓑ	ⓒ	ⓓ	133.	ⓐ	ⓑ	ⓒ	ⓓ
44.	ⓐ	ⓑ	ⓒ	ⓓ	89.	ⓐ	ⓑ	ⓒ	ⓓ	134.	ⓐ	ⓑ	ⓒ	ⓓ
45.	ⓐ	ⓑ	ⓒ	ⓓ	90.	ⓐ	ⓑ	ⓒ	ⓓ	135.	ⓐ	ⓑ	ⓒ	ⓓ

136. (a) (b) (c) (d)
137. (a) (b) (c) (d)
138. (a) (b) (c) (d)
139. (a) (b) (c) (d)
140. (a) (b) (c) (d)
141. (a) (b) (c) (d)
142. (a) (b) (c) (d)
143. (a) (b) (c) (d)
144. (a) (b) (c) (d)
145. (a) (b) (c) (d)
146. (a) (b) (c) (d)
147. (a) (b) (c) (d)
148. (a) (b) (c) (d)
149. (a) (b) (c) (d)
150. (a) (b) (c) (d)

151. (a) (b) (c) (d)
152. (a) (b) (c) (d)
153. (a) (b) (c) (d)
154. (a) (b) (c) (d)
155. (a) (b) (c) (d)
156. (a) (b) (c) (d)
157. (a) (b) (c) (d)
158. (a) (b) (c) (d)
159. (a) (b) (c) (d)
160. (a) (b) (c) (d)
161. (a) (b) (c) (d)
162. (a) (b) (c) (d)
163. (a) (b) (c) (d)
164. (a) (b) (c) (d)
165. (a) (b) (c) (d)

166. (a) (b) (c) (d)
167. (a) (b) (c) (d)
168. (a) (b) (c) (d)
169. (a) (b) (c) (d)
170. (a) (b) (c) (d)
171. (a) (b) (c) (d)
172. (a) (b) (c) (d)
173. (a) (b) (c) (d)
174. (a) (b) (c) (d)
175. (a) (b) (c) (d)
176. (a) (b) (c) (d)
177. (a) (b) (c) (d)
178. (a) (b) (c) (d)
179. (a) (b) (c) (d)
180. (a) (b) (c) (d)

▶ Paramedic Exam 1

1. During the initial phase of an acute stress reaction, which of the following physiological responses will occur?
   a. normal vital signs that remain unchanged
   b. increased vital signs that quickly return to normal
   c. increased pulse rate and pupillary dilatation
   d. lowered pulse rate and pupillary constriction

2. You use an end-tidal carbon dioxide detector as a tool to determine if endotracheal intubation has been correctly obtained. The absence of carbon dioxide in exhaled air after six ventilations indicates that the endotracheal tube has been
   a. correctly placed.
   b. placed in the esophagus.
   c. placed in the right mainstem bronchus.
   d. placed in the left mainstem bronchus.

3. In which of the following situations should a paramedic perform an initial assessment first?
   a. during cardiac arrest at a swimming pool
   b. when the patient is in a toxic environment
   c. when the scene is not yet secured by law enforcement
   d. during a rescue from a fully involved structure fire

4. The focused history and physical examination of a patient begins after you have
   a. controlled immediate threats to the patient's life.
   b. transported the patient to the hospital.
   c. secured the scene and gained access to the patient.
   d. contacted medical control for direction.

Answer questions 5–6 on the basis of the following information.

You arrive on the scene and find an elderly male complaining of severe abdominal and back pain. Upon further questioning, he states that the pain is "all over the left side." On palpation, you feel a pulsating mass in the abdomen.

5. This patient is most likely suffering from
   a. pulsating diaphragm lesions.
   b. acute arterial occlusion.
   c. acute pulmonary embolism.
   d. abdominal aortic aneurysm.

6. This patient's vital signs have been worsening steadily throughout the time he has been under your care. Treatment for this patient should include
   a. cardiac monitoring.
   b. two liters of crystalloid solution.
   c. dopamine administration.
   d. PASG/MAST application.

7. The hypoxic drive is regulated by
   a. low PaO_2.
   b. high PaO_2.
   c. high oxygen saturation percentage.
   d. low oxygen saturation percentage.

8. The posterior tibial pulse can be palpated near the
   a. arch of the foot.
   b. medial ankle bone.
   c. posterior knee.
   d. top of the foot.

9. Progressively deeper, faster breathing alternating gradually with shallow, slower breathing is called
    a. agonal respirations.
    b. Cheyne-Stokes respirations.
    c. Kussmaul's respirations.
    d. Biot's respirations.

10. Which patient should be transported immediately, with minimal on-scene care and any attempts at stabilization performed en route to the hospital?
    a. female, age 45, pulse 132, systolic BP 78
    b. male, age 60, pulse 115, respiratory rate 12
    c. female, age 28, systolic BP 96, respiratory rate 18
    d. male, age 54, pulse 98, diastolic BP 80

11. The collective change in vital signs associated with the late stages of increasing intracranial pressure consists of
    a. increasing pulse rate, shallow respirations, increasing blood pressure.
    b. slowing pulse rate, deep or erratic respirations, increasing blood pressure.
    c. rapid and shallow pulse, deep respirations, decreasing blood pressure.
    d. quickening pulse rate, shallow respirations, decreasing blood pressure.

12. If your patient has an open abdominal wound with a loop of bowel obtruding, you should treat this with
    a. a trauma dressing secured with triangular bandages.
    b. an occlusive dressing secured on only three sides.
    c. a wet sterile dressing and an occlusive dressing.
    d. a clean gauze dressing secured with sterile tape.

13. Which of the following patients is most critical in terms of age and mechanism of injury?
    a. an 86-year-old female with a fractured clavicle
    b. a 28-year-old male with a fractured femur
    c. a 43-year-old female with a fractured rib
    d. a 56-year-old male with a pelvic fracture

14. An unconscious patient who has one dilated pupil that is reactive to light is showing early signs of
    a. transient ischemic attacks.
    b. cerebral artery aneurysm.
    c. status epilepticus.
    d. increased intracranial pressure.

15. Your patient converses with you and answers most questions appropriately but is unsure of where she is or who you are even though you keep telling her your name. Her mental status is best described as
    a. unresponsive or unconscious.
    b. responsive to painful stimuli.
    c. responsive to verbal stimuli.
    d. awake and alert.

16. A harsh upper airway sound that can be heard when the patient inhales is called
    a. stridor.
    b. a cough.
    c. dyphonia.
    d. dyspnea.

17. You suspect that a patient has a complete airway obstruction when he
    a. cannot swallow.
    b. cannot cough.
    c. can only whisper.
    d. can exhale with some effort.

18. No breath sounds in one lung field may indicate which of the following conditions?
 a. pneumothorax
 b. partial airway obstruction
 c. flail chest
 d. pulmonary embolism

19. Why is ventilation of the pediatric patient with a bag-valve mask more difficult than ventilating an adult?
 a. The infant is more combative.
 b. The infant needs a lower concentration of oxygen.
 c. It is more difficult to create a good seal in an infant.
 d. The glottic opening is smaller in an infant.

20. The pharyngo-tracheal lumen airway should be removed if the patient
 a. vomits.
 b. becomes tachycardic.
 c. regains consciousness.
 d. has poor compliance.

21. What do oethostatic vital sign changes suggest for a patient with acute abdominal pain?
 a. The patient has appendicitis.
 b. The patient is hypovolemic.
 c. The patient has peritonitis.
 d. The patient is a diabetic.

22. A patient with an acute abdomen who shows no signs of hemorrhage and has stable vital signs should be positioned
 a. in whatever position is most comfortable for the patient.
 b. in supine position on a padded long backboard.
 c. in shock position with both lower legs elevated.
 d. sitting upright in a high Fowler's position.

23. Focused examination of the abdomen of a patient who is complaining of abdominal pain should consist of
 a. percussion on the entire abdomen.
 b. auscultation of the area of discomfort.
 c. gentle palpation of the entire abdomen.
 d. repeated tests for rebound tenderness.

24. Your patient is a 28-year-old diver who has been using scuba equipment. His diving partner states that he was unconscious when he surfaced after a dive. You should suspect
 a. Type I decompression sickness.
 b. Type II decompression sickness.
 c. air embolism.
 d. pneumomediastinum.

25. Drug dosages are lower in elderly patients than in young adults primarily because elderly patients
 a. weigh less on average than younger patients.
 b. have a slower rate of elimination of drugs.
 c. forget they took their medication and overdose.
 d. do not respond to drugs as well as the young.

26. Which statement about the pain that accompanies a myocardial infarction is incorrect?
 a. Patients often describe the pain as "crushing."
 b. The pain is present only during exertion or stress.
 c. The pain is relieved by sublingual nitroglycerin.
 d. Pain due to AMI radiates like anginal pain.

27. Which set of vital signs is consistent with left heart failure?
   a. BP 100/60, P 48 and regular, R 8 and shallow
   b. BP 130/80, P 68 and irregular, R 14 and normal
   c. BP 160/100, P 108 and irregular, R 26 and labored
   d. BP 170/110, P 76 and irregular, R 22 and shallow

28. Which of the following items is NOT standard equipment for performing an endotracheal intubation?
   a. laryngoscope
   b. suction equipment
   c. 5 cc syringe
   d. bite block

29. Which of the following signs or symptoms requires immediate corrective action in the pre-hospital setting?
   a. decreased level of consciousness
   b. night sweating in an AIDS patient
   c. pulse of 106 in a child
   d. resting heart rate of 56 in an athlete

Answer questions 30–33 on the basis of the following information.

You are called to the home of an elderly female who is having difficulty breathing. She has a history of chronic congestive heart failure.

30. Which vital-sign pattern is most likely for this patient?
   a. shallow rapid respirations, decreased pulse rate, cool clammy skin
   b. deep labored respirations, decreased pulse rate, hot dry skin
   c. shallow rapid respirations, increased pulse rate, cool clammy skin
   d. increased respiratory rate, decreased pulse rate, flushed dry skin

31. Which of the following are common medications associated with patients with chronic CHF?
   a. thiamine, nitroglycerine, and albuterol
   b. cortisone, digoxin, and theophylline
   c. furosemide, calcium, and nitroglycerine
   d. diuretics, potassium, and digoxin

32. You auscultate the patient's chest. What lung sounds would you would expect to hear from this patient?
   a. basilar wheezes in all lung fields bilaterally
   b. rales and/or rhonchi mainly in the lower lobes
   c. clear but diminished sounds in the upper lobes
   d. rubs with chest wall expansion in the bases

33. Which of the following best describes the pathophysiology of CHF?
   a. cardiac muscle failure resulting in pulmonary edema
   b. aortic valve failure resulting in pulmonary edema
   c. pneumonia resulting in pulmonary edema
   d. superior vena cava failure resulting in pulmonary edema

34. What is the purpose of performing the Sellick's maneuver?
   a. to visualize the upper airway structures during BVM
   b. to prevent the tongue from blocking the airway
   c. to protect a patient with possible spinal injury
   d. to prevent vomiting during attempts at intubation

35. Overinflating the pilot balloon in an endotracheal tube can cause
   a. displacement of the tube.
   b. return of the gag reflex.
   c. ischemia of the tracheal wall.
   d. damage to teeth and gums.

36. To ensure proper placement of the endotracheal tube, you should
   a. confirm placement of the tube by two different methods.
   b. suction the end of the tube and observe for vomitus or blood.
   c. check breath sounds in the chest before and after placement.
   d. visualize the open glottis and remove stylet before tube placement.

37. The digital intubation method is used for patients who
   a. have short anterior cords.
   b. are very old or very young.
   c. have arthritis in the neck.
   d. have suspected spinal injury.

38. Distended neck veins, diminishing unilateral breath sounds, and progressively worsening compliance are indications of
   a. esophageal intubation.
   b. endobronchial intubation.
   c. tension pneumothorax.
   d. hemopneumothorax.

39. When suctioning a patient, you should always
   a. begin suctioning after the catheter is placed in the airway.
   b. limit suctioning attempts to no more than 45 seconds each.
   c. hyperventilate the patient after every three suction attempts.
   d. insert the catheter while the suctioning apparatus is turned on.

40. Your patient exhibits cold, clammy skin, air hunger, distended neck veins, tracheal displacement, and absent breath sounds on one side. You should suspect
   a. tension pneumothorax.
   b. flail chest.
   c. massive hemothorax.
   d. pericardial tamponade.

41. What are the signs of circulatory overload in a patient who is receiving IV fluids?
   a. dyspnea, rales, and rhonchi
   b. agitation and clammy skin
   c. falling blood pressure
   d. Trauma Score lower than 10

42. What is your first action for an adult patient who is conscious but who has a complete airway obstruction?

a. Deliver rapid abdominal thrusts until cleared or unconsciousness results.

b. Use the jaw-thrust/chin-lift technique to confirm the obstruction.

c. Pinch the patient's nostrils and attempt to give two ventilations.

d. Ask the patient to lie down on the ground and attempt finger sweeps.

43. What is the treatment for someone who is suffering an exacerbation of either emphysema or chronic bronchitis and is not too hypoxic?

a. Transport this patient to the hospital rapidly, as there is little care that can be rendered for this condition in the prehospital setting.

b. Administer high-flow oxygen, establish an IV lifeline, place the patient on an EKG monitor, and administer bronchodilators.

c. Establish an airway, position the patient seated or semi-seated, administer low-flow oxygen, establish an IV lifeline, and transport.

d. Establish an airway, administer oxygen at the highest possible concentration, establish an IV lifeline, and transport rapidly.

44. What is the most commonly used drug in the prehospital setting for patients with asthma?

a. IV or IM corticosteroid

b. nebulized or SC epinephrine

c. inhaled or nebulized albuterol

d. IM or IV terbutaline

45. Which one of the following methods is recommended when measuring respiratory rate?

a. Use a Wright Meter to determine peak expiratory flow rate.

b. Tell the patient to remain quiet while you count his or her respirations.

c. Carry on a conversation with the patient to distract him or her while you count.

d. Count respirations while pretending to take a redial pulse.

Answer questions 46–47 on the basis of the following information.

You respond to a college fraternity where you encounter a 19-year-old male with a partially obstructed airway. According to witnesses, he was eating pizza and drinking beer when he began to cough and grab his throat. The patient is able to speak in a hoarse whisper only, and he has been coughing repeatedly for about 20 minutes.

46. What is the best treatment for this patient?

a. abdominal thrusts without back blows

b. back blows and chest thrusts

c. urge him to continue coughing

d. obstruction removal with forceps

47. To perform a needle cricothyrotomy, the patient should be placed

a. supine with head and neck in a slightly flexed position.

b. in the lateral recumbent position with head and neck hyperextended.

c. in the lateral recumbent position with head and neck in neutral position.

d. supine with head and neck hyperextended.

48. Which of the following conditions best suggests respiratory failure?
   a. change in mental status
   b. loud, audible stridor
   c. diaphoresis
   d. tachycardia (> 130)

49. Which of the following can complicate ventilation in a pediatric patient?
   a. hyperextension of the neck
   b. cricoid pressure
   c. a bag-valve mask without a pop-off valve
   d. ventilatory pressure that is higher than is used for adults

50. One breathing pattern is characterized by periods of apnea followed by periods in which respirations first increase then decrease in both depth and frequency. This pattern is called
   a. central neurogenic hyperventilation.
   b. apneustic respiration.
   c. Cheyne-Stokes breathing.
   d. diaphragmatic respiration.

51. What condition is the pathophysiological result of near drowning in sea water?
   a. ventricular fibrillation
   b. pulmonary edema
   c. pulmonary embolism
   d. metabolic alkalosis

Answer questions 52–56 on the basis of the following information.

You respond along with fire units to the scene of a structure fire. Firefighters have rescued a 25-year-old female who is unconscious and unresponsive to verbal or painful stimuli. The victim was located in a smoke-filled bedroom on the floor above the actual fire. Vital signs are: blood pressure 146/80; pulse 128,

strong and regular; and respiratory rate 40. The ECG monitor shows sinus tachycardia. Auscultation reveals generally clear lung sounds and mild expiratory wheezing. You note no burn injuries to the skin or clothing.

52. What would account for the patient's level of consciousness?
   a. She has a drug overdose resulting in unconsciousness.
   b. She has heat stroke from the hot environment.
   c. She is suffering from carbon monoxide poisoning.
   d. She is suffering from carbon dioxide poisoning.

53. Pulse oximetry readings should be scrutinized closely because elevated
   a. carbon monoxide levels can cause an inaccurately high reading of the percentage of oxygen saturation.
   b. carbon monoxide levels can cause an inaccurately low reading of the percentage of oxygen saturation.
   c. carbon dioxide levels can cause an inaccurately high reading of the percentage of oxygen saturation.
   d. carbon dioxide levels can cause an inaccurately low reading of the percentage of oxygen saturation.

54. Treatment for this type of toxic exposure should include which of the following?
   a. nasal cannula (low-flow) oxygen
   b. IV drip of sodium bicarbonate
   c. transport to a hyperbaric facility
   d. position of comfort transport

55. Other signs of this type of exposure include all of the following EXCEPT
   a. cyanotic skin.
   b. cherry-red skin.
   c. chest pain.
   d. hyperactivity.

56. Which of the following is a common source of the toxin that is responsible for this patient's condition?
   a. engine exhaust
   b. cellular respiration
   c. cellular metabolism
   d. well-ventilated space heaters

57. You have arrived on scene to find a 75-year-old female in respiratory distress. Your assessment reveals: BP 138/90, pulse 136/minute, and RR 34. Upon auscultation, you note diffuse bilateral wheezes in the apices and diminished breath sounds in the bases. Pulse oximetry is 82% on room air, and the patient appears fatigued. Which of the following treatment guidelines should you follow for this patient?
   1. Establish an IV at a KVO rate.
   2. Give two 20 cc/kg boluses before establishing an IV at a KVO rate.
   3. If possible, ventilate via BVM at a rate of 24/min to maximize oxygenation.
   4. Attempt orotracheal or nasotracheal intubation.
   5. Provide oxygen via a nonrebreather mask at 10 lpm.
   a. 1, 3, and 5
   b. 2, 3, and 4
   c. 1, 3, and 4
   d. 1, 3, 4, and 5

58. Which of the following is a disease that is associated with cigarette smoking and is related to, but distinct from, emphysema?
   a. chronic bronchitis
   b. congestive heart failure
   c. simple pneumothorax
   d. hemopneumothorax

59. What is the primary drug for the management of acute anaphylaxis?
   a. diphenhydramine HCL
   b. methylprednisolone
   c. terbutaline
   d. epinephrine

60. You have just started an IV lifeline, but the fluid is not flowing properly. What is the first thing you should do to troubleshoot this situation?
   a. Remove the cannula and try another site.
   b. Make sure the constricting band has been removed.
   c. Ensure that the right size drip-set is attached.
   d. Lower the IV bag below the level of the patient's arm.

61. Which of the following patients would benefit most from the application of the PASG/MAST?
   a. 10-year-old male, suspected spinal fracture, no blood loss
   b. 72-year-old female, suspected cardiogenic shock, no blood loss
   c. 40-year-old male, suspected lower extremity fracture, low blood pressure
   d. 67-year-old female, suspected ankle sprain, high blood pressure

62. Care for the patient with cardiac contusion is similar to care for the patient with which of the following conditions?
- **a.** closed abdominal trauma
- **b.** pericardial tamponade
- **c.** tension pneumothorax
- **d.** myocardial infarction

63. Which statement about use of Nitronox in the field is correct?
- **a.** Nitronox is a short-acting agent that is administered via inhalation.
- **b.** Nitronox is used to manage pain in patients with COPD and asthma.
- **c.** Nitronox may be given to patients with acute abdominal distension.
- **d.** Nitronox may be safely used for patients with head injury.

64. The most common cause of upper airway obstruction is
- **a.** anaphylaxis.
- **b.** croup.
- **c.** epiglottitis.
- **d.** relaxation of the tongue.

65. Which treatment for the care of a patient who is suffering from complications of dialysis is correct?
- **a.** If possible, obtain a blood pressure reading on the arm on which the shunt is located.
- **b.** Watch for narrow complex tachycardia to develop as the patient becomes hypoxic.
- **c.** Monitoring for dysrhythmias is frequently unnecessary in a hemodialysis patient.
- **d.** To prevent exacerbation of the problem, start an IV only if ordered by medical control.

66. Knee, femur, and hip dislocation and fracture caused by the knees hitting the firewall and absorbing initial impact are common in frontal collisions with a
- **a.** "down and under" pathway.
- **b.** "down and back" pathway.
- **c.** "up and over" pathway.
- **d.** "up and back" pathway.

67. A single-lead ECG tracing is useful for obtaining information about the heart. Which of the following can be determined from a single-lead ECG tracing?
- **a.** mechanical response of ventricles
- **b.** cardiac output and stroke volume
- **c.** timing of electrical impulse travel
- **d.** the presence of a myocardial infarct

68. What does the actual drawing of the QRS complex on an ECG tracing show?
- **a.** only ventricular repolarization
- **b.** ventricular depolarization and atrial repolarization
- **c.** ventricular repolarization and atrial depolarization
- **d.** impulse travel through the atrioventricular junction

69. A QRS complex is considered abnormal if it lasts longer than how many seconds?
- **a.** 0.04 seconds
- **b.** 0.08 seconds
- **c.** 0.10 seconds
- **d.** 0.12 seconds

70. What does the treatment for a patient whose ECG shows premature atrial contractions include?

    a. observation only as long as the patient remains asymptomatic

    b. vagal maneuvers and 6 mg adenosine rapid IV push over 1–3 seconds

    c. 1–1.5 mg/kg lidocaine via slow IV push, and consider sedation

    d. immediate synchronized cardioversion with 50–100 joules

71. Traumatic aortic rupture usually occurs as a result of transection of the aorta at the

    a. pulmonary artery.

    b. ligamentum teres.

    c. ligamentum nuchae.

    d. ligamentum arteriosum.

72. What is the clinical significance of a first-degree AV block?

    a. It signals the onset of rapid cardiovascular decompensation.

    b. It indicates that the heart rate may drop if action is not taken.

    c. It can lead to syncope and angina if not corrected quickly.

    d. It may foreshadow development of a more advanced dysrhythmia.

73. Wolff-Parkinson-White (WPW) syndrome is characterized by which of the following wave form abnormalities?

    a. QRS complex shorter than 0.12 seconds

    b. short P-R interval and long QRS complex

    c. lengthened and bizarre QRS complex

    d. inverted P waves and normal QRS complex

74. In which situation would you consider having the patient perform a Valsalva maneuver to slow the heart rate?

    a. male, age 34, paroxysmal junctional tachycardia

    b. male, age 68, idioventricular escape rhythm

    c. female, age 74, premature ventricular contractions

    d. female, age 39, ventricular tachycardia

75. Which rhythm is likely to foreshadow the development of other, more serious dysrhythmias?

    a. atrial fibrillation

    b. isolated premature atrial contractions

    c. accelerated junctional rhythm

    d. sinus dysrhythmia

76. What does a prolonged sinus tachycardia accompanying an acute myocardial infarction suggest?

    a. Cardiogenic shock may develop.

    b. Damage to the heart is minimal.

    c. Hypervolemia is the underlying cause.

    d. The diagnosis of MI is incorrect.

77. How should you position the patient to check for jugular vein distention?

    a. lying flat on his or her back

    b. sitting upright near 90 degrees

    c. standing up in anatomical position

    d. seated at a 45-degree angle

78. What does a carotid artery bruit indicate?

    a. good peripheral perfusion

    b. obstruction of blood flow

    c. jugular vein distention

    d. congestive heart failure

79. Hyperextension of the neck, followed by hyper-flexion, is common in
   a. rear-end impacts.
   b. rotational impacts.
   c. frontal impacts.
   d. lateral impacts.

80. The pain of stable angina is brought on by
   a. exercise or stress.
   b. imminent AMI.
   c. difficulty breathing.
   d. overuse of nitroglycerin.

81. In the care of a cardiac arrest patient, epinephrine is used to
   a. decrease the container size to increase BP.
   b. increase ventricular fibrillation amplitude.
   c. prevent anaphylaxis from lidocaine reactions.
   d. increase the effects of the other drugs.

82. A patient's signs and symptoms include orthopnea, spasmodic coughing, agitation, cyanosis, rales, jugular vein distention, and elevated blood pressure, pulse, and respirations. What condition should you suspect?
   a. left heart failure
   b. right heart failure
   c. myocardial infarction
   d. cardiogenic shock

83. Your patient is exhibiting the signs and symptoms of right-sided heart failure. There is no evidence of left-sided failure. In addition to ECG monitoring and high-flow oxygen, what additional treatments should he or she receive?
   a. IV of D5W with minidrip set, dopamine, and norepinephrine, and rapid transport
   b. IV of D5W with macrodrip set, morphine sulfate, and furosemide, and rapid transport
   c. IV of D5W with minidrip set, monitor vital signs closely, and normal transport
   d. IV of D5W with macrodrip set, shock position, PASG, and normal transport

84. What is sodium nitroprusside (Nipride) used in the treatment of?
   a. deep venous thrombosis
   b. myocardial infarction
   c. hypertensive emergency
   d. cardiogenic shock

85. Which of the following drugs is an antidys-rhythmic agent?
   a. furosemide
   b. lidocaine
   c. nitroglycerin
   d. isoproterenol

86. In performing emergency synchronized cardioversion, you would synchronize the electrical shock with which of the following wave forms?
   a. P wave
   b. R wave
   c. P-R interval
   d. QRS complex

87. The P wave on an ECG strip reflects what event inside the heart?
   a. atrial depolarization
   b. atrial repolarization
   c. ventricular depolarization
   d. ventricular repolarization

88. What does treatment for a patient who is experiencing stable angina consist of?
   a. oxygen and defibrillation if the QRS complex is wide
   b. rest, oxygen, and nitroglycerin administration
   c. reassurance, oxygen, ECG monitoring, and morphine sulfate
   d. seat patient upright, start IV, ECG, and furosemide

89. The wheezing associated with left-sided heart failure results from
   a. fluid in the lungs.
   b. chronic bronchitis.
   c. chest muscle tightness.
   d. chest wall expansion.

90. A patient is found in a back bedroom lying supine on the bed with a hunting knife embedded in her anterior chest, midline below the right breast. The patient is in obvious respiratory distress. She is cold, clammy, and diaphoretic with flat neck veins. You hear no breath sounds on the right side. This patient most likely is suffering from
   a. pneumothorax.
   b. pericardial tamponade.
   c. tension pneumothorax.
   d. hemothorax.

91. A primary reason for administering oxygen to a patient with AMI is to
   a. help limit the infarct size.
   b. prevent pulmonary edema.
   c. reduce anxiety and fear.
   d. treat ventricular dysrhythmias.

92. Which of the following is the most appropriate treatment for a seizing, head-injured adult patient?
   a. 5.0 mg of diazepam IM
   b. 5.0 mg of diazepam IVP
   c. nasal intubation with a 6.5 endotracheal tube
   d. direct laryngoscopy and intubation with a 7.5 endotracheal tube

Answer questions 93–96 on the basis of the following information.

You respond to a 22-year-old male who is complaining of rapid onset of chest pain. The patient states that the pain is tearing and sharp and that it started when he surfaced from a scuba dive from 60 feet down. The patient's diving partner states that the patient surfaced too rapidly.

93. What is this patient most likely suffering from?
   a. acute pulmonary edema
   b. nitrogen narcosis
   c. decompression sickness
   d. pulmonary embolism

94. What does treatment for this patient consist of?
   a. IV, high-flow oxygen, and rapid transport to the nearest emergency department
   b. IV, high-flow oxygen, and rapid transport to a recompression chamber
   c. IV, orotracheal intubation, and transport to the nearest emergency department
   d. IV, orotracheal intubation, and transport to a recompression chamber

95. Due to his rapid ascent, this patient may also be suffering from which other diving-related emergency?
a. nitrogen narcosis
b. acute pulmonary edema
c. decompression sickness
d. pneumonia

96. What is an additional possible problem associated with this injury?
a. an increased level of carbon dioxide in the interstitial spaces
b. nitrogen bubbles entering tissue spaces and smaller blood vessels
c. an increase in oxygen levels in the tracheal-bronchial tree
d. excess accumulation of lactic acid collecting in the alveolar space

97. The normal gestational period is
a. 50 weeks.
b. 40 weeks.
c. 30 weeks.
d. 20 weeks.

98. During delivery, a loop of umbilical cord presents from the birth canal. You should
a. cover the cord with a moist and sterile dressing.
b. have the mother stand to assist in delivery.
c. clamp the cord if possible and cut it.
d. reinsert the cord into the vaginal opening.

99. You would be likely to receive an order to administer intravenous thiamine to a patient who appeared to be
a. in status epilepticus.
b. in metabolic shock.
c. hyperventilating.
d. profoundly intoxicated.

100. During delivery, you notice that the amniotic fluid is discolored and has a foul odor. What should you do first?
a. Suction the upper airway using a meconium aspirator.
b. Intubate the child and give positive pressure ventilations.
c. Dry, warm, position, suction, and stimulate the child to breathe.
d. Provide five back blows and then five chest thrusts.

101. How should you control bleeding after the normal delivery of an infant?
a. Pack the vagina with sterile gauze.
b. Apply direct pressure to the genitalia.
c. Elevate the pelvis.
d. Perform fundal massage.

102. A greenstick fracture is one that is
a. open.
b. impacted.
c. partial.
d. comminuted.

103. What should you do to care for a patient with a suspected pelvic fracture?
a. Apply the PASG/MAST, titrate two IVs to effect, and monitor for signs of shock.
b. Immobilize the patient to a long spine board, start two IVs, and transport immediately.
c. Gently align lower limbs, soft splint with a blanket and cravat, and administer analgesics.
d. Do not immobilize, monitor distal pulse and sensation, and transport immediately.

104. Your patient has a chemical burn to her face and eyes. How should you treat this?
  a. Cover the eyes and face with a dry sterile dressing.
  b. Apply a paste made of baking soda and alcohol to the eyes.
  c. Apply a neutralizing agent to counteract any chemical reaction.
  d. Flush the area with clean cool water prior to and during transport.

105. Local cooling should be used to treat second degree minor burns that cover less than what percentage of total body surface area?
  a. 5% or less
  b. 10–15%
  c. 20–30%
  d. over 40%

106. A burn wound that blisters is an example of
  a. first-degree burn.
  b. second-degree burn.
  c. third-degree burn.
  d. chemical burn.

107. An adult who has burns over both sides of one arm and both sides of one leg would be estimated to have total burns over what percentage of body surface area?
  a. 9%
  b. 18%
  c. 27%
  d. 36%

108. Your patient is a comatose 56-year-old male. His breath smells fruity and sweet, and his respirations are very deep and rapid. After the initial assessment, you should provide which of the following treatments?
  a. Draw blood, start an IV of 0.9% NaCl, and give a 500 ml fluid bolus.
  b. Draw blood, start an IV of normal saline, and administer IM glucagon.
  c. Administer oxygen, start an IV of D5W, and transport immediately.
  d. Administer oxygen, monitor vital signs, and give 25 gm IV Dextrose 50%.

109. Signs of hypoglycemia include which of the following?
  a. nausea and vomiting; tachycardia; abdominal pain; deep, rapid respirations
  b. weak, rapid pulse; cold, clammy skin; headache; irritability; coma
  c. shallow, rapid breathing; low blood pressure; warm, dry skin; irritability
  d. decreased blood pressure, pulse, and respirations; loss of consciousness

110. Naloxone is given to patients who are suspected of having which of the following conditions?
  a. narcotic overdose
  b. Wernicke's syndrome
  c. Korsakoff's psychosis
  d. increased intracranial pressure

111. Patients who are found in a hazardous materials incident should be initially treated in which containment zone?
  a. hot
  b. warm
  c. cold
  d. moderate

112. A patient presents with symptoms of flushing, itching, hives, difficulty breathing, decreased blood pressure, and dizziness. What should you suspect?
   a. diabetic coma
   b. anaphylaxis
   c. acute appendicitis
   d. stroke

113. After administration of epinephrine, what drug may be given to help epinephrine stop an allergic reaction?
   a. oxygen
   b. diphenhydramine
   c. albuterol
   d. terbutaline

114. What is the reason for giving inhaled beta agonists to patients with severe allergic reactions?
   a. to increase heart rate and contractile force
   b. to block histamine receptors so edema is lessened
   c. to help suppress the inflammatory response
   d. to reverse bronchospasm and relax airways

115. A patient is covered with alpha-radioactive material after an accidental spill. An adequate level of shielding would be
   a. a lead apron.
   b. a concrete wall.
   c. a cloth uniform.
   d. aluminum foil.

116. What are the classic symptoms of narcotic overdose?
   a. altered mental status, euphoria, and dilated pupils
   b. excitability, hyperactivity, and hypertension
   c. respiratory depression and constricted pupils
   d. cardiac dysrhythmias and altered mental status

117. Your patient is a farmer who has employed a crop duster to spray his fields. The fields were sprayed earlier today and now the farmer has teary eyes, nausea and vomiting, diarrhea, and excessive salivation. What was he most likely poisoned with?
   a. organophosphates
   b. nitrogen-based fertilizer
   c. cyanide
   d. carbon monoxide

118. Your patient is a 26-year-old man who is awake and has a body temperature of 104° F. The patient also complains of muscle cramps and headache. A friend with whom he has been playing tennis reports that the patient has drunk only one liter of water in the past three hours. What should you suspect?
   a. heat stroke
   b. heat cramps
   c. heat exhaustion
   d. myocardial infarction

119. Which patient presents the signs and symptoms of moderate hypothermia?
   a. male, age 34, core temperature 85.8° F
   b. female, age 28, core temperature 88.8° F
   c. female, age 47, core temperature 95.8° F
   d. male, age 39, core temperature 96.4° F

120. What is the correct field treatment for a frostbitten body part?
   a. Transport the patient to the hospital.
   b. Rub the affected part with crushed ice or snow until warmed.
   c. Warm the affected part in water maintained at 100–106° F before transporting.
   d. Cover the frozen part tightly in wet occlusive dressings.

121. Which of the following statements regarding the complications in assessing elderly patients is true?
   a. Elderly patients are sometimes unable to describe their symptoms accurately.
   b. Elderly patients are likely to fake illnesses to get attention from their children.
   c. Elderly patients do not generally suffer from more than one disease at a time.
   d. Elderly patients generally cannot understand their medication regimens.

122. Signs and symptoms of radiation sickness include
   a. severe headache.
   b. excessive thirst.
   c. hair loss.
   d. hearing problems.

123. Your patient is a 46-year-old man with a long history of mental illness. He appears depressed and withdrawn. Suddenly, he begins to sob uncontrollably. What should you do?
   a. Administer a sedative to help him calm his emotions.
   b. Attempt to calm him by putting your arms around him.
   c. Maintain a quiet, listening, and non-judgemental attitude.
   d. Motion to your partner to go to the unit and get the restraints.

124. Depression is an example of a(n)
   a. psychiatric illness.
   b. psychosis.
   c. mood disorder.
   d. organic disease.

125. What would be the reason for a paramedic to give Benadryl (diphenhydramine) to a schizophrenic patient in the field?
   a. to help control their manic symptoms
   b. to help counteract catatonic symptoms
   c. to raise blood pressure and respiratory rate
   d. to counteract adverse medication reactions

126. Which of the following represents a significant mechanism of injury?
   a. A small child is in a 40 mph car accident.
   b. An adult falls from a 6-foot-high ledge.
   c. An adult pedestrian is hit by a bicycle.
   d. A child falls from a 6-foot-high ledge.

127. Your patient is a 10-year-old boy who has fallen off his bicycle. What should you do when obtaining the history of the accident?
   a. Insist on speaking only to the responsible adult.
   b. Suspect child abuse until the possibility is eliminated.
   c. Suspect abnormal musculoskeletal development.
   d. Obtain as much information as possible from the child.

Answer questions 128–132 on the basis of the following information.

You arrive to find a 6-year-old boy on the floor of his classroom, unconscious, incontinent, and responsive to pain only. The substitute teacher states that the child began to shake violently for approximately two minutes and has been unconscious ever since. She knows that he takes phenobarbital because she gave him one at lunch, but she is unable to provide further medical history.

128. This child most likely suffers from
   a. diabetes mellitus.
   b. diabetes insipidus.
   c. seizure disorder.
   d. status asthmaticus.

129. Phenobarbital is an example of what class or type of medication?
   a. synthetic form of insulin
   b. sedative or anticonvulsant
   c. hypoglycemic medication
   d. beta agonist agent

130. If this child is on medication, why did he have this episode at school?
   a. Medications only limit the number of seizures a person has; they do not always eliminate the seizures.
   b. Medication for this disorder does not control the amount of glucose available for cellular metabolism.
   c. This child may have had too much to eat, overriding the medication's ability to regulate blood sugar.
   d. The substitute teacher must have been mistaken in administering the medication to the child at lunch.

131. Treatment for this patient should include
   a. a 50% dextrose solution.
   b. a 25% dextrose solution.
   c. diazepam (Valium).
   d. oxygen and monitoring.

132. This patient should be transported to a hospital because
   a. he needs a lumbar puncture to determine if he has meningitis.
   b. medication levels need to be determined by laboratory analysis.
   c. glucose levels need to be determined by laboratory analysis.
   d. repeat episodes will continue without hospitalization.

133. Materials safety data sheets contain which of the following?
   a. evacuation radius
   b. melting and boiling point
   c. ingestion antidotes
   d. local reporting telephone numbers

134. What is the approximate weight of the average 6-year-old?
   a. 45 pounds, or 20 kg
   b. 56 pounds, or 25 kg
   c. 70 pounds, or 32 kg
   d. 75 pounds, or 34 kg

135. What is the paramedic's primary goal in cases of suspected child abuse?
   a. Gather up any physical evidence to take to the hospital.
   b. Ensure the abuser is arrested upon arrival at the hospital.
   c. Ensure that the child is removed from family custody.
   d. Make sure that the child receives necessary treatment.

136. All pediatric patients who have had seizures should be
   a. given diazepam rectally or IV or IM.
   b. transported to a hospital for evaluation.
   c. evaluated for signs of abuse or neglect.
   d. given acetaminophen to correct fever.

137. Your patient is ten months old. He has tachypnea and wheezing and a fever of 100.6° F. What do you suspect is wrong with your patient?
   a. asthma
   b. epiglottitis
   c. bronchiolitis
   d. croup

138. Cardiac arrest in young children is most commonly associated with which of the following?
   a. respiratory problems or diseases
   b. trauma from automobile accidents
   c. burn trauma from house fires
   d. underlying cardiac disease processes

139. Assessment and care of a patient who is a victim of sexual assault should include which of the following?
   a. Perform a complete vaginal exam.
   b. Ask detailed questions about the assault.
   c. Place sterile dressings on any wounds.
   d. Allow the patient to bathe and douche.

140. A patient begins to have a generalized seizure while running a marathon on a hot day. Which of the following procedures should you do first?
   a. Move the patient into the ambulance.
   b. Administer 5 mg of diazepam intravenously.
   c. Establish an airway and ventilate the patient.
   d. Place cold packs around the neck and under the arms.

141. Which statement characterizes normal physiologic changes that occur in vital signs during pregnancy?
   a. Blood pressure falls; pulse rate rises.
   b. Blood pressure falls; pulse rate falls.
   c. Blood pressure rises; pulse rate rises.
   d. Blood pressure rises; pulse rate falls.

142. You are recording vital signs for a 34-year-old woman who is eight months pregnant. Her blood pressure is 100/70, pulse rate is 80, and respirations are 17 per minute and normal. Upon auscultation of her chest, you hear a mild systolic flow murmur. How should you treat this patient?
   a. Transport her immediately to a facility with Ob/Gyn services for her imminent delivery.
   b. Establish an IV, administer high-flow oxygen, and monitor vital signs every two minutes.
   c. The murmur is not a finding of concern; document these findings on the patient care report.
   d. Continue to assess the patient for additional signs or symptoms of left-sided heart failure.

143. Your patient is a 29-year-old woman who is nine months pregnant with her third child. She reports the onset of painless bright red vaginal bleeding in the last half hour. How should you treat this patient?
   a. Perform a vaginal exam to determine if this is a placental abruption.
   b. Check for crowning, perineal bulging, or other signs of impending delivery.
   c. Wait for delivery and then transport both mother and child to the hospital.
   d. Treat her for signs and symptoms of shock and transport immediately.

144. Your patient is a 35-year-old woman who is eight months pregnant. You note that her blood pressure is 140/90 and edema is present all over her body. The patient is anxious and complains of seeing spots and having a headache. From this information, what condition should you suspect is present?
  a. gestational diabetes
  b. pre-eclampsia
  c. eclampsia
  d. hypertensive crisis

145. You are assisting in a delivery in the field. As the baby's head is born, you realize that the umbilical cord is wrapped around the baby's neck. What is your first step in the management of this problem?
  a. Attempt to slip the cord over the baby's head.
  b. Apply two clamps and cut the cord immediately.
  c. Moisten the cord and transport immediately.
  d. Position the patient as for a prolapsed cord.

146. You are assessing a neonate who has a pink body and blue extremities, a pulse rate of 90, positive grimace response, active motion, and irregular respiratory efforts. What is the Apgar score for this infant?
  a. 4
  b. 6
  c. 8
  d. 10

147. What is the order of care for a newborn born with evidence of meconium staining?
  a. Suction with the bulb syringe first, then remove remaining meconium under direct visualization.
  b. Suction with bulb syringe, then follow that with resuscitation with the bag-valve-mask unit.
  c. Report the presence of meconium to the medical control physician while administering oxygen.
  d. Deep suction the newborn with a nasogastric tube, followed by administration of high-flow oxygen.

148. Which of the following characteristics is the criterion for administering positive pressure ventilations to a newborn?
  a. Apnea was corrected with blow-by oxygen use.
  b. The heart rate rose from 90 to 110 in two minutes.
  c. Central cyanosis persists while oxygen is given.
  d. Meconium staining was noted during delivery.

Answer questions 149–151 on the basis of the following information.

You respond to the home of a 2-year-old girl who is experiencing labored and difficult breathing. The child's mother states that she has had a cold for the past several days and a seal-like bark for the past 20 minutes. Physical exam reveals she has a fever of 102° F and hot, dry skin. Inspiratory stridor is heard upon auscultation of lung sounds. Vital signs are blood pressure 100/70, pulse rate of 100, and respiratory rate of 40 that is labored and with sternal retractions noted.

149. This patient is most likely suffering from
   a. upper airway obstruction.
   b. epiglottitis.
   c. aspiration pneumonia.
   d. croup.

150. What is the appropriate treatment for this child?
   a. examination of the oropharynx with a tongue blade
   b. direct visualization of the vocal chords for swelling
   c. nebulized albuterol and cooling measures en route
   d. saline given by nebulizer treatment and oxygen

151. A related disease or condition that can result in rapid and total airway obstruction is
   a. bronchitis.
   b. epiglottitis.
   c. bronchiolitis.
   d. laryngitis.

152. The term *ethics* refers to
   a. professional standards of care.
   b. rules, standards, and morals.
   c. upgrading standards of care.
   d. moral code of conduct.

153. A tiered response system is one that does which of the following?
   a. dispatches responders at various levels, depending on the incident
   b. dispatches ALS responders to arrive first to all medical emergencies
   c. has ALS responders respond on fire trucks instead of ambulances
   d. uses chase vehicles staffed with ALS providers to drive ambulances

154. A victim is unresponsive after possible exposure to carbon monoxide in a closed garage. Which of the following procedures should you do first?
   a. Wait on properly trained personnel to enter and evacuate the garage.
   b. Open the windows of the garage to ventilate the environment.
   c. Provide high-flow oxygen to the patient via positive pressure ventilations.
   d. Remove the patient from the environment.

155. With whom does ultimate responsibility for patient care in the field always rest?
   a. the highest trained provider on scene
   b. the regional or state EMS director
   c. the medical control physician
   d. whomever provides online direction

156. What do you call a state law that defines the scope of practice and role of paramedics and other prehospital workers?
   a. delegation of authority
   b. good Samaritan law
   c. medical practice act
   d. durable power of attorney

157. Which of the following situations represents expressed consent?
   a. The patient says, "Help me. My chest hurts."
   b. The patient is eight years old with no parent present.
   c. The patient is unconscious and unresponsive.
   d. The patient says, "I don't need any help. Just let me die."

158. An intoxicated person refuses treatment or transport. How should you proceed?
   a. Do as the patient wishes and leave the scene immediately.
   b. Try to find a family member to get consent for treatment.
   c. Try to persuade the person to accept your assistance.
   d. Immediately document the refusal, then leave the scene.

159. Your radio report to the hospital about the patient's medical condition should include which of the following?
   a. the complete medical history
   b. name, age, race, sex, and weight
   c. the chief complaint
   d. estimated time of arrival on the scene

160. What is the function of a safety officer at a multicasualty incident?
   a. to teach the unit members to work together safely
   b. to decide when a scene is safe enough to enter
   c. to stand in for the transportation officer as necessary
   d. to ensure patient safety before the BLS unit arrives

161. Patients who have overdosed and have altered mental status are best transported
   a. supine.
   b. prone.
   c. left-lateral recumbent.
   d. full Fowler's.

162. At a mass-casualty incident (MCI) which sector should the incident commander establish first?
   a. triage sector
   b. treatment sector
   c. supply sector
   d. transportation sector

163. Which sector officer will coordinate with police to block streets and provide access at an MCI?
   a. triage officer
   b. transportation officer
   c. supply officer
   d. staging officer

164. What is the purpose of the START method?
   a. to coordinate the efforts of multiple response units to a MCI
   b. to ensure safe access of responding units to the MCI site
   c. to rapidly triage large numbers of patients quickly and efficiently
   d. to communicate with medical personnel as efficiently as possible

165. The first step in triage at an MCI is to
   a. direct the walking wounded away from the scene.
   b. assess the victims' respiratory status and pulse rate.
   c. assess the victims' hemodynamic status and AVPU.
   d. evaluate the victims' mental status and ABCs.

166. What does a yellow tag mean in the METTAG system?

   a. The patient does not need any care or transportation at this time.

   b. The patient is not critically injured and transport can be delayed.

   c. The patient is in critical condition and transport cannot be delayed.

   d. the patient is dead and should not receive any resuscitation efforts.

167. Continual re-experiencing of a traumatic event is a characteristic of which of the following?

   a. an anxiety disorder

   b. stress and burnout

   c. cumulative stress reaction

   d. delayed stress reaction

168. What communications system has the capability to send and receive voice and telemetry simultaneously?

   a. VHF

   b. multiplex

   c. UHF

   d. duplex

169. One of the best ways for EMS personnel to deal with job-related stress is to

   a. take sleeping pills at night as needed.

   b. take time away from family and friends.

   c. discuss the situation with coworkers.

   d. eliminate all physical exercises.

170. Ventilating a patient at 30 breaths per minute with a bag-valve mask and high-flow oxygen may result in

   a. an increase in intracranial pressure.

   b. a decrease in the normal serum blood pH.

   c. alkalizing the bloodstream.

   d. production of a tension pneumothorax.

171. You can reduce gastric distention during artificial ventilations by

   a. pressing on the stomach during ventilations.

   b. providing ventilations deep enough to cause chest rise only.

   c. positioning the patient at a 15-degree sideways incline during ventilations.

   d. squeezing the bag-valve mask quickly during ventilations.

172. To adequately ventilate a patient with a partial laryngectomy through a stoma, you should

   a. use more pressure to produce adequate chest rise.

   b. pinch the nose and close the mouth.

   c. suction the stoma with a soft-tip suction catheter first.

   d. use a special bag-valve mask designed to ventilate a stoma.

173. Which patient is most likely to require immediate transport?

   a. 25-year-old male, fractured wrist

   b. 45-year-old male, fractured pelvis

   c. 38-year-old female, fractured tibia

   d. 52-year-old female, fractured humerus

Answer questions 174–176 on the basis of the following information.

You respond to a 25-patient mass-casualty incident at a store. The 911 caller stated that she smelled something "funny" and then started to feel weak and nauseous. You are the second unit on the scene. The initial unit is nowhere to be seen, and they do not answer their radios.

174. What should you determine first in this situation?
a. whether the other crew is treating patients inside and needs your help
b. whether this is a potential hazardous-materials incident in progress
c. whether the other crew has been overcome and needs your immediate assistance
d. whether you need more oxygen and supplies than your ambulance carries

175. After you are instructed by the Haz-Mat team to begin treating decontaminated patients, you should
a. take universal precautions and wear protective equipment.
b. begin your efforts with the least symptomatic patient first.
c. get ready to treat the patients as you would at any other scene.
d. thoroughly question the first patient for purposes of documentation.

176. For which procedure is it necessary to wear a gown?
a. emergency childbirth
b. drawing blood
c. suctioning the airway
d. cleaning instruments

177. Which of the following requires intermediate-level disinfection through the use of a solution of bleach and water?
a. routine housecleaning measures in your station and bunkroom
b. any items that have come into contact with mucous membranes
c. any instruments that were used in any invasive procedures
d. all items that have come into contact with intact skin

178. Which infection is transmitted through contact with blood or body secretions?
a. hepatitis A
b. hepatitis B
c. varicella
d. tuberculosis

179. What is a major concern when dealing with a patient with organophosphate poisoning?
a. exposure of rescuers to the poison
b. life-threatening dysrhythmias
c. explosion or fire hazard
d. CVA or neurological effects

180. Which of the following medications is commonly used to treat patients who are victims of organophosphate poisoning?
a. adenosine
b. atropine sulfate
c. calcium chloride
d. flumanzenil

► Answers

1. c. Both good stress (*eustress*) and bad stress (*distress*) will initially cause sympathetic stimulation such as increased heart and respiratory rate, bronchodilation, dilated pupils, and increased blood flow to the skeletal muscles.

2. b. No carbon dioxide after six ventilations indicates either that the tube is in the esophagus or that the patient has been dead long enough that no carbon dioxide is being produced.

3. a. Before assessing airway, breathing, and circulation, it is necessary to remove the patient (and yourself) to a place of relative safety.

4. a. The purpose of the focused history and physical is to detect additional problems after you have controlled immediate threats to the patient's life. The ongoing assessment is typically performed during transport. Medical control may be consulted anytime during the call when you feel it is appropriate or whenever your protocols and standing orders require it.

5. d. This patient is exhibiting the classic signs and symptoms of an abdominal aortic aneurysm. Further palpation may cause the aneurysm to rupture, so be very careful in assessing this patient. The other choices will not cause abdominal pulsations to occur.

6. a. Cardiac monitoring should always be performed when you suspect an aneurysm is present. Rapid infusion of crystalloid solution is often indicated in the treatment of shock, but the fluid must be titrated to patient response. Dopamine is indicated for cardiogenic shock. Shock in this patient would be due to hypovolemia. Dopamine is contraindicated in the presence of uncorrected hypovolemia. PASG/MAST may be indicated for treatment of AAA in some jurisdictions; however, it is not a standardized treatment.

7. a. COPD patients can no longer rely upon normal regulatory mechanisms to control their respirations. The hypoxic drive measures for low levels of oxygen in the bloodstream to increase respiratory rate.

8. b. The posterior tibial pulse is assessed just below and posterior to where the ankle bone protrudes medially. The pulse located on the top of the foot is the dorsalis pedis. The popliteal pulse is located behind the knee.

9. b. Biot's breathing is an irregular pattern. Cheyne-Stokes respirations are regular and deep.

10. a. Indications for immediate transport include any signs or symptoms of shock; sustained pulse rate greater than 120 or less than 50; systolic BP less than 90; and respiratory rate less than 10 or greater than 29. Based only on these vital signs, the first patient appears to already be in shock.

11. b. This change in vital signs comprises Cushing's Reflex, a sign of increasing intracranial pressure. Cushing's Reflex is also sometimes called Cushing's Triad or Cushing's Response.

12. c. The most appropriate dressing for an evisceration is the application of a wet sterile dressing (which keeps the organs moist) and an occlusive dressing (which provides a barrier against further contamination and heat loss).

13. d. Each fracture has a potential blood loss of one or more units per fracture site. Because of its ring shape, the pelvis frequently has two or more fractures present. In addition, nerve and blood vessel damage and injury to genitourinary organ injuries can complicate the severity of this injury. Patients with pelvis fractures are always considered high-priority patients and should be rapidly stabilized and transported. If a patient has bilateral femur fractures, he or she is also a high-priority patient.

14. d. A unilaterally dilated pupil may be an early sign of increased intracranial pressure. As swelling increases in the brain, it puts pressure on the optic nerve that is located near the area of swelling.

15. c. The patient is responsive to verbal stimuli but is not alert because she is not oriented to her surroundings. This patient would be reported as V, when using the AVPU acronym (A = awake, V = verbal, P = painful, and U = unresponsive). You could use the additional scale of AAO or CAO to further characterize her mentation level. AAO stands for Awake, Alert, and Oriented. CAO stands for Counscious, Alert, and Oriented. Both are medically acceptable terms. You then judge if the patient is oriented to person, place, time, and sometimes a fourth factor, event. You would report your finding as one of the following: AAO×3, AAO×4, CAO×3 or CAO×4, depending on whether three or four factors were considered.

16. a. Stridor can usually be heard without a stethoscope, and emanates from the area of the throat.

17. b. Answers **c** and **d** both indicate some air exchange. Answer **a** has no relation to the air passageway.

18. a. The other three choices, while serious, generally do not cause complete collapse of a lung.

19. c. The bridge of the nose in a pediatric patient may make a mask seal more difficult to achieve. Additionally, the mask size needed to fit the pediatric patient's face may not be available.

20. c. If the patient is unconscious and vomits, the PTL will help prevent aspiration. Instead, if a gag reflex returns, the PTL will have to be removed before the patient vomits.

21. b. A positive tilt test in a patient with acute abdominal pain suggests that the patient is hypovolemic and may have impending shock.

22. a. Medical patients who are stable should be in a position of comfort.

23. c. Use only gentle palpation in the field. Properly performed auscultation for bowel sounds takes several minutes and is of little value to your overall treatment regimen. Correctly performed percussion requires a relatively quiet environment and an experienced hand to be of any diagnostic value. Continued assessment for rebound tenderness will aggravate the patient's discomfort and is unnecessary once you have determined the patient has abdominal distress.

24. c. Air embolism presents as neurological deficit (including unconsciousness) during or after ascent from a dive, or as sharp pain in the chest.

25. b. The dosage of many common medications is up to 50% lower in elderly adults primarily because of a decreased rate of elimination of the drug by the liver and kidneys.

26. c. The pain of MI is not generally relieved by sublingual nitroglycerin and intravenous morphine or nitroglycerin is usually necessary. It may have all of the same characteristics of angina, making a diagnosis by EMS providers relatively difficult.

27. c. A patient with left heart failure will present with elevated blood pressure, elevated and sometimes irregular pulse, and labored respirations.

28. c. Obturator cuffs on endotracheal tubes require more than 5 cc of air to create a good seal against the tracheal wall. A 10–12 cc syringe is a standard size.

29. a. Decreased level of consciousness can cause airway compromise and is an early sign of many medical and trauma conditions, including decreased tissue perfusion.

30. c. The vital signs given in this choice are most likely for a patient with CHF who is complaining of difficulty breathing.

31. d. Diuretics, potassium, and digoxin are the common medications used to treat CHF.

32. b. The pulmonary edema associated with CHF commonly results in rales and/or rhonchi, especially in the lower lobes.

33. a. CHF results from the cardiac muscle's inability to pump efficiently.

34. d. Sellick's maneuver is used to prevent patients from vomiting during intubation.

35. c. Excessive pressure against the delicate soft tissue of the lower airway may reduce blood flow to the site, causing ischemia.

36. a. To ensure proper placement, always confirm by two different methods: After watching the tube pass through the vocal cords, assess the chest for breath sounds in numerous locations and chest expansion, then check the proximal end of the tube for breath condensation. You may also use one of several commercial confirmation devices that monitor end-tidal CO_2 or provide an audible whistling sound to confirm air movement.

37. d. Because the digital method does not require hyperextendi53ng the patient's neck, it is used for patients with suspected spinal or cervical injury.

38. c. Excessive pressure inside the thoracic cavity due to the tension pneumothorax will result in all of the described symptoms.

39. a. Attempts at suctioning should be limited to no more than 5–10 seconds (depending upon the level of consciousness). You should ventilate the patient after each attempt, and you should not turn on the apparatus until the catheter is placed properly. In the case of a suction catheter that has a hole in the system that allows you to control if suction is being applied or not by occluding the opening, you should only suction upon withdrawal. This system may remain turned on at all times as long as you monitor closely when suction is actually being applied to the patient.

40. a. The signs and symptoms of tension pneumothorax, the presence of air in the pleural space and medialstinal shifting, are listed.

41. a. Dyspnea, rales, and rhonchi are classic signs of fluid overload, which is usually first manifested as pulmonary edema.

42. a. For the conscious patient, your first action would be abdominal thrusts.

43. c. Low-flow oxygen is appropriate for this patient if he or she is not too hypoxic. If a patient with emphysema or chronic bronchitis is hypoxic, he or she needs more oxygen.

44. c. Albuterol, a bronchodilator sold under the trade names Proventil and Ventolin, is frequently given via inhaler or nebulizer in the field.

45. d. Place your hand on the patient's wrist as if you were measuring his or her pulse and count for 30 seconds. This will prevent the patient from consciously changing the respiratory rate. Placing the wrist and hand over the patient's chest wall is called the *pledge of allegiance* method.

46. c. AHA standards dictate that a conscious patient with a partial obstructed airway should be dealt with by encouraging coughing and continuous monitoring of patient status. Interventions like the Heimlich maneuver are considered counterproductive as they may actually worsen the obstruction.

47. **d.** A hyperextended position will place the anatomical structures into a position that can be easily identified by palpation.

48. **a.** A patient in respiratory distress is compensating for the underlying condition, thereby preserving oxygenation to the brain. Once compensatory mechanisms have collapsed, the loss of gas exchange at the brain will result in a change in mental status.

49. **a.** Hyperextending the neck of a small child may result in a unintentional closure of the airway, due to the softer cartilage rings supporting the trachea.

50. **c.** Cheyne-Stokes respirations are characterized by periods of apnea lasting 10–60 seconds, followed by periods in which respirations gradually decrease, then increase, in depth and rate.

51. **b.** Because sea water is hypertonic, fluid is drawn from the bloodstream into the alveoli, causing pulmonary edema. Because of this, all near-drowning patients should be hospitalized and monitored for a short time.

52. **c.** This victim of smoke inhalation is exhibiting the classic signs and symptoms of carbon monoxide poisoning.

53. **a.** This is a common finding with the use of pulse oximetry in carbon monoxide poisoning. The CO molecule, which has a high affinity for hemoglobin, is bound to the molecule and is present for detection as "oxygen" in blood passing through the capillary beds resulting in fairly normal pulse oximetry readings. However, little, if any, of the oxygen is off-loaded from the hemoglobin molecule for use by the tissues.

54. **c.** If a hyperbaric chamber is available, this patient should be transported there immediately for "diving." Hyperbaric oxygen can dramatically improve outcomes for CO poisoning by reducing the time it takes for the CO molecule to unbind from the hemoglobin molecule. Low-flow oxygen and sodium bicarbonate are not indicated for carbon monoxide poisoning. The patient is unconscious, so position of comfort is not an issue. If you suspect the possibility of spinal injury, you should immobilize this patient to the long backboard.

55. **d.** Hyperactivity is not a sign of carbon monoxide exposure. Generally, patients are lethargic due to being hypoxic.

56. **a.** Engine exhaust is a common source of carbon monoxide. Improperly ventilated space heaters are another source. Cellular metabolism and cellular respiration result in the formation of carbon dioxide.

57. **c.** Because the patient appears fatigued, respiratory failure is imminent. Inadequate tidal volume may not permit good gas exchange without manual support.

58. **a.** In addition to emphysema, chronic bronchitis is associated with cigarette smoking. Either condition can lead to CHF. A simple pneumothorax can be caused by cigarette smoking, especially in young and thin males, but the disease process is unrelated to emphysema.

59. **d.** To manage acute anaphylaxis, epinephrine is the first medication used, followed by diphenhydramine. Epinephrine is a potent antihistamine and immediately reverses the physiological effects of the reaction (vasodilation, bronchoconstriction, and airway swelling), while diphenhydramine slows and stops the reaction itself.

60. **b.** Proper flow cannot be achieved if the constricting band (tourniquet) is not removed.

61. **c.** Indications for use of the PASG are to control bleeding, stabilize fractures, and raise blood pressure. Although its use is currently controversial, of the choices listed, **c** has the indications called for if PASG is to be used.

62. **d.** Patients with cardiac contusion can present with the symptoms of myocardial infarction, including life-threatening dysrhythmias. Care is similar to care of any cardiac patient.

63. **a.** Nitronox is a short-acting agent that the patient self-administers by mask. Its use is limited to patients who do not have the potential for having air filled spaces within their tissues, thus eliminating patients with COPD, pneumothoracies, or air-filled abdominal organs.

64. **d.** The lost of lingual control during unconsciousness occurs more commonly than the other conditions.

65. **d.** Fluid administration in dialysis patients should be under the direct authority of medical control. Dysrhythmias are common and if present, are generally caused by electrolyte imbalances. To prevent accidental damage to the shunt, a BP should never be assessed on the arm with the shunt.

66. **a.** "Up and over" refers to injuries sustained in the head, neck, and chest region. In the "down and under" pathway, the body slides forward and downward. This can be limited by the correct use of seat belts.

67. **c.** A single-lead ECG, used for routine monitoring, can be used to determine the heart rate, regularity, and the length of time it takes for the impulse to travel through the heart. It tells you nothing about the mechanical response of the heart, of which stroke volume is a part. You need additional lead views to verify the presence of an MI.

68. **b.** The QRS complex reflects the underlying ventricular depolarization and buried within it is the artial repolarization.

69. **d.** The QRS complex normally lasts 0.04 to 0.12 seconds; anything longer than 0.12 seconds is considered to be abnormal.

70. **a.** If the patient is asymptomatic, this arrhythmia requires observation only. Other treatments described are for patients with varying degrees of supraventricular tachycardia.

71. **b.** During significant deceleration forces, this ligament acts like a knife as the aorta swings violently toward the anterior.

72. **d.** First-degree AV block in itself calls for observation only; however, it may indicate the development of a more advanced heart block.

73. **b.** Wolff-Parkinson-White, a pre-excitation syndrome, is characterized by a short P-R interval and lengthened QRS complex. Often, a delta wave is present as well. This condition occurs in 3 of 1,000 individuals.

74. **a.** When PJT is caused by stress or excessive caffeine intake in a patient with no history of heart disease, the Valsalva maneuver can be successful at slowing the heart rate.

75. **c.** Because the underlying cause is usually ischemia, accelerated junctional rhythm can deteriorate into more serious dysrhythmias.

76. **a.** In a patient with acute MI, sinus tachycardia suggests that cardiogenic shock may develop.

77. **d.** Check for jugular vein distention with the patient elevated at a 45-degree angle. Most patients will have observable jugular veins when supine.

78. **b.** A bruit, noisy blood flow in a vessel, indicates partial obstruction due to plaque buildup or the presence of an embolus.

79. **a.** A strong force striking the car from behind causes the head to move backward. If the head restraint is not properly placed, it can actually act as a fulcrum, causing the neck to hyperextend. Then the head snaps forward, with the chin pointing toward the chest. This results in a severe hyperflexion of the neck.

80. a. Attacks of stable angina are brought on by exercise or by stress and are usually easily managed.

81. b. Epinephrine is used to coarsen dysrhythmias such as ventricular fibrillation, improving the chance of converting to a more viable rhythm.

82. a. Listed are classic signs and symptoms of left heart failure with pulmonary edema.

83. c. Right heart failure, unless it is accompanied by left heart failure with pulmonary edema, is not a true medical emergency and does not require rapid transport.

84. c. Sodium nitroprusside is used in the treatment of hypertensive emergency.

85. b. Lidocaine is a first-line drug in the treatment of dysrhythmias.

86. b. Emergency synchronized cardioversion is synchronized with the R wave in order to avoid firing during the relative refractory period, which could induce ventricular tachycardia.

87. a. The P wave reflects atrial depolarization at the beginning of the cardiac cycle.

88. b. The correct protocol for stable angina is rest, oxygen, and nitroglycerin.

89. a. The wheezing, due to bronchoconstriction of smooth muscle in the lung, is a reaction to fluid in the lung spaces.

90. d. Flat neck veins while the patient is supine indicate a lower than normal pressure inside the vasculature, most likely due to blood loss. This would indicate a hemothorax as the primary cause of the described signs and symptoms.

91. a. Oxygen can help limit the size of the infarct by increasing oxygen delivery to the heart muscle.

92. b. Diaxepam given through the IM route is ineffective. Oral intubation may be difficult to achieve through clenched teeth. Nasal intubation may raise intracranial pressure even higher.

93. d. A too-rapid ascent from a scuba dive may result in a pulmonary embolism due to lung overinflation.

94. b. An IV, 100% oxygen via a nonrebreather mask, and transport to a recompression chamber are essential for this patient.

95. c. Due to the depth of the dive and the rapid ascent, this patient may also be suffering from decompression sickness.

96. b. In this patient, nitrogen gas bubbles may have entered tissue spaces and blood vessels.

97. b. Full-term delivery usually occurs within the 40th week of pregnancy.

98. a. Covering the exposed cord will minimize drying of the cord. Additionally, you should try to insert two fingers into the birth canal and try to keep pressure from the baby's head away from the cord.

99. d. Intravenous thiamine is used to reverse the effects of acute thiamine deficiency, which may lead to seizures and encephalopathy in alcoholics.

100. a. Suction the newborn before stimulating it to breathe. Endotracheal suctioning may be warranted if meconium is noted in the upper airway.

101. d. Massaging the top of the uterus stimulates it to contract, and promotes control of normal postpartum bleeding.

102. c. A greenstick fracture is a partial fracture that is on only one side of the long bone. These fractures are noted most frequently in children, but may also be seen in adults.

103. a. This is the current field treatment regimen for pelvic fractures. The PASG/MAST is used as a air-splint to contain the fractured pelvis and prevent further injury.

104. d. The correct treatment for most chemical burns is to flush the area with cool water immediately and to continue this treatment even during transport.

105. b. Cooling of larger areas may lead to hypothermia. Note that you should cool for only approximately one minute.

106. b. Blister formation is characteristic of second-degree burns.

107. c. Using the rule of nines, this patient has burns over 27% of her body surface area (both sides of one arm = 9%; both sides of one leg = 18%).

108. a. This patient is showing signs and symptoms of diabetic ketoacidosis. Avoid the use of glucose administration if at all possible. At the minimum, you should obtain a glucometer reading before adminstering any glucose containing solutions. The fluid bolus will help dilute the glucose contained within his blood.

109. b. This option lists the classic signs of hypoglycemia.

110. a. Naloxone (Narcan) is a narcotic antagonist given to patients suspected of narcotic ingestion.

111. b. Major decontamination and treatment for life-threatening conditions should be conducted by properly protected personnel in the warm zone.

112. b. Hives, accompanied by difficulty breathing, strongly suggest anaphylaxis.

113. b. Epinephrine is the first-line drug for patients with severe allergic reactions. Oxygen, albuterol, and turbutaline are all respiratory drugs, but they do not have any antihistamine properties. Diphenhydramine (Benadryl) is an antihistamine and will stop the production of histamine, the chemical responsible for the exaggerated immune response.

114. d. Beta agonists such as albuterol help in the treatment of severe allergic reactions by relaxing the airway and thus relieving bronchospasm.

115. c. Alpha particles carry very little energy. A uniform is adequate protection against such a contaminant.

116. c. Respiratory depression and constricted pupils ("pinpoint pupils") are classic symptoms of narcotic overdose.

117. a. The symptoms of organophosphate absorption are described by the acronym SLUDGE: excessive salivation, lacrimation, urination, diarrhea, gastrointestinal distress, emesis.

118. c. The temperature of 104° F and the low fluid intake suggest heat exhaustion due to dehydration. Simple heat cramps are due to lactic acid build-up and do not usually have increased body temperatures. Normal mental status precludes heat stroke. This patient should be rehydrated and monitored for the onset of heat stroke.

119. b. Moderate hypothermia is characterized by a core temperature between 86 and 94° F.

120. a. The correct treatment is gradual warming in a water bath maintained between 100 and 106° F, although this treatment should not be attempted in the field because of the danger of refreezing. Pain management is essential because the procedure is extremely painful.

121. a. Because the elderly often suffer from multiple illnesses or diseases with overlapping symptoms and decreased sensory perception, they may be unable to describe their signs or symptoms. The elderly are not likely to fake illness.

122. c. Hair loss, nausea, and vomiting are common signs and symptoms of radiation sickness.

123. c. Allow the patient to express emotion and do not interrupt his expression with questions or comments. You should always be on your guard for safety issues when on a scene, but restraints are not necessary in this situation. It would not be advisable to touch this patient too closely as this may be perceived by him as an invasion of his space or privacy and is not a safe gesture.

124. c. Depression is a mood disorder; depressed patients feel hopeless and helpless and manifest many physical symptoms as well.

125. d. Benadryl is used to counter extrapyramidal reactions in patients who are taking antipsychotic drugs. Effects noted are involuntary movement, changes in muscle tone, and abnormal posture.

126. a. A 40 mph car accident is a significant mechanism of injury for a child but not for an adult unless other significant findings (lack of seatbelts, another person killed in the same car) are present.

127. d. With a child of this age, obtain as much information as possible from the patient him- or herself; this will allow the child to feel respected and mature. The adult caretaker can fill in relevant details.

128. c. The clinical presentation is one of seizures that could occur for a variety of reasons, including diabetes. However, the use of the drug phenobarbital is commonly associated with seizure disorders.

129. b. Phenobarbital is a sedative/anticonvulsant.

130. a. Anticonvulsants serve to limit the number of seizures a patient has, but they do not stop them from occuring altogether.

131. d. The medications listed in choices **a**, **b**, and **c** are not indicated for post-ictal patients who have stopped seizing.

132. b. This patient needs to be transported to a hospital because medication levels should be assessed by laboratory methods. Seizures may or may not continue to occur.

133. b. MSDS forms describe the physical properties of many chemicals and provide simple instructions for initial first aid, but not specific antidotes, if available.

134. a. The average 6-year-old weighs about 45 pounds.

135. d. In many states, medical personnel are legally required to report all cases of suspected abuse and neglect, but a paramedic's first responsibility is to ensure that the child is transported to the hospital to receive necessary treatment.

136. b. The cause of seizure activity can be determined only in the hospital.

137. c. Wheezing and tachypnea in a child younger than age 1 is most often due to bronchiolitis brought on by the RSV virus. Asthma in children this young often presents as coughing. Epiglottitis will often have a fever higher than 100.6° F and the epiglottis patient will be drooling as respiratory distress worsens. Croup will present with junky-sounding airways and the classic seal-barking cough.

138. a. Most childhood cardiac arrests are the result of preventable accidents that result in respiratory compromise.

139. c. Do not perform a vaginal exam, ask detailed questions about the assault in the field, or allow the patient to change clothes or bathe. You should not overly clean any wounds you encounter, but instead wrap them up with dry sterile dressings. Place any clothing or other evidence removed from the patient in a clean paper bag and take it with you to the hospital.

140. c. While the other procedures are applicable to the treatment of a possible heat stroke victim, securing the airway and ensuring respirations should occur first.

141. a. During pregnancy, a woman's blood pressure usually falls during the first two trimesters and her pulse rate rises.

142. c. A mild systolic murmur in a pregnant patient whose vital signs are normal is not a cause for concern.

143. d. Bright red bleeding in late pregnancy is assumed to be placenta previa, which is a true medical emergency that is life threatening to both mother and baby. Treat the mother for shock and transport immediately.

144. b. The patient shows signs and symptoms of pre-eclampsia (or toxemia of pregnancy) and should be transported to the hospital. The distinction between eclampsia and pre-eclampsia is the presence of seizures and/or coma.

145. a. First, attempt to slip the cord over the baby's head. If this is impossible, you should clamp the cord in two places and carefully cut it between the clamps, then continue with the delivery.

146. b. The score would consist of one point each for appearance, pulse rate, grimace, and respiratory effort, and two points for activity.

147. a. Do not resuscitate or stimulate further until the meconium is cleared from the respiratory tree by direct visualization of the cords.

148. c. Apnea and tachycardia may initially be present in the newborn, but once they are corrected, you do not need to continue to progress further into the inverted pyramid. Meconium staining is treated first with suction. The child may or may not require ventilatory support once it is cleared away.

149. d. This patient is exhibiting the classic signs and symptoms of croup.

150. d. A nebulized saline mist is the appropriate treatment for croup. Do not interfere with the airway in case there is any tissue swelling present.

151. b. Epiglottitis, a condition whereby the patient's airway can become totally obstructed, is related to croup.

152. b. *Ethics* refers to rules, standards, and morals that govern actions in a profession.

153. a. In a tiered system, responders are dispatched to calls depending upon the nature of the incident as stated by the 911 caller and evaluated by the dispatcher.

154. a. Safety first! Of the three extrication options, properly trained and protected rescuers can remove the patient safely.

155. c. No matter who is actually providing care or giving directions to the responder, ultimate responsibility always rests with the medical control physician.

156. c. A medical practice act defines the scope of practice and role of medical personnel.

157. a. Expressed consent means that the patient gives you permission to treat him or her, either verbally or in writing.

158. c. If a person who needs help refuses to accept it, you should try to persuade the person to accept aid and explain the consequences of refusing it. Only after doing so should you accept and document the refusal of care.

159. c. Although some details of the medical history, such as allergies, surgeries, and medications, are relevant, a detailed history is not. Do not say the patient's name over the radio. Estimated arrival at the hospital is important, but the time of your arrival on the scene is generally not important.

160. b. The function of the safety officer is to evaluate the scene and make the "go/no go" decision for the operation. The safety office is also responsible for continuing to monitor scene safety during the operation.

161. c. There is significant opportunity for the loss of airway control for this patient. A lateral recumbent position will allow passive draining of the airway in case of vomiting, as well as easy access for suctioning.

162. a. Triage must be done before treatment can be properly performed. In many cases, triage and scene assessment activities are in progress by the crew of the first arriving unit. If it is not ongoing, triage should be established first.

163. d. The staging officer's responsibilities include coordinating with police, ensuring access for vehicles, maintaining a log of available units, and coordinating requests for resources. The transportation office will establish the staging area if the incident commander has not already ordered one.

164. c. START stands for Simple Triage And Rapid Treatment and is designed to triage large numbers of patients as quickly as possible.

165. a. Regardless of the triage method utilized, the first step is to direct the walking wounded to a safe place where they can be cared for and reassessed.

166. b. A yellow tag indicates that while the victim's injuries are serious, they are not life threatening in the short term.

167. d. Delayed stress reaction, or post-traumatic stress disorder, is characterized by re-experiencing of the traumatic event and diminished responsiveness to everyday life, as well as physical and cognitive symptoms.

168. b. Duplex can send and receive voice only. UHF and VHF are bandwidth frequencies.

169. c. Sharing your feelings about a stressful event can help relieve them.

170. c. Hyperventilation may result in respiratory alkalosis, a harmful condition to the patient.

171. b. Quickly squeezing a BVM may cause enough pressure to force air into the esophagus. Pressing on the stomach may in fact compromise the airway by causing vomiting to occur.

172. b. A patient with a partial laryngectomy has an ability to exhale through the mouth and nose. Therefore, you will have to close them in order to direct air into the lungs while providing artificial ventilations.

173. b. Because of the possibility of severe blood loss, patients with fractures of the pelvis are most likely to need immediate transport.

174. b. This is a hazardous materials incident until proven otherwise. Do not rush in after fallen rescuers because you may become a victim, too.

175. a. Always wear personal protective equipment to help avoid becoming personally contaminated. Unless you are trained to work in the hot zone, you should not treat anyone until they are properly decontaminated.

176. a. Wearing a gown is considered part of your BSI precautions with emergency childbirth. It may be recommended in some circumstances when cleaning instruments or drawing blood, but is not generally needed.

177. d. Intermediate-level disinfection is used for all instruments and supplies that have come into contact with intact skin.

178. b. Hepatitis B is a blood-borne disease that is transmitted through contact with blood or body secretions.

179. a. Exposure to organophosphate is a major concern. Proper isolation procedures are paramount to rescuer safety. Dispose of all patient clothing according to Environmental Protection Agency guidelines.

180. b. A large dose of atropine sulfate is used to counteract cholinergic poisoning from organophosphates and carbamates.

Paramedic Practice Exam 2

CHAPTER SUMMARY
This is the second of four practice exams in this book based on the National Registry EMT-Paramedic written exam. Having taken one exam already, you should feel more confident in your ability to pick the correct answers. Use this test to see how knowing what to expect makes you feel more prepared.

L IKE THE FIRST exam in this book, this test is based on that of the National Registry of EMTs. It should not, however, look just like the first test you took, because now you know more about how the test is put together. You have seen how different types of questions are presented and are perhaps beginning to notice patterns in the order of questions. You see that questions on each area are grouped together. This pattern will help you develop your own test-taking strategy.

If you're following the advice of this book, you've done some studying between the first exam and this one. This second exam will give you a chance to see how much you've improved. We recommend that you review some more following the grading of this test as well. Don't just concentrate your efforts on the material you are weak in—factually dense material such as that on the NREMT-Paramedic exam calls for comprehensive reinforcement.

For this second exam, pay attention to the different types of questions and the relationship between questions on the same topic. Also, you might want to try timing yourself to get an idea of how long the actual test might take you. The answer sheet follows this page, and the test is followed by the answer key. Pay attention to the answer explanations in the key, especially for the questions you missed.

Exam 2

1.	ⓐ	ⓑ	ⓒ	ⓓ		46.	ⓐ	ⓑ	ⓒ	ⓓ		91.	ⓐ	ⓑ	ⓒ	ⓓ
2.	ⓐ	ⓑ	ⓒ	ⓓ		47.	ⓐ	ⓑ	ⓒ	ⓓ		92.	ⓐ	ⓑ	ⓒ	ⓓ
3.	ⓐ	ⓑ	ⓒ	ⓓ		48.	ⓐ	ⓑ	ⓒ	ⓓ		93.	ⓐ	ⓑ	ⓒ	ⓓ
4.	ⓐ	ⓑ	ⓒ	ⓓ		49.	ⓐ	ⓑ	ⓒ	ⓓ		94.	ⓐ	ⓑ	ⓒ	ⓓ
5.	ⓐ	ⓑ	ⓒ	ⓓ		50.	ⓐ	ⓑ	ⓒ	ⓓ		95.	ⓐ	ⓑ	ⓒ	ⓓ
6.	ⓐ	ⓑ	ⓒ	ⓓ		51.	ⓐ	ⓑ	ⓒ	ⓓ		96.	ⓐ	ⓑ	ⓒ	ⓓ
7.	ⓐ	ⓑ	ⓒ	ⓓ		52.	ⓐ	ⓑ	ⓒ	ⓓ		97.	ⓐ	ⓑ	ⓒ	ⓓ
8.	ⓐ	ⓑ	ⓒ	ⓓ		53.	ⓐ	ⓑ	ⓒ	ⓓ		98.	ⓐ	ⓑ	ⓒ	ⓓ
9.	ⓐ	ⓑ	ⓒ	ⓓ		54.	ⓐ	ⓑ	ⓒ	ⓓ		99.	ⓐ	ⓑ	ⓒ	ⓓ
10.	ⓐ	ⓑ	ⓒ	ⓓ		55.	ⓐ	ⓑ	ⓒ	ⓓ		100.	ⓐ	ⓑ	ⓒ	ⓓ
11.	ⓐ	ⓑ	ⓒ	ⓓ		56.	ⓐ	ⓑ	ⓒ	ⓓ		101.	ⓐ	ⓑ	ⓒ	ⓓ
12.	ⓐ	ⓑ	ⓒ	ⓓ		57.	ⓐ	ⓑ	ⓒ	ⓓ		102.	ⓐ	ⓑ	ⓒ	ⓓ
13.	ⓐ	ⓑ	ⓒ	ⓓ		58.	ⓐ	ⓑ	ⓒ	ⓓ		103.	ⓐ	ⓑ	ⓒ	ⓓ
14.	ⓐ	ⓑ	ⓒ	ⓓ		59.	ⓐ	ⓑ	ⓒ	ⓓ		104.	ⓐ	ⓑ	ⓒ	ⓓ
15.	ⓐ	ⓑ	ⓒ	ⓓ		60.	ⓐ	ⓑ	ⓒ	ⓓ		105.	ⓐ	ⓑ	ⓒ	ⓓ
16.	ⓐ	ⓑ	ⓒ	ⓓ		61.	ⓐ	ⓑ	ⓒ	ⓓ		106.	ⓐ	ⓑ	ⓒ	ⓓ
17.	ⓐ	ⓑ	ⓒ	ⓓ		62.	ⓐ	ⓑ	ⓒ	ⓓ		107.	ⓐ	ⓑ	ⓒ	ⓓ
18.	ⓐ	ⓑ	ⓒ	ⓓ		63.	ⓐ	ⓑ	ⓒ	ⓓ		108.	ⓐ	ⓑ	ⓒ	ⓓ
19.	ⓐ	ⓑ	ⓒ	ⓓ		64.	ⓐ	ⓑ	ⓒ	ⓓ		109.	ⓐ	ⓑ	ⓒ	ⓓ
20.	ⓐ	ⓑ	ⓒ	ⓓ		65.	ⓐ	ⓑ	ⓒ	ⓓ		110.	ⓐ	ⓑ	ⓒ	ⓓ
21.	ⓐ	ⓑ	ⓒ	ⓓ		66.	ⓐ	ⓑ	ⓒ	ⓓ		111.	ⓐ	ⓑ	ⓒ	ⓓ
22.	ⓐ	ⓑ	ⓒ	ⓓ		67.	ⓐ	ⓑ	ⓒ	ⓓ		112.	ⓐ	ⓑ	ⓒ	ⓓ
23.	ⓐ	ⓑ	ⓒ	ⓓ		68.	ⓐ	ⓑ	ⓒ	ⓓ		113.	ⓐ	ⓑ	ⓒ	ⓓ
24.	ⓐ	ⓑ	ⓒ	ⓓ		69.	ⓐ	ⓑ	ⓒ	ⓓ		114.	ⓐ	ⓑ	ⓒ	ⓓ
25.	ⓐ	ⓑ	ⓒ	ⓓ		70.	ⓐ	ⓑ	ⓒ	ⓓ		115.	ⓐ	ⓑ	ⓒ	ⓓ
26.	ⓐ	ⓑ	ⓒ	ⓓ		71.	ⓐ	ⓑ	ⓒ	ⓓ		116.	ⓐ	ⓑ	ⓒ	ⓓ
27.	ⓐ	ⓑ	ⓒ	ⓓ		72.	ⓐ	ⓑ	ⓒ	ⓓ		117.	ⓐ	ⓑ	ⓒ	ⓓ
28.	ⓐ	ⓑ	ⓒ	ⓓ		73.	ⓐ	ⓑ	ⓒ	ⓓ		118.	ⓐ	ⓑ	ⓒ	ⓓ
29.	ⓐ	ⓑ	ⓒ	ⓓ		74.	ⓐ	ⓑ	ⓒ	ⓓ		119.	ⓐ	ⓑ	ⓒ	ⓓ
30.	ⓐ	ⓑ	ⓒ	ⓓ		75.	ⓐ	ⓑ	ⓒ	ⓓ		120.	ⓐ	ⓑ	ⓒ	ⓓ
31.	ⓐ	ⓑ	ⓒ	ⓓ		76.	ⓐ	ⓑ	ⓒ	ⓓ		121.	ⓐ	ⓑ	ⓒ	ⓓ
32.	ⓐ	ⓑ	ⓒ	ⓓ		77.	ⓐ	ⓑ	ⓒ	ⓓ		122.	ⓐ	ⓑ	ⓒ	ⓓ
33.	ⓐ	ⓑ	ⓒ	ⓓ		78.	ⓐ	ⓑ	ⓒ	ⓓ		123.	ⓐ	ⓑ	ⓒ	ⓓ
34.	ⓐ	ⓑ	ⓒ	ⓓ		79.	ⓐ	ⓑ	ⓒ	ⓓ		124.	ⓐ	ⓑ	ⓒ	ⓓ
35.	ⓐ	ⓑ	ⓒ	ⓓ		80.	ⓐ	ⓑ	ⓒ	ⓓ		125.	ⓐ	ⓑ	ⓒ	ⓓ
36.	ⓐ	ⓑ	ⓒ	ⓓ		81.	ⓐ	ⓑ	ⓒ	ⓓ		126.	ⓐ	ⓑ	ⓒ	ⓓ
37.	ⓐ	ⓑ	ⓒ	ⓓ		82.	ⓐ	ⓑ	ⓒ	ⓓ		127.	ⓐ	ⓑ	ⓒ	ⓓ
38.	ⓐ	ⓑ	ⓒ	ⓓ		83.	ⓐ	ⓑ	ⓒ	ⓓ		128.	ⓐ	ⓑ	ⓒ	ⓓ
39.	ⓐ	ⓑ	ⓒ	ⓓ		84.	ⓐ	ⓑ	ⓒ	ⓓ		129.	ⓐ	ⓑ	ⓒ	ⓓ
40.	ⓐ	ⓑ	ⓒ	ⓓ		85.	ⓐ	ⓑ	ⓒ	ⓓ		130.	ⓐ	ⓑ	ⓒ	ⓓ
41.	ⓐ	ⓑ	ⓒ	ⓓ		86.	ⓐ	ⓑ	ⓒ	ⓓ		131.	ⓐ	ⓑ	ⓒ	ⓓ
42.	ⓐ	ⓑ	ⓒ	ⓓ		87.	ⓐ	ⓑ	ⓒ	ⓓ		132.	ⓐ	ⓑ	ⓒ	ⓓ
43.	ⓐ	ⓑ	ⓒ	ⓓ		88.	ⓐ	ⓑ	ⓒ	ⓓ		133.	ⓐ	ⓑ	ⓒ	ⓓ
44.	ⓐ	ⓑ	ⓒ	ⓓ		89.	ⓐ	ⓑ	ⓒ	ⓓ		134.	ⓐ	ⓑ	ⓒ	ⓓ
45.	ⓐ	ⓑ	ⓒ	ⓓ		90.	ⓐ	ⓑ	ⓒ	ⓓ		135.	ⓐ	ⓑ	ⓒ	ⓓ

136.	ⓐ	ⓑ	ⓒ	ⓓ	151.	ⓐ	ⓑ	ⓒ	ⓓ	166.	ⓐ	ⓑ	ⓒ	ⓓ
137.	ⓐ	ⓑ	ⓒ	ⓓ	152.	ⓐ	ⓑ	ⓒ	ⓓ	167.	ⓐ	ⓑ	ⓒ	ⓓ
138.	ⓐ	ⓑ	ⓒ	ⓓ	153.	ⓐ	ⓑ	ⓒ	ⓓ	168.	ⓐ	ⓑ	ⓒ	ⓓ
139.	ⓐ	ⓑ	ⓒ	ⓓ	154.	ⓐ	ⓑ	ⓒ	ⓓ	169.	ⓐ	ⓑ	ⓒ	ⓓ
140.	ⓐ	ⓑ	ⓒ	ⓓ	155.	ⓐ	ⓑ	ⓒ	ⓓ	170.	ⓐ	ⓑ	ⓒ	ⓓ
141.	ⓐ	ⓑ	ⓒ	ⓓ	156.	ⓐ	ⓑ	ⓒ	ⓓ	171.	ⓐ	ⓑ	ⓒ	ⓓ
142.	ⓐ	ⓑ	ⓒ	ⓓ	157.	ⓐ	ⓑ	ⓒ	ⓓ	172.	ⓐ	ⓑ	ⓒ	ⓓ
143.	ⓐ	ⓑ	ⓒ	ⓓ	158.	ⓐ	ⓑ	ⓒ	ⓓ	173.	ⓐ	ⓑ	ⓒ	ⓓ
144.	ⓐ	ⓑ	ⓒ	ⓓ	159.	ⓐ	ⓑ	ⓒ	ⓓ	174.	ⓐ	ⓑ	ⓒ	ⓓ
145.	ⓐ	ⓑ	ⓒ	ⓓ	160.	ⓐ	ⓑ	ⓒ	ⓓ	175.	ⓐ	ⓑ	ⓒ	ⓓ
146.	ⓐ	ⓑ	ⓒ	ⓓ	161.	ⓐ	ⓑ	ⓒ	ⓓ	176.	ⓐ	ⓑ	ⓒ	ⓓ
147.	ⓐ	ⓑ	ⓒ	ⓓ	162.	ⓐ	ⓑ	ⓒ	ⓓ	177.	ⓐ	ⓑ	ⓒ	ⓓ
148.	ⓐ	ⓑ	ⓒ	ⓓ	163.	ⓐ	ⓑ	ⓒ	ⓓ	178.	ⓐ	ⓑ	ⓒ	ⓓ
149.	ⓐ	ⓑ	ⓒ	ⓓ	164.	ⓐ	ⓑ	ⓒ	ⓓ	179.	ⓐ	ⓑ	ⓒ	ⓓ
150.	ⓐ	ⓑ	ⓒ	ⓓ	165.	ⓐ	ⓑ	ⓒ	ⓓ	180.	ⓐ	ⓑ	ⓒ	ⓓ

► Paramedic Exam 2

1. Your patient is a 27-year-old male who has fallen from a 24-foot ladder. As you are approaching and forming your general impression, you note that he is conscious and talking. What should you do first?
   a. Look at his chest to begin assessing the airway.
   b. Manually stabilize his neck in a neutral position.
   c. Palpate for a radial pulse in an uninjured arm.
   d. Palpate for a carotid pulse on one side of his neck.

2. In a motor vehicle crash, which of the following would be most important to understand in relation to the force of collision and the potential for injury?
   a. speed at time of impact
   b. weight of the vehicle
   c. road conditions at the scene
   d. condition of the vehicle's tires

3. You note snoring sounds during your initial assessment of a semiconscious trauma patient. What is your next step?
   a. Manually stabilize the cervical spine.
   b. Perform the chin-lift/jaw-thrust maneuver.
   c. Perform the head-tilt/chin-lift maneuver.
   d. Measure and insert an oropharyngeal airway.

4. A patient with left shoulder pain may have a
   a. bowel obstruction.
   b. pelvic fracture.
   c. pneumothorax.
   d. ruptured spleen.

5. With the START triage method, several vital signs are quickly assessed to determine the order to care for and transport patients. According to the START method, which of the following patients would receive immediate treatment to support hemodynamic status without further assessment?
   a. male, radial pulse present, skin warm and dry
   b. female, radial pulse present, capillary refill time 1 sec
   c. male, radial pulse present, skin pale, and cyanotic
   d. female, radial pulse present, capillary refill time 0.5 sec

6. A patient in compensatory hemorrhagic shock would most likely present with which set of vital signs?
   a. pulse 120 and BP 122/86 mmHg
   b. pulse 80 and BP 118/70 mmHg
   c. pulse 64 and BP 72/50 mmHg
   d. pulse 58 and BP 212/120 mmHg

7. A patient has fallen off a 20-foot ladder, striking his back on a railing. He is experiencing pain at the injury site and a loss of bladder control. Which part of the spinal cord is most like affected by this mechanism?
   a. coccyx
   b. cervical
   c. sacral
   d. lumbar

8. An unrestrained driver of a small car struck a tree at high speed. He has a distended abdomen that is tender when palpated. Vital signs are pulse, 120 beats per minute; respirations, 20 per minute; and blood pressure, 116/90 mmHg. What would be the most likely cause of the abdominal tenderness?
   a. bacterial peritonitis
   b. abdominal muscle strain
   c. organ damage
   d. seat belt injury

9. Where would you expect to see a wound that is described as distal to the knee?
   a. hip
   b. stomach
   c. thigh
   d. calf

Answer questions 10–13 on the basis of the following information.

You respond to a 63-year-old male who is complaining of sudden onset of extreme substernal chest pain that, he says, "feels like my insides are tearing." The patient states that the pain radiates to the middle of his back between his shoulder blades.

10. Which condition is this patient most likely suffering from?
   a. dissecting aortic aneurysm
   b. abdominal aortic aneurysm
   c. acute arterial occlusion
   d. acute pulmonary embolism

11. Which of the following is a predisposing factor for this patient's condition?
   a. hypotension
   b. hypertension
   c. angina pectoris
   d. myocardial infarction

12. Which of the following medications may be ordered by medical control to treat this patient?
   a. dopamine
   b. atropine sulfate
   c. morphine sulfate
   d. isoproterenol

13. Progression of this condition may cause
   a. stroke, pericardial tamponade, acute myocardial infarction.
   b. acute arterial occlusion, acute pulmonary embolism, encephalitis.
   c. deep venous thrombosis, varicose veins, arterial atherosclerotic disease.
   d. arterial atherosclerotic disease, pulmonary embolism, acute arterial occlusion.

14. Your patient has survived a vehicle rollover in which another passenger in the vehicle died. He is alert and not complaining of pain. His vital signs are: pulse, 100; systolic BP, 90; respirations, 28. What additional procedures are required prior to initiating transport?
   a. Complete a detailed physical exam and stabilize his injuries, and then transport.
   b. Quickly immobilize him using the long back board as a splint, and then transport.
   c. Perform a focused physical exam, splint all extremity fractures, and then transport.
   d. Immobilize first, complete a focused physical exam of any injuries, and then transport.

15. Which statement about motorcycle crashes is correct?
   a. They seldom result in severe trauma, unless operated at high speeds.
   b. Helmet use can reduce the incidence and severity of head injury.
   c. Helmet use can reduce the incidence and severity of spinal injury.
   d. Leather clothing cannot protect the rider against soft-tissue injury.

16. What is a positive Battle's sign an indication of?
   a. basilar skull fracture
   b. orbital skull fracture
   c. subarachnoid hemorrhage
   d. cervical spinal trauma

17. A contrecoup contusion is a brain injury that
   a. results from cerebral edema at the site of impact.
   b. causes subdural or epidural hematoma formation.
   c. is on the opposite side of the head from the impact site.
   d. results from open skull fracture and brain bruising.

18. Your patient is a car crash victim who was unconscious prior to your arrival, but is now awake. As you examine the patient, you notice that he is becoming disoriented. What should you suspect?
   a. basilar skull fracture
   b. epidural hematoma formation
   c. concussion with awakening
   d. inner-ear injury

19. Your trauma patient opens her eyes, pulls her hand away when pinched, and speaks only in garbled sounds. What is her Glasgow Coma Scale score?
   a. 5
   b. 7
   c. 9
   d. 11

20. Your trauma patient is agitated and apprehensive. She is increasingly cyanotic, and breath sounds are rapidly diminishing over her left lung. She is exhibiting signs and symptoms of shock. You should suspect
   a. hemothorax.
   b. tension pneumothorax.
   c. cardiac tamponade.
   d. flail chest.

21. A child has third-degree burns over the front of her trunk and the entire front of her right leg. According to the rule of nines, what percentage of her body surface area is affected?
   a. $18\frac{1}{2}$%
   b. $22\frac{1}{2}$%
   c. 25%
   d. 33%

22. Your patient is a 34-year-old woman who has been in an automobile crash. Her respiratory rate is 34 with normal chest wall expansion; systolic blood pressure is 78; capillary refill is delayed; and her Glasgow Coma Scale score is 10. This patient's Revised Trauma Score score is
   a. 5.
   b. 6.
   c. 9.
   d. 10.

23. Which group of vital sign changes is associated with Cushing's reflex?
   a. decreased blood pressure, decreased pulse rate, decreased respiratory rate, decreased temperature
   b. increased blood pressure, decreased pulse rate, decreased respiratory rate, increased temperature
   c. decreased blood pressure, increased pulse rate, increased respiratory rate, decreased temperature
   d. increased blood pressure, increased pulse rate, increased respiratory rate, increased temperature

24. Which of the following is the best way to examine a patient with abdominal pain?
   a. Begin palpation at the spot indicated as being the most painful.
   b. Begin palpation of all four quadrants ending with the painful area.
   c. Begin auscultation and percussion away from the site of the pain.
   d. Begin auscultation and percussion at the site of the pain.

25. You suspect that a trauma patient has a pelvic injury. She is cool and diaphoretic, with a heart rate of 134 and blood pressure of 100/72. Which of the following procedures is most appropriate in the management of her condition?
   a. two large bore IVs run wide open
   b. application of the PASG
   c. transport in a position of comfort
   d. perform the detailed assessment prior to transport

26. Your medical patient is a 58-year-old woman who complains of severe abdominal pain. The tilt test is positive. In which position should you place this patient for transport?
   a. high Fowler's position
   b. left lateral recumbent position
   c. right-sided fetal position
   d. supine position with knees flexed

27. What does *ascites* refer to?
   a. chronic alcoholism
   b. fluid in the abdomen
   c. severe abdominal pain
   d. a ruptured aortic aneurysm

28. Which type of hepatitis is spread via the fecal or oral route?
   a. hepatitis A
   b. hepatitis B
   c. hepatitis C
   d. hepatitis D

29. Your patient is a 60-year-old woman who has fallen down her front steps and has possibly fractured her ankle. Which assessment finding may be considered abnormal in this patient?
   a. altered mental status
   b. respirations regular
   c. pulse 68 and regular
   d. blood pressure 128/86

30. Which of the following drugs does NOT commonly cause toxicity in elderly patients?
   a. lidocaine
   b. nitroglycerin
   c. digitalis
   d. theophylline

31. Which dysrhythmia is considered normal in an athletic adult?
   a. sinus bradycardia
   b. sinus arrest
   c. atrial fibrillation
   d. first-degree AV block

32. Which statement about the vital signs of a patient with an AMI is correct?
   a. Respiratory and pulse rates will be elevated, while blood pressure will be depressed.
   b. Vital signs are insignificant because management depends on the underlying heart rhythm.
   c. Vital signs vary greatly since they are related to the area and extent of cardiac damage.
   d. Elevated respiratory and pulse rates are generally associated with a favorable prognosis.

33. A patient has been stabbed in the back. Which of the following signs would most likely make you suspect that the patient has a kidney injury?
   a. abdominal tenderness
   b. hematuria
   c. thirst
   d. ecchymosis to the flank

34. Your patient is a 24-year-old female who shows signs and symptoms of pelvic inflammatory disease. What is the goal of prehospital care for this patient?
   a. Begin definitive therapy on the scene prior to initiating your transport.
   b. Perform a complete physical exam to identify associated medical problems.
   c. Make the patient as comfortable as possible and transport to the hospital.
   d. Begin the identification of all the patient's previous sexual contacts.

35. Which of the following factors would normally cause a decrease in a patient's respiratory rate?
   a. anxiety
   b. sleep
   c. fever
   d. hypoxia

36. While ventilating a patient with a bag-valve mask, you note decreasing compliance. How should you react to this finding?
   a. Stop using the bag-valve mask and intubate the patient.
   b. Request permission to sedate the patient with morphine.
   c. Assess the cause of this finding and try to correct it.
   d. Continue ventilation with BVM; this is a normal finding.

37. What would a pulse oximetry reading of 88 percent indicate for your patient with acute respiratory distress?
   a. normal oxygenation
   b. mild hypoxia
   c. moderate hypoxia
   d. severe hypoxia

38. The primary use of the Magill forceps in the field is to
   a. directly remove a visible foreign body obstruction.
   b. open the airway of a patient with suspected neck trauma.
   c. move the tongue aside during attempts at intubation.
   d. aid in removal of an esophageal obturator airway in the field.

39. Which of the following signs most likely indicates imminent birth?
- **a.** painful uterine contractions
- **b.** urge to have a bowel movement
- **c.** ruptured membranes
- **d.** dilation of the cervix

40. Which of the following is a sign of esophageal intubation?
- **a.** air leak heard over the trachea
- **b.** breath sounds absent on the left
- **c.** bilateral chest wall expansion
- **d.** abdominal movement with ventilation

Answer questions 41–42 on the basis of the following information.

You are called to the home of a 68-year-old female who is complaining of severe dyspnea. She states that it started about 45 minutes ago and has been getting progressively worse. She has a cardiac history but denies chest pain at this time. Her breathing is very congested. During your assessment, you notice accessory muscle use and rales bilaterally.

41. Which of the following conditions is this patient most likely suffering from?
- **a.** pulmonary embolism
- **b.** acute pulmonary edema
- **c.** pneumonia
- **d.** lung cancer

42. In addition to oxygen, this patient should also be treated with which of the following medications?
- **a.** albuterol
- **b.** dopamine
- **c.** lidocaine
- **d.** morphine sulfate

43. A pregnant patient complains of painful, irregular labor contractions. The patient states that she is 37 weeks pregnant and her amniotic membranes ruptured two days ago. Based on this information, you would
- **a.** perform a field delivery.
- **b.** initiate immediate transport.
- **c.** inform the patient that she is experiencing Braxton-Hicks contractions.
- **d.** tell the patient to call when her contractions become regular.

44. What is the primary treatment of metabolic acidosis?
- **a.** having the patient rebreathe his own carbon dioxide
- **b.** ventilating the patient adequately with oxygen
- **c.** administering sodium bicarbonate IV 1.0 mEq/kg
- **d.** determining and treating the underlying cause

45. Which drug is an example of a beta 2 agonist?
- **a.** aminophylline
- **b.** ipratropium
- **c.** labetalol
- **d.** albuterol

46. What is the condition that is present when the pleural space expands because air enters from an interior wound?
- **a.** a closed pneumothorax
- **b.** an open pneumothorax
- **c.** a tension pneumothorax
- **d.** traumatic asphyxia

47. Which of the following statements is true in regard to the prehospital management of a very ill neonate?
   a. Early placement of a tracheal tube is critical in early respiratory distress.
   b. High-flow oxygen carries a risk of oxygen toxicity.
   c. Interventions should be performed for 30 seconds prior to re-evaluation.
   d. Allow the parent to hold the infant during treatment.

48. What does the term *stridor* refer to?
   a. a rattling sound associated with fluid in the upper airway
   b. a whistling sound heard upon expiration in asthma patients
   c. a gurgling sound resulting from fluid in the lower airways
   d. a high-pitched sound upon inspiration from airway obstruction

49. A patient who is 37 weeks pregnant is having contractions and states that her water broke about 20 minutes ago. The vaginal exam reveals that the baby's foot is present in the birth canal. Your next action would be to
   a. move the patient to the cot and initiate rapid transport.
   b. turn the mother onto her stomach and prepare for a field delivery.
   c. apply downward pressure on the symphysis pubis to delay delivery.
   d. place the mother on her left side and prepare for a field delivery.

50. What is the primary treatment for a patient with chronic emphysema who is NOT severely hypoxic?
   a. ventilating with high-flow oxygen via mask
   b. administering low-flow oxygen via cannula
   c. nasotracheal intubation and high-flow oxygen
   d. orotracheal intubation and high-flow oxygen

51. Epinephrine 1:1,000 may be indicated in
   a. asthma.
   b. epiglottitis.
   c. pertussis.
   d. emphysema.

52. You are on the scene of a vehicle crash involving a bus. As triage officer, the first patient you encounter is sitting on the ground, conscious, confused, and breathing 40 times per minute. She states that she was thrown out of her seat and struck the side of her head. Your next action would be to
   a. apply oxygen by nonrebreather mask.
   b. check the radial pulse rate.
   c. classify the patient as "Immediate" (red).
   d. apply a "Hold" (green) triage tag.

Answer questions 53–55 on the basis of the following information.

You are called to the home of a 17-year-old female who was found by her parents hanging from a rope in the garage. The patient was cut down by her father approximately six minutes prior to your arrival, but she is unconscious and unresponsive to pain or voice. She is breathing spontaneously but has coarse inspiratory stridor.

53. What is the most probable cause of the inspiratory stridor?
- **a.** a trachea that is crushed or torn
- **b.** a cervical spine lesion from trauma
- **c.** bronchoconstriction due to trauma
- **c.** a foreign-body airway obstruction

54. Upon examination of the patient's upper chest and neck, you note the presence of a large swollen area that extends from her throat to her shoulder. When you press on this area, you feel crackles under the skin. What is this condition called?
- **a.** traumatic asphyxia
- **b.** laryngeal crepitus
- **c.** subcutaneous emphysema
- **d.** subcutaneous embolism

55. Which of the following is an appropriate treatment for this patient?
- **a.** crychothyrotomy or trastracheal jet insufflation
- **b.** airway management by the least invasive means
- **c.** larygoscopy to determine the extent of damage
- **d.** administer epinephrine to reverse airway swelling

56. Your partner and you are evaluating a patient experiencing a behavioral emergency. Your patient is visibly upset and is pacing back and forth. He is verbally confrontational, and his hands are in fists. At times, he displays aggressive actions, both physical and verbal. Which of the following actions is most appropriate for this situation?
- **a.** Observe the scene for danger.
- **b.** Conduct a patient assessment.
- **c.** Obtain information from bystanders.
- **d.** Physically restrain the patient.

57. A critically traumatized 18-year-old male is entrapped. It will be at least 15 minutes before he is freed. The community hospital is 20 minutes away by ground. A medical helicopter can be to the scene in eight minutes. A Level I trauma center is one hour away by ground. Given the situation, which is the best mode of transport for this patient?
- **a.** Transport the patient by ground to the community hospital, and then transfer the patient to the trauma center by air.
- **b.** Transport the patient by ground to the Level I trauma center.
- **c.** Fly the patient from the scene to the community hospital.
- **d.** Fly the patient from the scene to the Level I trauma center.

58. What is the first sign of laryngeal edema in a patient suffering from anaphylaxis?
- **a.** wheezing
- **b.** coughing
- **c.** hoarseness
- **d.** dyspnea

59. What does the disease process of emphysema cause within the lung tissues?
- **a.** a build-up of fluid due to increased capillary permeability
- **b.** deflation of a portion of the lung due to the rupture of a bleb
- **c.** bronchoconstriction due to increased airway resistance
- **d.** a loss of elasticity in the alveoli due to prolonged insult

Answer questions 60–65 on the basis of the following information.

You are called to the home of a 78-year-old male who is having difficulty breathing. The patient is sitting upright in a tripod position and you note profound accessory muscle use. His skin is pale, cool, and clammy. Vital signs are: blood pressure, 180/72; heart rate, 90; and respiratory rate, 40. Breathing is shallow and labored with a coarse rattling sound during expiration. Auscultation reveals coarse rales to the nipple line with no air movement in the bases. The patient can speak only in one- or two-word sentences. Family members inform you that the patient was sleeping when this episode began and that this has happened several times since his AMI one year ago. He has mild pedal edema and neck veins are nondistended. His family first noticed the patient having dyspnea about 25–30 minutes ago.

60. This patient is exhibiting the signs and symptoms of which of the following diseases?
   a. chronic bronchitis
   b. emphysema
   c. congestive heart failure
   d. status asthmaticus

61. Which medication should be used for this patient?
   a. albuterol
   b. nitrous oxide
   c. dobutaine
   d. morphine sulfate

62. A patient with the symptoms and history described may exhibit which of the following symptoms prior to an acute onset?
   a. orthostatic hypotension
   b. paroxysmal nocturnal dyspnea
   c. cough and fever
   d. headache

63. Priorities for the management of this patient include all of the following EXCEPT
   a. decreasing venous return to the heart.
   b. increasing venous return to the heart.
   c. decreasing myocardial oxygen demand.
   d. improving oxygenation and ventilation.

64. This patient would most likely benefit from which of the following?
   a. moving him to a supine position
   b. assisting him in walking to the ambulance
   c. having him breathe deeply into a paper bag
   d. giving him intermittent positive pressure ventilation

65. If this patient were experiencing right-side heart failure, you would expect to find all of the following symptoms EXCEPT
   a. tachycardia.
   b. profound peripheral edema.
   c. jugular venous distention.
   d. syncope.

66. When performing water related rescues, use of personal flotation device is required when
   a. the water is greater than three feet deep.
   b. rough water is present.
   c. the rescuer weighs less than 150 pounds.
   d. the rescuer enters any and all water.

67. An isotonic solution is one that
   a. has an electrolyte composition like that of blood plasma.
   b. is used only in patients who are severely dehydrated.
   c. has a higher solute composition than the body cells.
   d. has a lower solute composition than the body cells.

68. What is the most common cause of cardiogenic shock?
   a. cervical spinal cord injury
   b. severe allergic reaction
   c. left ventricular failure
   d. internal or external hemorrhage

69. The use of PASG/MAST is indicated for which of the following conditions?
   a. to control uterine bleeding in a pregnant patient with abruptio placentae
   b. to prevent shock in a patient with uncontrollable bleeding in the neck
   c. to support the respiratory efforts of a patient with severe dyspnea
   d. to stabilize lower-extremity fractures in a hypotensive patient

70. A patient has been violently beaten. Which of the following statements is true surrounding the care provided by EMS?
   a. Evidence preservation is the first priority.
   b. Latex gloves will prevent you from smudging fingerprints.
   c. Statements made by the patient should be recorded in the report.
   d. Bloody clothing should be placed in plastic bags.

71. Which statement about use of the PASG/MAST during the treatment of a shock patient with an impaled object in the abdomen is correct?
   a. Do not use the PASG/MAST for the treatment of any patient with an impaled object.
   b. Inflate the lower compartments of the PASG/MAST, then re-evaluate for abdominal use.
   c. Request medical direction before inflating the legs of the PASG/MAST in this situation.
   d. Remove the object following medical consultation, and then inflate the abdominal section only.

72. When administering IV fluids to a trauma patient it is critical to continuously monitor which vital sign?
   a. breath sounds
   b. capillary refill
   c. blood pressure
   d. pupillary response

73. Why is morphine sulfate used in the management of AMI patients?
   a. to help distinguish between angina pectoris and AMI
   b. to relieve pain and reduce myocardial oxygen demand
   c. to decrease the likelihood of ventricular dysrhythmias
   d. as an alternative therapy for patients allergic to lidocaine

74. Paroxysmal nocturnal dyspnea (PND) is commonly a sign of which of the following conditions?
   a. myocardial infarction
   b. ruptured aortic aneurysm
   c. left side heart failure
   d. right side heart failure

75. Management of left-side heart failure includes high-flow oxygen, IV of crystalloid solution, ECG monitoring, and the administration of which pharamcological agents?
 a. beta blockers and furosemide
 b. morphine sulfate and nitroglycerin
 c. nifedipine and sodium nitroprusside
 d. labetalol and norepinephrine

76. You are inserting the tracheal tube when you begin to hear the sound of the patient's breathing. Your next action would be to
 a. inflate the distal cuff and secure the tube.
 b. wait for the patient to inhale and insert the tube further.
 c. pull back on the tube and secure with tape.
 d. attach an end-tidal CO_2 detector to confirm placement.

77. What is the initial electrical treatment for a patient with third-degree AV block who is symptomatic?
 a. insertion of a demand pacemaker
 b. unsynchronized cardioversion
 c. transcutaneous cardiac pacing
 d. synchronized cardioversion

78. A patient suspected of having an abdominal aortic aneurysm will receive oxygen, an IV, ECG monitoring, and rapid transport as part of his or her treatment. What else should you do when treating such a patient?
 a. apply the PASG/MAST garment
 b. carefully palpate the abdomen
 c. administer dopamine or dobutamine
 d. administer SL nifedipine

79. A 52-year-old male has been ejected from a car. He is apneic, with a slow pulse palpated at the femoral artery. Which of the following procedures would best manage this patient's airway?
 a. Nasotracheally intubate the patient.
 b. Ventilate with the bag mask and attach to high-flow oxygen.
 c. Apply a nonrebreather mask with high-flow oxygen.
 d. Perform immediate orotracheal intubation.

80. Vagal maneuvers are used to treat which type of dysrhythmias?
 a. premature atrial contractions
 b. ventricular tachycardia
 c. atrial fibrillation or flutter
 d. paroxysmal supraventricular tachycardia

81. Which part of the ECG tracing reflects repolarization of the ventricles?
 a. P wave
 b. QRS complex
 c. R wave
 d. T wave

82. The length of the normal P-R interval is
 a. 0.04–0.12 seconds.
 b. 0.12–0.20 seconds.
 c. 0.20–0.28 seconds.
 d. 0.28–0.36 seconds.

83. A 3-year-old female is unresponsive and not breathing. Parents state that she was eating grapes when she suddenly made a high-pitched whistling noise and turned blue. Your immediate action would be
 a. provide back blows and chest thrusts.
 b. start cardiopulmonary resuscitation.
 c. perform endotracheal intubation.
 d. perform abdominal thrusts.

84. Your patient postures in response to painful stimuli and has snoring respirations. Which of the following would best establish an airway?
  a. modified jaw thrust
  b. tongue jaw lift
  c. head-tilt/neck-lift
  d. neutral plus position

85. In a patient with ventricular tachycardia, the QRS complex is
  a. absent during the cardiac cycle.
  b. 0.04 and 0.12 seconds in duration.
  c. greater than 0.12 seconds and bizarre in shape.
  d. shorter than 0.04 seconds and flattened.

86. A patient with nonperfusing ventricular tachycardia would receive the same treatment as a patient with which other rhythm?
  a. ventricular fibrillation
  b. perfusing ventricular tachycardia
  c. atrial tachycardia
  d. asystole

87. Which of the following indicates that an AMI patient is developing cardiogenic shock?
  a. increasing pain
  b. narrowing pulse pressure
  c. falling blood pressure
  d. sinus bradycardia

88. Which of the following are signs and symptoms of right-side heart failure?
  a. tachycardia, peripheral edema, and jugular vein distention
  b. bradycardia, carotid bruits, and falling blood pressure
  c. respiratory distress, hypoxia, and cyanosis
  d. chest pain, pulmonary edema, and anxiety

89. Which of the following is often the first sign of the onset of the development of a potentially lethal dysrhythmia in an MI patient?
  a. changing pulse rate
  b. increasing pain
  c. loss of consciousness
  d. narrowing pulse pressure

90. Why are easing anxiety and relieving pain considered major goals for prehospital care of MI patients?
  a. The onset of either may signal the development of a lethal dysrhythmia.
  b. Anxiety and pain often mask underlying symptoms of cardiogenic shock.
  c. They may prevent the patient from cooperating with additional treatments.
  d. Both anxiety and pain increase heart rate and myocardial oxygen demand.

91. Dopamine can be used to
  a. decrease oxygen demand.
  b. increase cardiac output.
  c. reduce blood pressure.
  d. prevent dysrhythmias.

92. A patient is short of breath after impact with the steering wheel in a motor vehicle crash. Breath sounds are diminished on the left. Which of the following conditions is most likely the cause of the patient's complaint?
  a. simple pneumothorax
  b. tension pneumothorax
  c. pulmonary contusion
  d. cardiac tamponade

93. Which of the following is a possible cause of pulseless electrical activity?
   a. right-side heart failure
   b. tachycardia
   c. hypovolemia
   d. hypokalemia

94. Some treatments for suspected MI patients mask the elevated cardiac enzyme levels that are used to diagnose MI in the hospital setting. To prevent this, you should NOT administer
   a. transcutaneous pacing.
   b. any drugs via the IM route.
   c. any nebulized beta agonists.
   d. diazepam or morphine sulfate IV.

95. Your patient is a 67-year-old male who is complaining of chest pain. The chest pain continues after two doses of nitroglycerin. He reports a history of angina and says that all his previous attacks have been relieved by nitroglycerin. How should you treat this patient?
   a. Take a detailed history to determine why this episode is different.
   b. Treat the patient as though he is having an AMI and transport rapidly.
   c. Look for signs and symptoms of decreased perfusion or cardiogenic shock.
   d. Assume that his medication has expired and give two more doses from yours.

96. What is the most common complication of an acute myocardial infarction?
   a. the onset of cardiogenic shock
   b. occurrence of unstable angina
   c. the onset of a dysrhythmia
   d. increased intermittent chest pain

97. In addition to oxygen, what is the first-line pharmacologic agent used for the treatment of malignant PVCs?
   a. lidocaine
   b. bretylium
   c. procainamide
   d. magnesium sulfate

98. Which of these following rhythms might indicate a need for cardioversion?
   a. atrial fibrillation at a rate of 120
   b. junctional tachycardia at a rate of 120
   c. wandering atrial pacemaker at a rate of 120
   d. ventricular tachycardia at a rate of 120

99. Your patient, who has had a recent tracheostomy, tried to remove himself from the ventilator and dislodged the trach cannula. Subcutaneous emphysema is now evident. What should you do next?
   a. Remove the tracheostomy and attempt to reinsert it.
   b. Remove the tracheostomy tube and insert an endotracheal tube.
   c. Deflate the tracheostomy cuff and ventilate around it with a BVM.
   d. Continue to ventilate the patient through the tracheostomy tube.

Answer questions 100–102 on the basis of the following information.

You are called by the police department to a neighborhood where you encounter a male patient approximately 20–30 years old. The police officer states that neighbors called because the patient was "freaking out." Witnesses say they saw him smoking something just before he started acting in a bizarre manner. During your assessment, you notice that the patient is hyperactive and anxious. His pupils are dilated, and he is hypertensive and tachycardic.

100. This patient is most likely experiencing
   a. insulin shock.
   b. cocaine ingestion.
   c. narcotic ingestion.
   d. delirium tremens.

101. The appropriate treatment for this patient consists of oxygen, IV, ECG monitoring, and
   a. transport.
   b. naloxone.
   c. activated charcoal.
   d. syrup of ipecac.

102. When treating this patient, you should be prepared for which of the following complications?
   a. tachycardia and septic shock
   b. CNS depression and hypoglycemia
   c. dysrhythmias and seizures
   d. bradycardia and tachypnea

103. Your patient is in respiratory distress. He is exhibiting jugular venous distension. Crackles are auscultated throughout his lung fields. He is tachycardic, hypertensive, and tachypneic. Which of the following sets of treatment is indicated for this patient's presentation?
   a. oxygen, morphine sulfate IM, intravenous line at 30 cc/hour, and 40 mg furosemide IV
   b. oxygen, intravenous line at 30 cc/hour, nitroglycerin sL, and 40 mg furosemide IV
   c. oxygen, saline lock, and 2 mg morphine sulfate IV
   d. oxygen, sublingual nitroglycerin, and 40 mg furosemide IM

104. A patient is complaining of chest pressure and shortness of breath. He has jugular venous distension and pedal edema. His lung sounds are clear and equal. Which of the following conditions is most likely causes these findings?
   a. left-sided heart failure
   b. right-sided heart failure
   c. pulmonary embolus
   d. cardiac asthma

105. Your patient has a suspected hand injury. How can you best immobilize the hand in the position of function?
   a. Tape it flat against the chest with the fingers extended outward together.
   b. Put the arm into a sling and swathe and allow the hand to dangle naturally.
   c. Place a roll of gauze bandage into the palm and secure the hand to a splint.
   d. Secure the hand to a padded splint with the hand clenched into a fist.

106. When splinting a limb with a suspected fracture, one caregiver applies the splint while another
   a. holds the limb and monitors distal pulse, motor, and sensation.
   b. calms, reassures, and provides emotional support to the patient.
   c. checks for limb alignment and administers high-flow oxygen.
   d. gets the stretcher or other supplies and monitors vital signs.

107. You are caring for a patient whose finger was just cut off in an accident. What should you do with the amputated finger?
   a. Place the severed finger in a plastic bag and immerse the bag in cold water.
   b. Immerse the severed finger directly into a pail of ice cold normal saline solution.
   c. Bandage the severed finger in sterile gauze and place it in a plastic bag with ice.
   d. Bandage the hand with the severed finger placed back into its normal position.

108. Which of the following is NOT characteristic of a mild or moderate pit viper envenomation?
   a. bruising located around the wound site
   b. systemic effects like nausea or vomiting
   c. localized edema at the wound site
   d. little or no pain felt by the patient

109. How should you treat a patient who has sustained dry lime burns to the hand and arm?
   a. Use a neutralizing acid to offset the effect of the chemical burn.
   b. Brush the lime away and then flood the skin with cool water.
   c. Immediately immerse the injured limb in a pail of cold water.
   d. Use alcohol to dissolve the lime, and then flood with cool water.

110. A patient in a very early stage of hypoglycemia may complain of
   a. drowsiness.
   b. dry mouth.
   c. nausea.
   d. hunger.

111. Diabetic patients may develop hypoglycemia if they take too much insulin or if they
   a. exercise too much with limited food intake.
   b. overeat and do not exercise enough.
   c. sit in a chair for prolonged periods of time.
   d. inject their insulin directly into a vein.

112. With which of the following conditions is central neurogenic hyperventilation commonly associated?
   a. diabetes mellitus
   b. CNS trauma
   c. pulmonary edema
   d. COPD

113. A patient is in respiratory distress. She has a valid DNR order. Which of the following treatments is correct?
   a. Nothing should be done to the patient in this situation.
   b. Provide oxygen and a nebulized albuterol treatment.
   c. Administer 2 L of oxygen via a nasal cannula.
   d. Initiate a direct laryngoscopy and intubation.

114. You have secured the airway and immobilized the cervical spine for your patient with an altered mental status. What is your next priority of care?
   a. Draw blood for glucose assessment and establish an IV.
   b. Assess DCAP-BTLS looking for any hidden injuries.
   c. Administer naloxone via the IV and IM glucagon.
   d. Hyperventilate with O2 and administer dexamethasone.

115. You are called to the home of a 36-year-old man who is having a seizure. His wife reports that he has not taken his "seizure pills" lately and that he has now had three seizures in a row without regaining consciousness. You have secured the airway and are now ventilating with the bag-valve mask. What should you do next?
   a. Draw blood, administer dextrose, and transport immediately.
   b. Monitor blood glucose level and administer naloxone and thiamine.
   c. Secure the patient to a long spine board until the seizures are over.
   d. Begin an IV, monitor cardiac rhythm, and administer diazepam.

116. What is the primary treatment for severe anaphylaxis in an adult?
   a. 0.3–0.5 mg of epinephrine 1:10,000 given intravenously
   b. 0.1–0.3 mg of epinephrine 1:10,000 given subcutaneously
   c. 0.3–0.5 mg of epinephrine 1:1,000 given intravenously
   d. 0.1–0.3 mg of epinephrine 1:1,000 given subcutaneously

117. An adult patient has overdosed on an unknown medication as a suicidal gesture. She is alert, oriented, and refusing treatment and transport. What is your most appropriate next action?
   a. Obtained a signed refusal from the patient
   b. Advise the patient that she will die if not treated.
   c. Restrain her and transport to the emergency department.
   d. Consult with medical direction to transport the patient.

118. Which of the following patients is considered to be at high risk for a heat-related emergency?
   a. 29-year-old amputee
   b. 48-year-old police officer
   c. 17-year-old athlete
   d. 78-year-old diabetic

119. A late sign of hypoxia in children is
   a. tachypnea.
   b. hypotension.
   c. tachycardia.
   d. bradycardia.

120. What is the most important treatment consideration for a patient who is suffering from decompression sickness?
   a. Have suction equipment ready because vomiting is common.
   b. Monitor the ECG and be prepared to defibrillate as necessary.
   c. Provide high-concentration oxygen with a nonrebreather mask.
   d. Administer Nitronox or morphine sulfate as needed to control pain.

121. When interviewing patients who are distraught or potentially violent, you should do all of the following EXCEPT
   a. remove the patient from the crisis situation as quickly as possible.
   b. encourage the patient to explain the situation in his or her own words.
   c. firmly tell the patient whenever he or she is distorting reality.
   d. avoid arguing with or shouting at the person who is distraught.

122. What term best describes a patient who talks nonstop and is restless and overactive?
   a. manic
   b. depressed
   c. demented
   d. schizophrenic

123. Lifting improperly may most likely result in an injury to which part of the back?
   a. cervical
   b. thoracic
   c. lumbar
   d. sacral

124. After experiencing a sudden syncopal episode, a 41-year-old female is complaining of pleuritic chest pain and shortness of breath. Her vital signs are RR = 28, P = 126, and BP = 88/60. The pulse oximeter reads 89% on high-flow oxygen. Her breath sounds are clear. Which of the following conditions best describes the patient's signs and symptoms?
   a. pulmonary embolism
   b. pulmonary edema
   c. chronic bronchitis
   d. acute asthma

125. What is the management for a patient with a head injury and an unusual respiratory pattern?
   a. positioning in the left lateral recumbent position
   b. administration of oxygen and methyprednisolone
   c. rapid transport because of possible brain stem injury
   d. intubation and hyperventilation to reduce ICP

Answer questions 126–127 on the basis of the following information.

You respond to a 56-year-old male who appears to be intoxicated. He is belligerent and disoriented and has a laceration on his forehead. You have made several attempts to convince him of the need for treatment, but he refuses treatment or transport.

126. Given this situation, you should
   a. let him sign a refusal form and return to service.
   b. call medical direction for advice and guidance.
   c. transport the patient against his will in restraints.
   d. bandage the laceration, then leave the scene.

127. Regardless of any of the options considered in the previous question, the patient continues to insist he does not need medical attention. In this situation, which of the following is most important?
   a. Obtain a signed refusal form and return to service as soon as possible.
   b. Continue to insist that the patient accompany you to the hospital for care.
   c. Properly document your advice to the patient and his continued refusal.
   d. Restrain the patient in the supine position and transport him immediately.

128. You are called to treat a patient who is unconscious and responsive to painful stimuli only. Which of the following treatment modalities is appropriate for this patient?
   a. 25 gm of 50% dextrose slow IV push, 2 mg naloxone IV, and transport to a detoxification center
   b. blood glucose test, dextrose (if indicated), thiamine, monitor, oxygen, IV, and rapid transport
   c. oxygen, IV fluid bolus titrated to a systolic BP of 100–110 mmHg, naloxone, and rapid transport
   d. 1,000 cc Ringer's lactate IV, oxygen, ECG monitoring, and transport to an emergency department

129. During a basketball game, an 18-year-old male is complaining of sudden shortness of breath and sharp chest pain that increases with inspiration. He is alert, warm, and diaphoretic. His vital signs are RR = 24, P = 100, and BP = 122/84. His breath sounds are diminished in the lower right lung field. He denies any medical history, does not smoke, and takes no medication. Which of the following conditions best describes the patient's signs and symptoms?
   a. pulmonary embolism
   b. simple pneumothorax
   c. asthma
   d. COPD

130. A 64-year-old male complains of weakness and dizziness. He is anxious, with a patent airway with adequate breathing. The pulse is rapid and skin cool and diaphoretic. Auscultation of the lung reveals bilateral rales. His vital signs are pulse, 156; respirations, 28 per minute; blood pressure, 82/60 mmHg; and SpO$_2$ 92%. His EKG reveals narrow QRS complexes that are strangely irregular. P waves are difficult or impossible to find. The best treatment for this patient is to
   a. decrease the atrial rate.
   b. restore a normal sinus rhythm.
   c. decrease the ventricular rate.
   d. increase cardiac contractility.

131. A patient with a history of emphysema is short of breath, tachycardic, and confused. Which of the following actions would be most appropriate?
   a. Provide low levels of oxygen to prevent respiratory arrest or depression caused by high-flow oxygen in this COPD patient.
   b. Provide positive pressure ventilations with a BVM on room air only.
   c. Minimal oxygen is required if saturation readings from the pulse oximeter are greater than 85%.
   d. Provide high-flow oxygen and support ventilations as you would with non-COPD patients.

132. Why are children particularly prone to head injuries?
a. because they have small airways in comparison to their head size
b. because they have large tongues in relation to their airway size
c. because of an inability to balance and use their small muscle groups
d. because of their larger sized heads in relation to their body size

133. Your patient is a 4-year-old girl who awoke in the middle of the night with a cough that her mother describes as sounding "like a dog barking." The patient feels more comfortable sitting up. Vital signs are: respirations, 26/min; pulse, 100; temperature, 101° F. On physical exam, you hear stridor on inspiration. From this scenario, you should suspect which condition?
a. airway obstruction
b. croup
c. epiglottitis
d. asthma

134. What volume of fluid bolus should be given initially to a severely dehydrated child?
a. 20 mL/kg
b. 30 mL/kg
c. 40 mL/kg
d. 50 mL/kg

Answer questions 135–138 on the basis of the following information.

You are called to the home of a 21-year-old female in active labor. She is two weeks from her expected due date and is having contractions of 1.5 minutes duration, which are three minutes apart. This is her second pregnancy. Her first child was delivered vaginally at full term.

135. What is your first course of action for this patient?
a. Place her on the gurney in high Fowler's or comfortable position and examine her for crowning.
b. Place her in the left-lateral recumbent position, apply oxygen, and transport her immediately.
c. Call her obstetrician and advise him or her that the birth will soon take place at the scene.
d. Place her in position of comfort with a sanitary napkin over her vagina and transport rapidly.

136. Your patient suddenly tells you she feels something slippery between her legs. Upon visual examination, you notice a two-inch segment of the umbilical cord protruding from the vagina. What is this condition called?
a. prolapsed cord
b. abruptio umbilicus
c. placenta previa
d. abruptio previa

137. Which of the following is not an appropriate treatment option for this patient?
a. Provide high-flow oxygen and rapidly transport the mother in the knee-chest position.
b. Take pressure off the cord by placing your fingers into the vagina and gently lifting the infant.
c. Wrap the cord in a moist sterile dressing, provide supplemental oxygen, and transport quickly.
d. Leave the cord as it is, place the mother in the right-lateral recumbent position, and transport.

138. You are ready to transport this patient. If the umbilical cord is still exposed, how can you use it to evaluate the infant's perfusion?
   a. Gently feel the cord for pulsations to determine the infant's heart rate.
   b. Determine the infant's temperature by feeling the cord for changes.
   c. Look at the umbilical cord for color changes with blue indicating hypoxia.
   d. Attach a pulse oximetry lead to the cord and determine the oxygen saturation.

139. You arrive at the scene of an imminent delivery in the field. The First Responder, who called for assistance, reports that the patient is a 32-year-old female who is "G4, P3." What does this mean?
   a. The patient is pregnant for the seventh time and has three living children.
   b. The patient's cervix has dilated a total of four centimeters in three hours.
   c. The patient has been pregnant four times and delivered three live children.
   d. The patient has had four rounds of contractions timed three minutes apart.

140. Your patient is a 28-year-old female who reports that she is nine weeks pregnant. She is complaining of severe abdominal pain, shoulder pain, and vaginal bleeding. Vital signs are within normal limits and a physical exam reveals tenderness in the lower-left quadrant. What should you suspect is occuring?
   a. uterine rupture
   b. ectopic pregnancy
   c. spontaneous abortion
   d. abruptio placentae

141. What does the term *effacement* refer to?
   a. the direction the fetus is facing during the birth
   b. the position of the fetus in the uterus prior to birth
   c. thinning of the cervix during the first stage of labor
   d. opening of the cervix during the last stage of labor

142. Your patient is a 33-year-old woman who is nine months pregnant. She complains of severe abdominal pain and abdominal tenderness. She reports there is no vaginal bleeding at this time. What should you should suspect?
   a. abruptio placentae
   b. placenta previa
   c. threatened abortion
   d. preeclampsia

143. Which of the following signs and symptoms would be present in a pregnant patient with pre-eclampsia?
   a. high blood pressure, normal pulse rate, and respiratory rate
   b. high blood pressure, headaches, edema, and visual disturbances
   c. high blood pressure, edema, excessive weight gain, and seizures
   d. high blood pressure, abdominal pain, and bright-red bleeding

144. When does the third stage of labor begin?
   a. when contractions are five minutes apart
   b. when the cervix is fully dilated
   c. immediately upon the birth of the baby
   d. as the placenta is delivered

145. What is the correct procedure for cutting the umbilical cord after the birth of the baby?
  a. Milk the cord of all blood and cut it no more than 5 cm from the infant.
  b. Clamp the cord close to the infant and cut it between the infant and the clamp.
  c. Clamp the cord in two places and cut it near the infant and near the placenta.
  d. Clamp the cord in two places 5 cm apart and cut it between the clamps.

146. What is the appropriate range for the heart rate of a healthy neonate immediately after birth?
  a. 80–100 beats per minute
  b. 100–120 beats per minute
  c. 120–150 beats per minute
  d. 150–180 beats per minute

147. What does the presence of meconium on the neonate or in the amniotic fluid indicate?
  a. The infant may have been distressed.
  b. The infant was born prematurely.
  c. The infant will need resuscitation.
  d. The infant has congenital anomalies.

148. You would perform chest compressions on any newborn whose heart rate is less than how many beats per minute?
  a. 120
  b. 100
  c. 80
  d. 60

149. Medications and drugs are most often delivered to a newborn through the use of which circulatory vessel?
  a. umbilical artery
  b. umbilical vein
  c. ductus arteriosus
  d. jugular vein

Answer questions 150–152 on the basis of the following information.

You respond to a 2-year-old female who is postictal following seizure activity. The patient's parents report that the child was sleeping when she began to shake and turn blue. She has had a runny nose, but she has had no medications lately. There is no history of seizures.

150. This patient is most likely suffering from which condition?
  a. juvenile diabetes
  b. a hypoglycemic seizure
  c. an anaphylactic seizure
  d. a febrile seizure

151. Which of the following vital signs would you expect this patient to have?
  a. increased body temperature, tachycardia, and tachypnea
  b. normal temperature, normal blood pressure, and bradycardia
  c. increased temperature, increased blood pressure, and bradycardia
  d. normal body temperature, tachycardia, and bradypnea

152. What would be the appropriate treatment if this patient continues in a prolonged postictal state?
  a. Obtain blood glucose readings and administer 25% dextrose as needed.
  b. Instruct the parents to give acetaminophen or ibuprofen every four hours.
  c. Remove the child's excess clothing, administer oxygen and an IV, and transport.
  d. Administer high-concentration oxygen, diazepam, and naloxone, and transport.

153. You are assessing a patient with a history of pneumonia. His pulse oximetry reading is 86%. He denies shortness of breath. Which of the following statements is most accurate?
   a. The patient is not hypoxic.
   b. The pulse oximeter is incorrect.
   c. Administer oxygen therapy.
   d. Eighty-six percent is a normal pulse oximeter reading.

154. Which situation would constitute a moral dilemma for a paramedic?
   a. a female rape victim who insists on being cared for only by a female paramedic or EMT
   b. a patient who has sustained a potentially serious head injury but refuses care or transport
   c. a patient who signed a Do Not Resuscitate order who is now unconscious and dying
   d. a patient who is found unconscious with no family member present to authorize care

155. An emphysemic patient experiences a sudden onset of respiratory distress and sharp chest pain. His skin is warm and nondiaphoretic. His breath sounds are diminished on the left side. Your strongest suspicion is
   a. asthma.
   b. pneumonia.
   c. pneumothorax.
   d. chronic bronchitis.

156. You are called to a physician's office to care for a patient who is experiencing symptoms of a myocardial infarction. The physician tells you that she will stabilize the patient herself and that she is assuming responsibility for care. She does, however, wish for you to transport the patient to the hospital. How should you proceed?
   a. Defer to the on-scene physician and take her to the hospital with you.
   b. Request online medical direction from your jurisdictional physician.
   c. Ignore her request and assume responsibility for the patient immediately.
   d. Insist that the on-scene physician communicate with medical control.

157. What does a Type II ambulance usually consist of?
   a. conventional cab-and-chassis truck
   b. standard van usually with a raised roof
   c. special cab-forward van with an integral body
   d. modified fire engine that can provide transport

158. What do you call a legal document that specifies what type of treatment a patient does and does not want to receive?
   a. a Do Not Resuscitate order
   b. an administrative tort
   c. an advance directive
   d. a durable power of attorney

159. At what age is a person considered capable of giving consent to treatment?
   a. 15
   b. 16
   c. 18
   d. 21

160. An unconscious patient has sonorous respirations. This condition should be corrected
   a. simultaneously with the physical exam.
   b. on completion of the initial assessment.
   c. on assessing for the presence of a pulse.
   d. before evaluating the respiratory status.

161. What is the process of transmitting physiological data from the field to the hospital over the phone lines called?
   a. modulation
   b. biotelemetry
   c. multiplexing
   d. trunking

162. You have gained access to a 34-year-old truck driver who has become entrapped after a vehicle rollover accident. The vehicle appears safe for the time being and there is no danger of fire or explosion. What should you do while waiting for rescue workers to arrive on the scene?
   a. Quickly remove the patient from the car and place him on a long board.
   b. Explain to the patient the need for waiting for rescuers to arrive on scene.
   c. Explain technical aspects of the rescue to the patient using medical terminology.
   d. Tell the patient you will be right back, and leave him to get needed supplies.

163. You are the first paramedic unit to arrive on the scene of a multi-injury bus crash. What is your first responsibility?
   a. Assume command of the incident and give a preliminary report to dispatch.
   b. Wait until an incident commander arrives on scene and then follow his or her direction.
   c. Extract patients from the bus and triage them into categories by color or priority.
   d. Review and evaluate the efficiency of site operations up until your arrival.

164. A patient presents with shallow breaths at a rate of six per minute. What should you do next?
   a. Initiate IV therapy.
   b. Check for carotid and radial pulses.
   c. Administer positive-pressure ventilation with a BVM.
   d. Identify the specific cause of the respiratory distress.

165. Under the START triage method, which patient would receive immediate respiratory treatment without further assessment?
   a. male, no respiratory effort
   b. female, respirations 12/min
   c. male, respirations 28/min
   d. female, respirations 38/min

166. What does a red tag mean in the METTAG triage system?
   a. The victim is dead.
   b. The victim has critical injuries.
   c. The victim has minor injuries.
   d. The victim is not injured.

167. What is another term for a cumulative stress reaction?
   a. burnout
   b. fight-or-flight reaction
   c. flashback
   d. anxiety

168. What is one of the most helpful things you can do to alleviate stress in the first day or two after a critical incident?
   a. Take a tranquilizer or sleeping aid so you can sleep.
   b. Go on vacation to get away from the painful memories.
   c. Get lots of rest and also engage in strenuous exercise.
   d. Work longer shifts to keep your mind off the incident.

169. On reaching the scene of a single-motor-vehicle accident, you note that the driver is pinned behind the steering wheel. You also note the presence of two sets of spider-web patterns on the windshield. What does this alert you to?
- **a.** Look for a second victim in this accident.
- **b.** Suspect multiple injuries for this driver.
- **c.** Assume a high-speed collision has occured.
- **d.** Expect that hit-and-run injuries have occured.

170. Which patient is likely to need rapid transport to a trauma center rather than assessment and stabilization on the scene?
- **a.** male, age 56, ejected from a crashed vehicle with a flail chest
- **b.** female, age 60, burns to 10% BSI on her chest and abdomen
- **c.** male, age 28, fell 10 feet from a platform onto a pile of mulch
- **d.** female, age 46, struck by car traveling 10 mph, no penetrating injuries

171. A male patient is complaining of crushing chest pressure and shortness of breath. His vital signs include RR = 20, P = 54, and BP = 132/74. The EKG shows a sinus bradycardia with a first-degree AV block. Which of the following treatments would be most appropriate?
- **a.** atropine 0.5 mg IV
- **b.** transcutaneous pacing
- **c.** nitroglycerin 0.4 mg sL
- **d.** dopamine 10 mcg/kg/min

172. For which procedure is it necessary to wear a mask and protective eyewear?
- **a.** endotracheal intubation
- **b.** starting a peripheral IV
- **c.** giving an IM or SC injection
- **d.** cleaning a contaminated ambulance

173. What is the most common job-related source of HIV infections among healthcare workers?
- **a.** assisting at emergency childbirth
- **b.** direct contact with a patient's skin
- **c.** an accidental needle stick
- **d.** breathing contaminated air

174. What is the leading cause of death among the elderly?
- **a.** metastatic cancer
- **b.** respiratory disease
- **c.** accidents and falls
- **d.** cardiac disease

175. What should you do when confronted with a patient whom you suspect to be a victim of elder abuse?
- **a.** Ask the patient if he or she wants or needs your help.
- **b.** Quietly confront the family with your suspicions.
- **c.** Report your suspicions to the appropriate authority.
- **d.** Search the family's medical records for prior signs of abuse.

176. Your patient is two years old. How can you reassure her before listening to her chest with your stethoscope?
- **a.** Explain in detail exactly how the stethoscope works.
- **b.** Gain her trust by letting her listen to your chest first.
- **c.** Hold up the stethoscope so she can see it won't hurt her.
- **d.** Let her take the stethoscope apart so she isn't afraid.

177. Your patient is a 9-year-old who has a suspected broken arm. Which of the following is appropriate for you to do as you stabilize the patient and prepare him for transport?
   a. Allow him to assist in his own care by holding the splint.
   b. Let him pick what kinds of bandages and splints you use.
   c. Offer him a candy bar or other snack if he doesn't cry.
   d. Calm and reassure him and explain what you are doing.

178. There are many factors to consider when assessing a patient for suicide risk. Which of the following accurately accounts for one suicide risk factor?
   a. Young women commit suicide more often than young men do.
   b. Generally, men attempt suicide more often than women do.
   c. Caucasian males over 85 years of age have the highest suicide rate.
   d. Suicide is the leading cause of death in Hispanic women under 30.

179. What sort of communication system would you need to be able to carry on a two-way conversation with a physician while also transmitting telemetry?
   a. simplex transmission system
   b. duplex transmission system
   c. multiplex transmission system
   d. quadriplex transmission system

180. Which of the following is NOT a component of the START triage method?
   a. circulation assessment
   b. respiration assessment
   c. mentation/level of consciousness
   d. neuro-muscular function

► Answers

1. **b.** The airway is always given first priority, but in this case, since the patient is talking, the first step in his assessment and care would be to stabilize the cervical spine as you begin your ABC assessment.

2. **a.** Kinetic energy = mass (weight) × velocity (speed)^2/2. This means that speed plays a greater role in the force changes during a motor vehicle crash. While the other items are important when evaluating an accident scene, speed has the greatest influence on the potential for damage and injury.

3. **b.** Snoring indicates that the airway is partially obstructed by the patient's tongue. Clear the airway first by positioning with the chin-lift/jaw-thrust maneuver or by inserting a nasopharyngeal airway. An oropharyngeal airway is not indicated due to the patient's LOC. Cervical stabilization takes place prior to beginning your ABC assessment and head tilt/chin lift is not advisable due to the possibility of c-spine injury.

4. **d.** Bleeding within the abdominal cavity can irritate the abdominal surface of the diaphragm, causing referred pain to the shoulder.

5. **c.** The START method quickly reviews three categories to determine patient priority: respirations, pulse, and mental status. After respiratory status is assessed, the basis for judging a patient's hemodynamic status is presence or absence or a radial pulse or skin color and temperature. This patient is showing signs of shock.

6. **a.** By definition, compensatory shock means that in the presence of a hypoperfusing state, the body maintains its blood pressure to the brain. One way to maintain this condition is to increase heart rate. Answer **a** satisfies both of these conditions.

7. **c.** Nerves that assist in bladder control exit from the sacral spine, located above the coccyx.

8. **c.** Organ damage from the mechanism of injury may result in inflammation and bleeding, resulting in the compensatory vital signs.

9. **d.** *Distal* refers to a location that is further from the trunk of the body than the reference point.

10. **a.** This patient is exhibiting classic signs and symptoms for a dissecting aortic aneurysm. The tearing sensation occurs as the intimal linings of the aorta are separated as blood collects between the tissues.

11. **b.** Hypertension is present in 75–85% of dissecting aortic aneurysm cases.

12. **c.** Morphine sulfate is the appropriate medication for this patient. Medications that increase cardiac rate, output, function, or contractile force are contraindicated while the dissection is occuring.

13. **a.** These are all consequences of further dissection. Other conditions also include syncope, heart failure, and absent or reduced pulses and death.

14. **b.** Even though the patient's condition appears to be stable, the mechanism of injury indicates that serious underlying injuries, such as internal bleeding, may be present. Immobilize him quickly using the long board as a full body splint. Transport immediately in this case. You can perform additional assessments or treatments while en route.

15. **c.** Use of a helmet can protect the rider against head injury but not against spinal injury. Leather clothing is helpful in reducing the amount of soft tissue injury. Because the

energy of the accident is mostly absorbed into the rider, severe trauma is noted even with low-speed crashes.

16. a. Battle's sign is noted as discoloration of the mastoid area behind the ear. It is an indication that blood has collected there following a basal skull fracture. Periorbital ecchymosis (raccoon's eyes) is noted with facial and orbital trauma and fractures. Subarachnoid bleeding may have no external manifestations or signs.

17. c. A contrecoup injury is an injury to the brain opposite the impact site; it results from the brain's rebounding movement against the skull wall following the initial impact. The coup injury is noted at the site of the actual impact.

18. b. The symptoms are indicative of a mass-forming lesion in the head, such as an epidural or subdural hematoma. When a patient has a simple concussion, his or her mental status will continue to improve with time.

19. c. The score is 9: 2 points for eye opening, 5 points for motor response, and 2 points for speech.

20. b. The signs and symptoms of tension pneumothorax are given.

21. c. According to the rule of nines as applied to pediatric injuries, the front or back of the trunk each represents 18% of the body surface and the front of one leg represents 7% with the entire leg counting for 14%.

22. c. Using the Revised Trauma Score, 3 points for the GCS, 3 points for the systolic blood pressure, and 3 points for the respiratory rate.

23. b. This option lists the vital sign changes associated with Cushing's syndrome.

24. b. Palpate all quadrants of the abdomen, ending where the patient says it hurts. Because of the need for a quiet environment and several

minutes to perform this successfully, you should not perform abdominal auscultation or percussion in the field.

25. b. The use of the MAST/PASG as a splint in the stabilization of suspected pelvic fractures is indicated for this patient. Since the systolic blood pressure is greater than 90–100 mmHg, any IV fluid should be restricted to a slow, or "keep open," rate. This may reduce any additional bleeding from the dilution of clotting factors.

26. d. A positive tilt test (decrease in blood pressure or increase in pulse rate when the patient moves from supine to sitting position) indicates the possibility of internal bleeding. In hypovolemia, the supine position maintains good blood flow to the brain without compromising the airway.

27. b. Ascites refers to an accumulation of fluid in the abdomen.

28. a. Hepatitis A is spread by the fecal-oral route and is most commonly acquired from eating contaminated food. Hepatitis B, C, and D are all blood-borne diseases.

29. a. Altered mental status is an abnormal finding in healthy elderly patients. The pulse rate does decrease somewhat with age but should remain within the normal range of 60–100. Blood pressure often increases with age and respiration rates increase sightly as patients use less of their lung tissues.

30. b. All the other drugs listed are commonly associated with toxicity in elderly patients.

31. a. Sinus bradycardia, or a heartbeat slower than 60 BPM, is often considered normal, particularly in an athletic adult.

32. c. Vital signs in MI patients depend on the location and extent of underlying heart damage and the patient's response to the insult.

33. b. Frank blood in the urine is a strong sign of injury to the kidney. Abdominal tenderness is unlikely since the kidneys are located in the retroperitoneal space. Bruising may provide indirect information about organ involvement but is not as specific as hematuria.

34. c. The goal of prehospital care for patients with PID is to provide comfort. There is no need to perform a vaginal exam or ask any questions regarding sexual contacts.

35. b. A patient will breathe more slowly when asleep than when awake; all the other factors listed increase respiratory rate.

36. c. Compliance refers to how easily air flows into and out of the lungs. If compliance is decreasing, look for the cause by first reassessing (with look, auscultate, and feel) the airway and head position and then looking for signs that the patient is developing a tension pneumothorax; once you find the cause, try to correct it.

37. d. A pulse oximetry reading around 90% for a patient in a normal atmosphere indicates that severe hypoxia is present. It corresponds to a PaO2 reading of around 60 mmHg. Normal PaO2 is between 80 and 100 mmHg. Normal pulse oximetry readings are from 93% to 100% with 93–95 considered the lower end of normal.

38. a. Magill forceps are used to remove an obstructing foreign body that is visible during laryngoscopy after abdominal thrusts have been unsuccessful.

39. b. When the fetus is close to the entrance of the birth canal, the head presses down on the internal anal sphincter, resulting in the urge to have a bowel movement. Painful uterine contractions can start well in advance of physical delivery.

40. d. Right side-only breath sounds are a sign of right mainstem intubation, ruling out b. Air leak over the trachea may be the sign of an improperly inflated cuff, ruling out a. Bilateral chest wall expansion is a normal finding, ruling out c. These findings point to the need

to have a good baseline assessment of lung sounds and respiratory status prior to performing any interventions.

41. b. Rapid onset, rales, accessory muscle use, and dyspnea are classic symptoms for a patient with acute pulmonary edema.

42. d. Morphine sulfate would be an appropriate treatment for acute pulmonary edema. It increases peripheral venous capacitance and decreases venous return, improving ventilation and decreasing myocardial oxygen demand.

43. b. Immediate transport is indicated for this patient's condition. Without the intact protective amniotic sac, the fetus is at risk of being infected.

44. b. Treatment of metabolic acidosis consists mainly of adequate ventilation. Administration of sodium bicarbonate is rarely needed. Rebreathing CO_2 is a treatment for respiratory alkalosis caused by simple hyperventilation. Identification of the cause of acidosis is not as critical as identifying that it is present and beginning corrective measures to prevent its worsening.

45. d. Albuterol is a beta agonist that is used to cause bronchodilation in patients with asthma and other respiratory emergencies. Aminophylline is a methylxanthine in the same class as theophylline. Ipratropium is an anticholinergic bronchodilator. Labetalol is an alpha and beta adrenergic blocker.

46. a. Closed pneumothorax occurs when air enters the pleural space from an interior wound. An open pneumothrax occurs when the chest wall is open so that air can enter directly into the chest from the outside. A tension pneumothorax develops when a simple pneumothorax becomes large enough to cause pressure and structural changes within the chest.

47. c. Interventions during a neonatal resuscitation should be assessed often, so that changes are noted as soon as they occur. The parents should not hold the infant, although it may be helpful to have them close by.

48. d. Stridor is a sound made during inspiration and is associated with croup and upper airway obstruction.

49. a. A single limb presentation is considered nondeliverable vaginally and requires rapid cesarean section to successfully deliver the infant. Rapid transport is indicated.

50. b. Patients with emphysema or chronic bronchitis benefit from administration of low-flow oxygen and constant monitoring.

51. a. As a bronchodilator, epinephrine 1:1,000 is sometimes indicated in younger (< 35 years old) asthma patients.

52. c. A patient who is conscious and breathing over 30 times per minute is classified as "Immediate." There is no need to check for the presence or rate of the pulse. While she may need oxygen therapy, now is not the time to do so.

53. a. The inspiratory stridor most likely indicates an edematous crushed or torn trachea.

54. c. This patient's symptoms indicate subcutaneous emphysema.

55. b. It will be difficult to determine the actual extent of injury, so the least invasive airway technique is appropriate. Monitor vital signs and pulse oximetry readings to determine if perfusion is adequate.

56. a. Given the circumstances, not enough personnel are available to restrain this patient if he becomes violent. Conducting a hands-on assessment may not be possible given the state of the patient's behavior. Constantly being aware of your surroundings will provide the greatest level of safety.

57. d. Aeromedical transport offers the advantage of rapid transport to specialized facilities such as the Level I trauma center. The amount of time needed to extricate the patient, coupled with the time to transport the patient to either the closest hospital or the trauma center by ground, is too much. Flying the patient directly to the trauma center is most appropriate.

58. c. The first sign of laryngeal edema is usually a hoarse voice.

59. d. Patients with emphysema have a loss of elasticity in the alveoli due to prolonged insult. Bleb formation results in decreased ability of the alveoli to expand and contract and an overall decreased surface area of the lungs. Ruptured blebs do not result in lung "deflation."

60. c. This patient is exhibiting the classic signs and symptoms of congestive heart failure. His history of AMI indicates that he may have permanent damage to the heart and raises the possibility that he is now having an acute episode of failure.

61. d. Oxygen, morphine, nitroglycerin, and furosemide are all used in the treatment of CHF patients.

62. b. Proxysmal nocternal dyspnea (PND), dyspnea upon exertion, and increased dyspnea are all signs of worsening CHF.

63. a. Priorities for managing this patient are indicated by choices **b**, **c**, and **d**.

64. d. Increased ventilatory pressures assist in driving off some of the pulmonary edema.

65. d. Choices **a**, **b**, and **c** are all typically associated with CHF; syncope is not.

66. **d.** No matter the competency level of the rescuer, personal safety is absolute.

67. **a.** Isotonic solutions such as Ringer's lactate or normal saline have electrolyte compositions similar to that of blood plasma although they lack the large protein molecules found within blood.

68. **c.** Cardiogenic shock results most often from left ventricular failure following acute MI.

69. **d.** Third-trimester pregnancy, impaled objects, and dyspnea are all contraindications for use of the PASG/MAST. In addition, the PASG/MAST is contraindicated with any uncontrolled bleeding occuring above the site of the garment.

70. **c.** Managing the patient's injury is the first priority of the EMS provider. Any statements made by the patient should be recorded as possible evidence of the crime.

71. **a.** PASG/MAST use is not indicated when there is an impaled object in the abdomen if you suspect there is any uncontrollable bleeding.

72. **a.** Breath sounds are particularly important to monitor during IV fluid administration because of the danger of fluid overload, which will initially manifest as pulmonary edema.

73. **b.** Morphine relieves pain, decreases venous return, and reduces the oxygen demand of the myocardium.

74. **c.** Left-side heart failure with pulmonary edema is often associated with PND. PND manifests as difficulty breathing when the patient lies flat. As the condition worsens, many patients will report the need to sleep sitting up in a recliner.

75. **b.** The accepted protocol for management of left-side heart failure is given.

76. **b.** As the tip of the nasotracheal tube reaches the glottic opening, you should hear the respiratory effort of the patient. Insertion of the tube past the vocal cords is timed to the inhalation phase in order to minimize resistance against the tube itself.

77. **c.** The preferred field treatment is transcutaneous pacing. Definitive treatment is pacemaker insertion. Drug therapy indicated for this patient is aimed at increasing cardiac output by improving contractility, force of contractions, or increasing rate.

78. **a.** Treat the patient for shock and transport rapidly. Do not palpate the abdomen. This is one of the few medical conditions that may still benefit from the use of PASG/MAST as the garment may tamponade any bleeding that may be occurring. Medications which stimulate the cardiovascular system should be avoided.

79. **b.** This patient needs immediate oxygenation and ventilation. Using a bag-valve mask will accomplish this task most effectively.

80. **d.** PSVTs (paroxysmal supraventricular tachycardia) may be managed by vagal maneuvers, such as the Valsalva maneuver or ice-water immersion.

81. **d.** The T wave reflects repolarization of the ventricles.

82. **b.** The length of a normal P-R interval is 0.12–0.20 seconds, or 3–5 small boxes on the ECG strip.

83. **d.** This child is likely too heavy to perform back blows and chest thrusts. Since her airway is likely to be blocked, initial attempts to dislodge a foreign body are warranted.

84. **a.** A modified jaw thrust would tighten the muscle bed on the floor of the mouth, causing the tongue to move away from the posterior oropharynx.

85. **c.** Patients with ventricular dysrhythmias often manifest lengthened and bizarre QRS complexes.

86. a. Treatment for both conditions consists of immediate defibrillation; continued treatment includes CPR and drugs. Additional therapy depends upon whether a normal rhythm is initiated.

87. c. Falling blood pressure, especially a systolic pressure lower than 80 mm Hg, together with decreasing level of consciousness, is a sign of cardiogenic shock in an AMI patient. Reflex tachycardia may develop as the patient's body attempts to compensate for the shock.

88. a. The classic signs and symptoms of right-side heart failure are given.

89. a. A change in the pulse rate may be the first sign that a dysrhythmia is developing; this is why recording baseline vital signs is particularly important.

90. d. Anxiety and pain can increase the heart rate and, therefore, the oxygen demand of the myocardium.

91. b. Dopamine is a potent sympathomimetic agent, and in cases of cardiogenic shock, it may be used to increase cardiac output.

92. a. The question does not provide any indication of a tension pneumothorax. A pulmonary contusion or cardiac tamponade should affect lung sounds.

93. c. Pulseless electrical activity may occur secondary to a variety of conditions and carries a grave prognosis. Comon causes, as listed in the AHA PEA algorithm, include pulonary embolus, tension pneumothorax, acidosis, cardiac tamponade, hypovolemia, hypoxia, hypothermia, hyperkalemia, AMI, and drug overdose. Hypokalemia may cause dysrhythmias but does not usually cause PEA. Tachycardia is not considered a cause of PEA simply because the definition of PEA is a pulseless patient with a rhythm that you would normally expect to find a pulse with. (In other words, tachycardia without a pulse is PEA.)

94. b. Intramuscular injections can injure muscle tissues, causing the release of enzymes that may mask the cardiac enzymes that are looked for to confirm a diagnosis of MI.

95. b. A patient with angina whose pain does not respond to nitroglycerin is most likely suffering from MI and should be transported without delay.

96. c. The most common complication of MI is dysrhythmia, and some dysrhythmias are or become life threatening. Cardiogenic shock may develop following an AMI, especially when the site of infarction is the left ventricle. Angina is a complication of arterslerosis and coronary artery vasoconstriction or vasospasm.

97. a. Lidocaine is the first drug used to treat malignant PVCs or nonmalignant PVCs in patients who are symptomatic or who have a history of cardiac disease. All the other agents are used if V fib or V tach develops, or they may be used to treat PVCs after a trial of lidocaine has been unsuccessful.

98. d. Based on rhythm alone, ventricular tachycardia is the most likely to require cardioversion. The other rhythms most likely will remain asymptomatic at a heart rate of 120.

99. b. If the trach tube has been dislodged, it may not be easy to reinsert, so rest it in its original position. Placing an endotracheal tube into the stoma and inflating the cuff will help rapidly establish a patient's airway.

100. b. Dilated pupils, hyperactivity, tachycardia, and hypertension are classic signs of cocaine use. Narcotic use would result in lethargy, stupor, and respiratory depression.

101. a. Transport is the only other treatment required for this patient. Be prepared to provide respiratory support if needed. Naloxone is used with narcotic ingestion to restore respirations and is not indicated in this patient. Activated charcoal and ipecac are indicated for poisoning or overdose via the oral route. This patient was reported to have inhaled (smoked) something that appears to be a stimulant.

102. c. Dysrhythmias and seizures are both serious possible complications of stimulation effects from cocaine use.

103. b. This patient appears to be experiencing acute pulmonary edema. Of the choices provided, **b** has both the correct doses and routes of the indicated medications.

104. b. Reduced pumping capacity of the right ventricle causes blood flow to "back up" into the systemic vascular system, causing congestion as evidenced by the pedal edema and JVD. Lung fields that are past the cardiac insufficiency remain free from fluid.

105. c. The neutral position, or position of function, for the hand is achieved by using a gauze roller bandage (or similar material) placed inside the palm with the fingers curled around it. The hand, wrist, and forearm should then be splinted with a board, wire ladder, or vacuum type splint.

106. a. Immobilization of a suspected fracture is best accomplished with two rescuers. After positioning the limb properly, one EMS provider applies the splint, while the other holds the limb in position and monitors the distal pulse, motor, and sensory responses.

107. a. Do not allow the severed digit to get wet because the tissues will begin to draw in the hypotonic fluid and will swell up, which may make reimplantation impossible. The cold environment will help reduce oxygen demand by the cells of the severed digit and will help keep it alive longer.

108. d. Pit viper envenomation is generally very painful. Little or no pain is characteristic of coral snake (neurotoxic) envenomation.

109. b. Brush away as much of the lime as possible, then flood the burned area with water. Neutralizing chemicals are generally not recommended because the use of one chemical to neutralize another usually results in the release of heat and the formation of a third chemical.

110. d. The earliest manifestations of hypoglycemia are hunger, anxiety, and restlessness.

111. a. Hypoglycemia develops in patients with diabetes when they take too much insulin or get too much exercise for the amount of food they eat.

112. b. Central neurogenic hyperventilation is characterized by rapid, deep, noisy breathing and is associated with lesions of the central nervous system. Cheyne-Stokes is the pattern commonly seen with diabetic emergencies.

113. b. "Do Not Resuscitate" is not the same as "do not treat." Under these conditions, management of the condition is warranted.

114. a. The first priority for patients with altered mental status of unknown cause is a blood glucose determination to rule out hypoglycemia as a potential cause.

115. d. For a patient in status epilepticus, treatment consists of establishing an IV, monitoring cardiac rhythm, and administering diazepam to stop the seizures.

116. a. This is the standard adult dosage and route for a patient with severe anaphylaxis. The SC route is recommended unless the patient is in life-threatening distress. Services may recommend the use of 1:1,000 instead 1:10,000.

117. d. This patient may not have the right to refuse treatment and transport due to the actions she has taken. Consulting with medical direction on how to best approach this patient may be helpful.

118. d. The very young, the very old, those under-nourished, and those with chronic illness are all predisposed to heat illnesses for a variety of reasons.

119. d. Bradycardia in a child is an ominous sign of a hypoxic brain.

120. c. Provide oxygen at 100% concentration and intubate if the patient is not breathing spontaneously.

121. c. The purpose of the interview is to calm the patient and to obtain as much information as possible, not to tell the patient what you think. There is a time to reorient patients to reality, but first you must work to calm them down and gain their trust.

122. a. A patient who is displaying manic symptoms is restless or extremely active and talks constantly. The patient may be extremely suspicious or violent. If the patient has bipolar disorder, he or she may swing between periods of mania and depression.

123. c. The lumbar spine will be most impacted from an unevenly distributed load; the cervical spine is also at risk for injury, although such injuries are less likely.

124. a. The patient's presentation points to a pulmonary embolism as the likely cause. The other conditions are not normally associated with sudden syncope, and adventitious lung sounds like crackles or wheezes should be evident, unlike the patient's clear ones.

125. c. Unusual respiratory patterns indicate the possibility of brain-stem injury and call for rapid transport of the patient. Hyperventilation should be used only when you

strongly suspect herniation is occuring. It is not indicated for the routine treatment of increasing ICP. You should ventilate the patient at a normal rate with 100% oxygen.

126. b. Medical direction should be sought if at all possible for any suspected substance abuse patient refusing treatment or transport. Because you are required to be an advocate for the patient, it is never advisable to simply transport someone against their will, even if you suspect impairment due to drug or alcohol use. It is also not advisable to allow them to sign a refusal form when it is obvious that they are in need of medical attention. Treating the patient, then leaving the scene without transport, leaves you open to legal liability and a possible charge of abandonment.

127. c. It is important in this situation to make a complete documentation of the patient's refusal to accept treatment. Documentation should include the steps you took to convince him to seek medical attention, the potential consequences of his refusal, and your assessment findings.

128. b. This choice gives the most appropriate treatment protocol for this patient. Because he is unconscious, he may be treated under implied consent. Treatment in this case is aimed at ruling out the most treatable cause for coma—diabetes.

129. b. While it is possible that he could have a pulmonary embolism, the more likely culprit is a simple pneumothorax. He has few risk factors for a PE, and lung sounds usually remain present unless a large area of pulmonary tissue is not perfused for some period of time.

130. a. The patient is experiencing an unstable atrial fibrillation. He is hypotensive and tachypneic. In this situation, it is imperative to capture the atrial rate as soon as possible. The ventricular rate will decrease once the atria are under control.

131. d. This patient is unstable and requires immediate care. High-flow oxygen will be needed to help care for this patient.

132. d. A child's relatively large head leads to a disproportionate number of head injuries. When they fall, they tend to lead with their heads. They do have underdeveloped muscles and reflexes, resulting in more trips and falls than adults, but their biggest problem is the oversized head.

133. b. The signs, symptoms, and assessment findings of croup are described. The "seal-bark cough" is a classic presentation with croup.

134. a. Give a severely dehydrated child an initial bolus of 20 cc/kg of normal saline or Ringer's solution. Reassess for response and repeat with 10 or 20 cc/kg boluses as long as the child continues to improve and you do not detect any signs of fluid overload.

135. a. In this situation, the first step would be to examine the patient for crowning to determine if you need to assist with delivery on the scene or if you can attempt to transport her.

136. a. The protruding umbilical cord is known as a prolapsed cord.

137. d. Choices **a**, **b**, and **c** are all appropriate treatment options for this patient. If you opt to position the patient for transport, you should place her in the left-lateral recumbent position to improve uterine blood flow and return.

138. a. The umbilical vein, found within the umbilical cord, provides oxygenated blood to the infant. The vein is large enough for you to feel the pulsations as blood flows from the placenta to the fetus. If the cord cools down,

an arterial vasospasm may occur, resulting in the cessation of blood flow to the infant, but the cord temperature does not correlate to the infant's temperature, ruling out **b**. The umbilical cord has various color gradations from red to purplish and the relationship between color and oxygen level is difficult to determine, ruling out **c**. Pulse oximetry is not appropriate for fetal monitoring in the method described, ruling out **d**.

139. c. G4, P3 refers to a woman who has been pregnant four times and delivered three live infants.

140. b. The signs and symptoms of an ectopic pregnancy are given. Most ectopic pregnancies implant within the fallopian tube and have attained a large enough size around nine weeks to rupture the tube, resulting in intense pain and bleeding. The bleeding may or may not be present from the vagina. Most cases of spontaneous abortion are undetected by the mother, who often doesn't even know she is pregnant, and present as an "abnormal menstrual cycle."

141. c. *Effacement* refers to the stretching and thinning of the cervix, which occurs during the first stage of normal labor.

142. a. The signs and symptoms of abruptio placentae, or premature separation of the placenta, are given.

143. b. Patients with pre-eclampsia (or toxemia of pregnancy) manifest all the signs and symptoms of the hypertensive disorders of pregnancy except seizures. Once the patient begins to experience seizures, the condition has changed from pre-eclampsia to eclampsia.

144. c. The third stage of labor begins with the birth of the fetus and ends with the delivery of the placenta.

145. d. Clamp the cord in two places, approximately 5 cm apart, and cut the cord between the clamps. Generally, you want to place the first clamp several (5–7) inches away from the infant.

146. d. Heart rate at birth is normally 150–180 beats per minute, slowing to 130–140 within a few minutes.

147. a. The presence of meconium indicates that the fetus may have been distressed before birth.

148. d. Chest compressions are required when a newborn's heart rate is less than 60, or between 60 and 80 after 30 seconds of positive-pressure ventilation. Remember to perform each intervention for approximately 30 seconds, then reassess for the need to continue resuscitation.

149. b. The umbilical vein, located in the umbilical cord, is used for this purpose. If the cord is left untreated at the hospital, it may be cannulated for a week or even longer. It enters immediately into the hepatic circulation.

150. d. Fever-induced seizures are common in young children with only minor illnesses. Once a child has a febrile seizure, he or she is prone to repeat episodes, which can occur at lower temperatures than the first seizure.

151. a. Increased body temperature, tachycardia, and tachypnea are common in a child who is recently postictal from febrile seizures.

152. c. Oxygen, an IV, and transport is an appropriate treatment for this patient. Remove excess clothing from the patient to passively cool him or her, but do not allow the patient to get chilled. Sponge the child with room temperature water if the temperature is excessively high. Never use alcohol on the skin as a cooling agent. Alcohol can be absorbed directly through the skin.

153. c. Eighty-six percent is close to the bottom of the oxygen saturation curve, meaning that, by this point, most of the hemoglobin in the blood are not carrying oxygen.

154. b. This situation constitutes a dilemma because the paramedic would have to choose between the duty to provide care and the duty to obtain consent. If a patient has a signed DNR order, you should honor his or her order. When a patient is unconscious, you treat him or her under the doctrine of implied consent. The rape victim is simply requesting an all-female crew, and you should try to accommodate her wishes.

155. c. The patient's rapid onset reduces the possibility of pneumonia. No information indicates any other medical condition such as asthma or chronic bronchitis. Patients with emphysema are prone to experiencing simple pneumothorax.

156. a. Paramedics should defer to a physician who is present on scene provided this individual is assuming responsibility for the continued care of this patient. Make sure you know the rules and regulations for your jurisdiction regarding on-scene physicians.

157. b. A Type II ambulance is an integral unit consisting of a standard van, usually with a raised roof.

158. c. The living will and DNR order are both examples of legal documents called advanced directives. They specify the kind of healthcare a person does and does not want to receive in the event of their imminent death.

159. c. In most states, consent for treatment must be obtained from all patients who are 18 years old or older. This can be modified in situations of extenuating circumstances, such as when an underage minor is pregnant or has legal custody of a minor child in his or her care.

160. d. Snoring respirations are indicative of an airway issue and should be corrected before further assessment is completed.

161. b. Transmitting physiological data over phone lines is called biotelemetry.

162. b. Unless the scene is unsafe or the patient is in danger of further injury, you should not attempt an emergency extrication at this time. Dialogue with the patient should be in terminology that is understandable to him. Avoid using jargon or overly technical terms. Leaving a patient before turning him over to personnel of equal or higher rank constitutes abandonment. Also, it is important to provide psychological support to a patient who is entrapped.

163. a. The first paramedic unit to arrive at the scene of a mass-casualty incident would immediately assume command and transmit a report to dispatch, alerting them to the need for more units. As other units begin to arrive, they may be detailed to perform triage or some other duty.

164. c. The respiratory rate is too slow and must be corrected immediately with ventilatory assistance.

165. d. In the START system, a patient with respirations greater than 30 per minute would receive immediate attention. Patient **a** would not receive any care beyond the initial opening of the airway. Patients **b** and **c** would receive additional assessment before treatment.

166. b. When using the METTAG system, a red tag indicates a patient with critical injuries who needs rapid transport.

167. a. A cumulative stress reaction refers to a person's reaction to the continuous, long-term effects of stress. It is also called burnout. The fight-or-flight response is part of the stress reaction brought on by stimulation of the sympathetic nervous system. A flashback occurs when someone has a vivid memory of a previous incident.

168. c. Rest, alternating with strenuous exercise, is helpful in relaxing you after a stressful incident. It is not a good idea to try to avoid thinking about the incident by going on vacation, taking sleeping pills, or throwing yourself into work. You should talk to mental health professionals or peer counselors.

169. a. The spider-web pattern is made when a victim's head hits the windshield. Two spider-web patterns indicate that there is a second victim somewhere on the scene.

170. a. All the others do not have critical mechanisms, so they should not receive rapid transportation.

171. c. Although his heart rate is slow, the patient is not hypotensive. The other three answer choices address symptomatic bradycardia, not the situation this patient presents in.

172. a. Commonly accepted infection-control guidelines call for all personnel to wear masks and protective eyewear for any procedure that carries the risk of splashing of blood, vomitus, or other fluids.

173. c. Accidental needle sticks are the most common source of work-related HIV and Hepatitis B infections in healthcare workers.

174. d. Because cardiac disease is so common, you should administer medications commonly prescribed for other types of emergencies with extreme caution.

175. c. Report your suspicions promptly. Many states have laws requiring you to report any suspicions of child abuse, elder abuse, or domestic violence.

176. b. Toddlers can often be reassured by being allowed to handle unfamiliar objects. They will not understand detailed explanations and should not be allowed to disassemble equipment.

177. d. Respect the teenager's feelings by explaining the purpose and result of your actions and by providing reassurance.

178. c. Women attempt suicide more often, but men are more successful at it. Also, men choose more deadly means. About 60% of the people who successfully commit suicide have a history of previous attempts.

179. c. A multiplex system allows for a two-way conversation and simultaneous transmission of telemetry readings.

180. d. Neuro-muscular function is not part of the START algorithm. START assesses respirations, pulse, and mental status.

5 ▶ Paramedic Practice Exam 3

CHAPTER SUMMARY

This is the third of four practice exams in this book based on the National Registry EMT-Paramedic written exam. Use this test to identify which types of questions are still giving you problems.

YOU ARE NOW becoming very familiar with the format of the National Registry EMT-Paramedic exam. Your practice test-taking experience will help you most, however, if you have created a situation that closely mirrors the day of the official test.

For this third exam, simulate a real test. Find a quiet place where you will not be disturbed. Have with you two sharpened pencils and a good eraser. Complete the test in one sitting, setting a timer or a stopwatch. You should have plenty of time to answer all of the questions when you take the real exam, but you want to practice working quickly without rushing.

The answer sheet you should use is on the next page. After the exam is an answer key, which will help you see where you need to concentrate further study. When you've finished the exam and scored it, turn back to Chapter 1 to see which questions correspond to which areas of your paramedic training—then you'll know which parts of your textbook to concentrate on before you take the fourth exam.

Exam 3

1.	ⓐ	ⓑ	ⓒ	ⓓ	46.	ⓐ	ⓑ	ⓒ	ⓓ	91.	ⓐ	ⓑ	ⓒ	ⓓ
2.	ⓐ	ⓑ	ⓒ	ⓓ	47.	ⓐ	ⓑ	ⓒ	ⓓ	92.	ⓐ	ⓑ	ⓒ	ⓓ
3.	ⓐ	ⓑ	ⓒ	ⓓ	48.	ⓐ	ⓑ	ⓒ	ⓓ	93.	ⓐ	ⓑ	ⓒ	ⓓ
4.	ⓐ	ⓑ	ⓒ	ⓓ	49.	ⓐ	ⓑ	ⓒ	ⓓ	94.	ⓐ	ⓑ	ⓒ	ⓓ
5.	ⓐ	ⓑ	ⓒ	ⓓ	50.	ⓐ	ⓑ	ⓒ	ⓓ	95.	ⓐ	ⓑ	ⓒ	ⓓ
6.	ⓐ	ⓑ	ⓒ	ⓓ	51.	ⓐ	ⓑ	ⓒ	ⓓ	96.	ⓐ	ⓑ	ⓒ	ⓓ
7.	ⓐ	ⓑ	ⓒ	ⓓ	52.	ⓐ	ⓑ	ⓒ	ⓓ	97.	ⓐ	ⓑ	ⓒ	ⓓ
8.	ⓐ	ⓑ	ⓒ	ⓓ	53.	ⓐ	ⓑ	ⓒ	ⓓ	98.	ⓐ	ⓑ	ⓒ	ⓓ
9.	ⓐ	ⓑ	ⓒ	ⓓ	54.	ⓐ	ⓑ	ⓒ	ⓓ	99.	ⓐ	ⓑ	ⓒ	ⓓ
10.	ⓐ	ⓑ	ⓒ	ⓓ	55.	ⓐ	ⓑ	ⓒ	ⓓ	100.	ⓐ	ⓑ	ⓒ	ⓓ
11.	ⓐ	ⓑ	ⓒ	ⓓ	56.	ⓐ	ⓑ	ⓒ	ⓓ	101.	ⓐ	ⓑ	ⓒ	ⓓ
12.	ⓐ	ⓑ	ⓒ	ⓓ	57.	ⓐ	ⓑ	ⓒ	ⓓ	102.	ⓐ	ⓑ	ⓒ	ⓓ
13.	ⓐ	ⓑ	ⓒ	ⓓ	58.	ⓐ	ⓑ	ⓒ	ⓓ	103.	ⓐ	ⓑ	ⓒ	ⓓ
14.	ⓐ	ⓑ	ⓒ	ⓓ	59.	ⓐ	ⓑ	ⓒ	ⓓ	104.	ⓐ	ⓑ	ⓒ	ⓓ
15.	ⓐ	ⓑ	ⓒ	ⓓ	60.	ⓐ	ⓑ	ⓒ	ⓓ	105.	ⓐ	ⓑ	ⓒ	ⓓ
16.	ⓐ	ⓑ	ⓒ	ⓓ	61.	ⓐ	ⓑ	ⓒ	ⓓ	106.	ⓐ	ⓑ	ⓒ	ⓓ
17.	ⓐ	ⓑ	ⓒ	ⓓ	62.	ⓐ	ⓑ	ⓒ	ⓓ	107.	ⓐ	ⓑ	ⓒ	ⓓ
18.	ⓐ	ⓑ	ⓒ	ⓓ	63.	ⓐ	ⓑ	ⓒ	ⓓ	108.	ⓐ	ⓑ	ⓒ	ⓓ
19.	ⓐ	ⓑ	ⓒ	ⓓ	64.	ⓐ	ⓑ	ⓒ	ⓓ	109.	ⓐ	ⓑ	ⓒ	ⓓ
20.	ⓐ	ⓑ	ⓒ	ⓓ	65.	ⓐ	ⓑ	ⓒ	ⓓ	110.	ⓐ	ⓑ	ⓒ	ⓓ
21.	ⓐ	ⓑ	ⓒ	ⓓ	66.	ⓐ	ⓑ	ⓒ	ⓓ	111.	ⓐ	ⓑ	ⓒ	ⓓ
22.	ⓐ	ⓑ	ⓒ	ⓓ	67.	ⓐ	ⓑ	ⓒ	ⓓ	112.	ⓐ	ⓑ	ⓒ	ⓓ
23.	ⓐ	ⓑ	ⓒ	ⓓ	68.	ⓐ	ⓑ	ⓒ	ⓓ	113.	ⓐ	ⓑ	ⓒ	ⓓ
24.	ⓐ	ⓑ	ⓒ	ⓓ	69.	ⓐ	ⓑ	ⓒ	ⓓ	114.	ⓐ	ⓑ	ⓒ	ⓓ
25.	ⓐ	ⓑ	ⓒ	ⓓ	70.	ⓐ	ⓑ	ⓒ	ⓓ	115.	ⓐ	ⓑ	ⓒ	ⓓ
26.	ⓐ	ⓑ	ⓒ	ⓓ	71.	ⓐ	ⓑ	ⓒ	ⓓ	116.	ⓐ	ⓑ	ⓒ	ⓓ
27.	ⓐ	ⓑ	ⓒ	ⓓ	72.	ⓐ	ⓑ	ⓒ	ⓓ	117.	ⓐ	ⓑ	ⓒ	ⓓ
28.	ⓐ	ⓑ	ⓒ	ⓓ	73.	ⓐ	ⓑ	ⓒ	ⓓ	118.	ⓐ	ⓑ	ⓒ	ⓓ
29.	ⓐ	ⓑ	ⓒ	ⓓ	74.	ⓐ	ⓑ	ⓒ	ⓓ	119.	ⓐ	ⓑ	ⓒ	ⓓ
30.	ⓐ	ⓑ	ⓒ	ⓓ	75.	ⓐ	ⓑ	ⓒ	ⓓ	120.	ⓐ	ⓑ	ⓒ	ⓓ
31.	ⓐ	ⓑ	ⓒ	ⓓ	76.	ⓐ	ⓑ	ⓒ	ⓓ	121.	ⓐ	ⓑ	ⓒ	ⓓ
32.	ⓐ	ⓑ	ⓒ	ⓓ	77.	ⓐ	ⓑ	ⓒ	ⓓ	122.	ⓐ	ⓑ	ⓒ	ⓓ
33.	ⓐ	ⓑ	ⓒ	ⓓ	78.	ⓐ	ⓑ	ⓒ	ⓓ	123.	ⓐ	ⓑ	ⓒ	ⓓ
34.	ⓐ	ⓑ	ⓒ	ⓓ	79.	ⓐ	ⓑ	ⓒ	ⓓ	124.	ⓐ	ⓑ	ⓒ	ⓓ
35.	ⓐ	ⓑ	ⓒ	ⓓ	80.	ⓐ	ⓑ	ⓒ	ⓓ	125.	ⓐ	ⓑ	ⓒ	ⓓ
36.	ⓐ	ⓑ	ⓒ	ⓓ	81.	ⓐ	ⓑ	ⓒ	ⓓ	126.	ⓐ	ⓑ	ⓒ	ⓓ
37.	ⓐ	ⓑ	ⓒ	ⓓ	82.	ⓐ	ⓑ	ⓒ	ⓓ	127.	ⓐ	ⓑ	ⓒ	ⓓ
38.	ⓐ	ⓑ	ⓒ	ⓓ	83.	ⓐ	ⓑ	ⓒ	ⓓ	128.	ⓐ	ⓑ	ⓒ	ⓓ
39.	ⓐ	ⓑ	ⓒ	ⓓ	84.	ⓐ	ⓑ	ⓒ	ⓓ	129.	ⓐ	ⓑ	ⓒ	ⓓ
40.	ⓐ	ⓑ	ⓒ	ⓓ	85.	ⓐ	ⓑ	ⓒ	ⓓ	130.	ⓐ	ⓑ	ⓒ	ⓓ
41.	ⓐ	ⓑ	ⓒ	ⓓ	86.	ⓐ	ⓑ	ⓒ	ⓓ	131.	ⓐ	ⓑ	ⓒ	ⓓ
42.	ⓐ	ⓑ	ⓒ	ⓓ	87.	ⓐ	ⓑ	ⓒ	ⓓ	132.	ⓐ	ⓑ	ⓒ	ⓓ
43.	ⓐ	ⓑ	ⓒ	ⓓ	88.	ⓐ	ⓑ	ⓒ	ⓓ	133.	ⓐ	ⓑ	ⓒ	ⓓ
44.	ⓐ	ⓑ	ⓒ	ⓓ	89.	ⓐ	ⓑ	ⓒ	ⓓ	134.	ⓐ	ⓑ	ⓒ	ⓓ
45.	ⓐ	ⓑ	ⓒ	ⓓ	90.	ⓐ	ⓑ	ⓒ	ⓓ	135.	ⓐ	ⓑ	ⓒ	ⓓ

136.	ⓐ	ⓑ	ⓒ	ⓓ
137.	ⓐ	ⓑ	ⓒ	ⓓ
138.	ⓐ	ⓑ	ⓒ	ⓓ
139.	ⓐ	ⓑ	ⓒ	ⓓ
140.	ⓐ	ⓑ	ⓒ	ⓓ
141.	ⓐ	ⓑ	ⓒ	ⓓ
142.	ⓐ	ⓑ	ⓒ	ⓓ
143.	ⓐ	ⓑ	ⓒ	ⓓ
144.	ⓐ	ⓑ	ⓒ	ⓓ
145.	ⓐ	ⓑ	ⓒ	ⓓ
146.	ⓐ	ⓑ	ⓒ	ⓓ
147.	ⓐ	ⓑ	ⓒ	ⓓ
148.	ⓐ	ⓑ	ⓒ	ⓓ
149.	ⓐ	ⓑ	ⓒ	ⓓ
150.	ⓐ	ⓑ	ⓒ	ⓓ

151.	ⓐ	ⓑ	ⓒ	ⓓ
152.	ⓐ	ⓑ	ⓒ	ⓓ
153.	ⓐ	ⓑ	ⓒ	ⓓ
154.	ⓐ	ⓑ	ⓒ	ⓓ
155.	ⓐ	ⓑ	ⓒ	ⓓ
156.	ⓐ	ⓑ	ⓒ	ⓓ
157.	ⓐ	ⓑ	ⓒ	ⓓ
158.	ⓐ	ⓑ	ⓒ	ⓓ
159.	ⓐ	ⓑ	ⓒ	ⓓ
160.	ⓐ	ⓑ	ⓒ	ⓓ
161.	ⓐ	ⓑ	ⓒ	ⓓ
162.	ⓐ	ⓑ	ⓒ	ⓓ
163.	ⓐ	ⓑ	ⓒ	ⓓ
164.	ⓐ	ⓑ	ⓒ	ⓓ
165.	ⓐ	ⓑ	ⓒ	ⓓ

166.	ⓐ	ⓑ	ⓒ	ⓓ
167.	ⓐ	ⓑ	ⓒ	ⓓ
168.	ⓐ	ⓑ	ⓒ	ⓓ
169.	ⓐ	ⓑ	ⓒ	ⓓ
170.	ⓐ	ⓑ	ⓒ	ⓓ
171.	ⓐ	ⓑ	ⓒ	ⓓ
172.	ⓐ	ⓑ	ⓒ	ⓓ
173.	ⓐ	ⓑ	ⓒ	ⓓ
174.	ⓐ	ⓑ	ⓒ	ⓓ
175.	ⓐ	ⓑ	ⓒ	ⓓ
176.	ⓐ	ⓑ	ⓒ	ⓓ
177.	ⓐ	ⓑ	ⓒ	ⓓ
178.	ⓐ	ⓑ	ⓒ	ⓓ
179.	ⓐ	ⓑ	ⓒ	ⓓ
180.	ⓐ	ⓑ	ⓒ	ⓓ

▶ Paramedic Exam 3

1. Which organs are contained in the right upper quadrant of the abdomen?
   a. spleen, tail of pancreas, stomach, left kidney, and part of the colon
   b. liver, gall bladder, head of pancreas, part of duodenum, and part of the colon
   c. appendix, ascending colon, small intestine, right ovary, and fallopian tube
   d. small intestine, descending colon, left ovary, and fallopian tube

2. Chest pain associated with stable angina may be caused by
   a. a buildup of lactic acid and CO_2.
   b. an occluded coronary artery.
   c. cardiac dysrhythmias.
   d. cardiac cell death.

3. Your patient is a 65-year-old female complaining of chest pressure. The EKG shows a wide complex tachycardia at a rate of 200 beats per minute. The patient's vital signs are P = 200, RR = 26, and BP 90/60. Which of the following answers is the best treatment for this patient?
   a. lidocaine 0.5–1.0 mg/kg IVP
   b. synchronized cardioversion at 100 joules
   c. defibrillation at 200 joules
   d. amiodarone 150 mg IVP, push slowly

4. What does the *P* of the AVPU algorithm mean?
   a. response to painful stimuli
   b. perception of the environment
   c. level of pain they are feeling
   d. radial pulse rate and rhythm

5. What are the components of the focused history and physical exam?
   a. ABC and LOC assessment and vital signs
   b. SAMPLE history and focused examination
   c. head-to-toe check and treatment of injuries
   d. vital signs and detailed physical exam

6. What does pulse pressure refer to?
   a. diastolic blood pressure reading × the systolic reading
   b. systolic × the diastolic blood pressure reading
   c. difference between the systolic and diastolic readings
   d. systolic blood pressure as measured by a Doppler device

7. A 56-year-old male experienced a syncopal episode and is now complaining of intense chest pressure. His vital signs are RR = 26, P = 110, and BP = 80/64. Crackles can be auscultated in both lower lung fields. Which of the following conditions best defines the patient's presentation?
   a. congestive heart failure
   b. cardiogenic shock
   c. cardiac arrest
   d. malignant hypotension

8. An elderly male is complaining of a sudden onset of severe pain in his right leg. The affected extremity is cool to the touch and pale. The temperature and pulse in the patient's left leg is normal. You suspect
   a. varicose arteries.
   b. arterial occlusion.
   c. pulmonary embolism.
   d. deep-vein thrombosis.

Answer questions 9–11 on the basis of the following information.

You arrive at a golf course to find a 45-year-old male unconscious and responsive to pain, but only with movement. The patient was struck in the head by a golf ball traveling at high velocity. His eyes are closed; pupil examination reveals his left pupil is 2 mm, and the right is 8 mm and not reactive to light. This patient moves upper extremities to localized pain and moves lower extremities spontaneously. He is breathing full deep respirations at a rate of 24 per minute.

9. You would expect the vital signs of this patient generally to follow which of the following groupings?
   a. RR increased, HR decreased, BP decreased
   b. RR increased, HR decreased, BP increased
   c. RR decreased, HR decreased, BP decreased
   d. RR decreased, HR increased, BP increased

10. Treatment of this patient would include which of the following?
   a. spinal immobilization to a long board with cervical collar
   b. IV fluid boluses titrated to a systolic BP of 100–110 mmHg
   c. opening the patient's airway using the head-tilt/chin-lift technique
   d. placing the patient in the sniffing position to facilitate airflow

11. A patient with a closed head injury should be closely monitored for all of the following EXCEPT
   a. hypovolemic shock.
   b. respiratory alkalosis.
   c. hypoxic seizures.
   d. hemopneumothorax.

12. Your patient, a car accident victim, complains of seeing "a dark curtain" in front of one eye. What should you suspect?
   a. optic nerve damage
   b. retinal detachment
   c. orbital fracture
   d. conjunctival hemorrhage

13. Treatment for a patient in cardiogenic shock and complaining of chest pressure should include
   a. adenosine IV push.
   b. furosemide IV push.
   c. dopamine infusion.
   d. nitroglycerin sL.

14. What do the signs and symptoms of traumatic asphyxia include?
   a. paradoxical chest motion, pain on inspiration, and increased respiratory rate
   b. dyspnea, bloodshot eyes, distended neck veins, and a cyanotic upper body
   c. agitation, air hunger, distended neck veins, shock, and tracheal displacement
   d. shock, cyanosis, absent breath sounds over one lobe, and flat neck veins

15. An adult patient has burns covering her head and upper back. Using the rule of nines, this patient's burns cover what percentage of her body surface area?
   a. 9%
   b. 18%
   c. 27%
   d. 36%

16. How would you classify a burn that is pearly white and almost painless?
   a. first-degree burn
   b. second-degree burn
   c. third-degree burn
   d. chemical burn

17. Which of the following conditions indicates the need for rapid transport?
   a. isolated penetrating trauma by a knife in the upper forearm
   b. a pedestrian struck by a motor vehicle traveling about 10 mph
   c. first-degree and second-degree burns to the entire chest wall
   d. a pulse rate 130, blood pressure 90/60, and respiratory rate 36/min

18. What is the Glasgow Coma Scale Score for a patient who opens her eyes in response to pain, speaks incomprehensibly, and withdraws in response to pain?
   a. 6
   b. 7
   c. 8
   d. 9

19. Your patient is a 23-year-old man who complains of abdominal pain. The patient states that the pain began suddenly and was originally located only in the area around the umbilicus. Now, however, it has moved to the right lower quadrant. The patient also complains of nausea and vomiting, and he has a fever of 102° F. Examination displays rebound tenderness. What condition should you suspect?
   a. diverticulitis
   b. gastritis
   c. peptic ulcer
   d. appendicitis

20. A 42-year-old male complains of sudden, intense pain that is centered in his lower back. He is pale, cool, and diaphoretic, especially below the level of his umbilicus. He is tachycardic and hypotensive. Which of the following conditions best describes the patient presentation?
   a. myocardial infarction
   b. abdominal aortic aneurysm
   c. pancreatitis
   d. kidney stones

21. What is the typical presentation of a patient with esophageal varices?
   a. acute abdominal pain
   b. painless hematemesis
   c. melena and hemoptysis
   d. pain radiating to the jaw

22. What does the initial symptom of infection with HIV primarily consist of?
   a. mild fatigue and fever
   b. encephalopathy
   c. Kaposi's sarcoma
   d. pneumocytis carinii

23. A 63-year-old male is complaining of substernal chest pain radiating to his left arm and jaw. He is diaphoretic and cool to the touch. The cardiac monitor shows sinus tachycardia. The patient's vital signs are BP = 136/70, P = 118, and RR = 16. You have administered oxygen and established an IV. What should you do now?
   a. Defibrillate immediately with 200 joules.
   b. Prepare to administer atropine IV push.
   c. Sedate the patient and then proceed with synchronized countershock at 50 joules.
   d. Administer sublingual nitroglycerin and evaluate the patient's response to the medication.

24. Your patient is a 78-year-old woman who is complaining of diffuse abdominal pain, nausea, and vomiting. Physical examination reveals abdominal distention and absent bowel sounds. You should suspect she has which of the following conditions?
   a. bowel obstruction
   b. aortic aneurysm
   c. esophageal varices
   d. gastrointestinal bleeding

25. Atypical signs and symptoms of myocardial infarction that are commonly seen in elderly patients include all of the following EXCEPT
   a. confusion and fatigue.
   b. syncope.
   c. tearing chest pain.
   d. neck pain.

26. Which breathing pattern is characteristic of diabetic ketoacidosis or other types of metabolic acidosis?
   a. ataxic breathing
   b. Biot's breathing
   c. Cheyne-Stokes breathing
   d. Kussmaul's breathing

27. Normal vesicular breath sounds are usually described as having which of the following characteristics?
   a. medium pitch, medium loudness, with equal inspiratory and expiratory phases
   b. high pitch, soft, with a long inspiratory phase and a long expiratory phase
   c. low pitch, soft, with a long inspiratory phase and a short expiratory phase
   d. medium pitch, soft, with a short inspiratory phase and a long expiratory phase

28. What is the purpose of the OPQRST mnemonic?
   a. to obtain the medical history
   b. to assess the neurologic status
   c. to assess the respiratory status
   d. to define the major complaint

29. Your patient is age 70. He complains of chest pain that began while he was raking leaves. You perform an initial assessment and a focused history and physical examination and administer oxygen and nitroglycerin. The patient then states that he feels much better. What is he most likely suffering from?
   a. stable angina
   b. unstable angina
   c. myocardial infarction
   d. cardiac arrest

30. A 25-year-old female complains of diffuse lower abdominal pain, vaginal discharge, and low-grade fever. Which of the following conditions best describes the patient's presentation?
   a. pelvic inflammatory disease
   b. ectopic pregnancy
   c. kidney infection
   d. ovarian cyst

31. What do the signs and symptoms of hypertensive crisis include?
   a. pitting edema, tachycardia, tachypnea, and venous congestion
   b. paralysis, seizures, headache, and altered level of consciousness
   c. severe respiratory distress, apprehension, cyanosis, and diaphoresis
   d. restlessness, confusion, blurred vision, nausea, and vomiting

32. Why are vital sign changes not a good early indicator of shock in a young healthy adult?
   a. Patients often display false-positive vital sign readings during shock.
   b. The vital signs are often too low to be measured accurately during shock.
   c. The body attempts to compensate by maintaining normal vital signs.
   d. Signs and symptoms of shock are based on neurological findings only.

33. During an emergency delivery, the newborn's head presents in the canal. After suctioning, how can you assist with the delivery of the anterior shoulder?
   a. Gently pull on the infant's head.
   b. Gently guide the infant's head upward.
   c. Gently guide the infant's head downward.
   d. Rotate the infant's head to the transverse position.

34. The physiological cause of the anxiety and restlessness that make up the classic early signs of shock are a direct result of which of the following phenomena?
   a. the release of catecholamines
   b. the decrease in cardiac output
   c. the rise in blood pressure
   d. the constriction of arterioles

Answer questions 35–37 on the basis of the following information.

You arrive to find a 65-year-old male in acute respiratory distress. You hear wheezes from across the room, and you note extreme accessory muscle use. The patient has assumed a tripod position and is breathing through pursed lips. Your physical exam reveals a barrel chest and stained fingernails. Vital signs are blood pressure, 160/90; pulse, 100, strong and irregular with atrial fibrillation on the cardiac monitor; and respiratory rate, 40, with shallow and labored breathing. Ausculation of the chest reveals wheezes and diminished lung sounds throughout all fields.

35. What is this patient most likely suffering from?
   a. chronic bronchitis
   b. anaphylaxis
   c. asthma
   d. emphysema

36. Which of the following medications would NOT be used to treat this patient's condition?
   a. methylpredniosolone
   b. epinephrine 1:1,000
   c. meperidine
   d. metaproterenol

37. Why is this patient breathing through pursed lips?
   a. to provide positive pressure to inflate the alveoli
   b. to minimize mouth movement during ventilation
   c. to try and retain carbon dioxide in the lung fields
   d. to "blow off" carbon dioxide to increase blood pH

38. Under what circumstance could the pulse oximetry reading show a falsely elevated reading in a patient?
   a. when the patient is exposed to radioactivity
   b. when the patient is exposed to carbon monoxide
   c. when the patient is exposed to pyrexins
   d. when the patient is exposed to carbon tetrachloride

39. Which statement about airway obstruction caused by the tongue is incorrect?

 a. The tongue is the most common cause of airway obstruction in an unconscious patient.

 b. Airway blockage does not depend on the position of the patient's head, neck, and jaw.

 c. The esophagus and epiglottis can contribute to airway blockage in an unconscious patient.

 d. The tongue can block the airway only when the patient is recumbent or supine.

40. Which technique should you use to open the airway of a trauma patient?

 a. the head-tilt/chin-lift

 b. the jaw thrust

 c. the head tilt/neck-lift

 d. the sniffing position

41. What is bronchiolitis caused by?

 a. either infection or allergy

 b. mycobacterium tuberculosis

 c. the respiratory syncytial virus

 d. an exacerbation of asthma

Answer questions 42–44 on the basis of the following information.

Your patient is a 30-year-old female who is complaining of a generalized rash and dyspnea after eating shellfish. The patient has small itchy, red welts all over her body and says her tongue feels like it is swollen. She complains of difficulty moving air in and difficulty catching a full breath. This patient's vital signs show a blood pressure of 110/60; a pulse of 100, strong and regular; and a respiratory rate of 36. Her breathing is somewhat shallow and labored.

42. This patient is exhibiting the signs and symptoms of

 a. an allergic reaction.

 b. a partial airway obstruction.

 c. anaphylactic shock.

 d. epiglottitis or croup.

43. Medications used to treat this patient may include which of the following?

 a. isoproterenol

 b. haloperidol

 c. hydroxyzine

 d. dopamine

44. This patient needs close monitoring because she could progress into which of the following conditions?

 a. bradycardia

 b. complete airway obstruction

 c. anaphylactic shock

 d. respiratory distress

45. After placing an endotracheal tube, you note that breath sounds are much stronger on the right side of the chest than on the left. What does this suggest?

 a. The ET tube has been inserted into the right mainstem bronchus.

 b. The patient has developed a pneumothorax on the right side.

 c. The ET tube has not been inserted far enough into the trachea.

 d. The patient has probably aspirated vomitus into the trachea.

46. You have just delivered a baby girl. Evaluation reveals that the infant cries loudly and has a heart rate of 140, her body is pink but the extremities are blue, and she is actively moving all extremities. Her APGAR score is
a. 7.
b. 8.
c. 9.
d. 10.

47. Causes of third trimester bleeding include
a. ectopic pregnancy, pre-eclampsia, uterine rupture.
b. eclampsia, spontaneous abortion, placenta previa.
c. ectopic pregnancy, uterine rupture, pelvic inflammatory disease.
d. abruptio placentae, placenta previa, uterine rupture.

48. What is an assessment finding of pulsus paradoxus associated with?
a. emphysema
b. congestive heart disease
c. COPD
d. myocardial infarction

49. The term *tracheal tugging* refers to which of the following?
a. the use of accessory muscles during respiration
b. retraction of intercostal muscles during inspiration
c. cyanosis and nasal flaring with exhalation
d. retraction of neck tissues during respiration

50. A dull sound heard during chest percussion may be associated with which condition?
a. pneumothorax
b. emphysema
c. pneumonia
d. bronchitis

51. Pulse oximetry allows you to continuously record which of the following?
a. pulse rate and oxygen saturation
b. respiratory rate and oxygen saturation
c. pulse rate and hemoglobin level
d. respiratory rate and hemoglobin level

52. Your patient is a 66-year-old man who is extremely thin but has a noticeably distorted barrel-shaped chest. He reports a history of dyspnea that has recently gotten worse. You note that he purses his lips when breathing, but hypoxia is not apparent. In addition to monitoring vital signs, breath sounds, and the ECG, starting an IV, and transporting the patient, what other treatments should you give to this patient?
a. Administer high-flow oxygen via BVM ventilation.
b. Administer low-flow oxygen and a bronchodilator.
c. Administer oxygen via non-rebreather mask and furosemide.
d. Orally intubate the patient and assist ventilations.

53. A 28-year-old woman is complaining of a sudden onset of severe abdominal pain that radiates to her shoulder. Her BP = 88/60, P = 110, and R = 20. Her skin is cool, pale, and clammy. She states that her last normal menstrual period was 6–8 weeks ago. Which of the following conditions best describes the patient presentation?
a. uterine rupture
b. ectopic pregnancy
c. abruptio placentae
d. postpartum hemorrhage

54. What respiratory pattern is characteristic of Kussmaul's respiration?
   a. an increase in both rate and depth
   b. an increase in respiratory rate only
   c. a decrease in both rate and depth
   d. decrease in respiratory rate only

55. Which of the following factors increases the amount of energy necessary for the patient to expend for respiration?
   a. loss of pulmonary surfactant
   b. decrease in airway resistance
   c. increase in pulmonary compliance
   d. a decrease in body temperature

56. What does it mean if the pH of normal urine is 6.0 and the pH of distilled water is 7.0?
   a. Urine is twice as acidic as distilled water.
   b. Urine is ten times as acidic as distilled water.
   c. Urine is twice as alkaline as distilled water.
   d. Urine is ten times as alkaline as distilled water.

57. Your patient is a 6-year-old child who is conscious but not breathing because of an airway obstruction. What is the first thing you should do for this patient?
   a. Give five back blows followed by five chest thrusts.
   b. Visualize the airway and perform a finger sweep.
   c. Perform subdiaphragmatic abdominal thrusts.
   d. Open the airway with a head-tilt/chin-lift.

58. You should attempt to remove foreign material from a patient's airway with forceps only in what situation?
   a. You do not have access to laryngoscopy equipment.
   b. You have tried but failed to suction the airway.
   c. You are unable to insert an endotracheal tube.
   d. You are able to visualize the obstruction directly.

Answer questions 59–63 on the basis of the following information.

Your patient is a 29-year-old female complaining of the sudden onset of severe shortness of breath and chest pain. She indicates that she is recovering from surgery to her left femur after an automobile crash.

59. What is this patient most likely suffering from?
   a. medication reaction
   b. myocardial infarction
   c. cerebral vascular accident
   d. pulmonary embolism

60. You would expect to find which of the following in this patient?
   a. tracheal deviation
   b. bradycardia
   c. pulses paradoxes
   d. bradypnea

61. This patient's physiological problems are most likely due to what cardiac problem?
a. the right side of the heart pumping against increased resistance
b. the left side of the heart pumping against decreased resistance
c. the right side of the heart pumping against decreased resistance
d. the left side of the heart pumping against increased resistance

62. Proper management of this patient includes which of the following?
a. IV fluid boluses
b. low-flow oxygen
c. ventilatory assistance
d. transport in shock position

63. Which of the following conditions is a common cause of this patient's problem?
a. placement of a central line
b. ruptured cerebral aneurism
c. myocardial tissue damage
d. taking anticoagulant drugs

64. Which of the following combinations are the only two situations in which a prehospital provider should place a gloved hand into the vagina?
a. shoulder dystocia and prolapsed cord
b. prolapsed cord and breech presentation
c. placental abruption and breech presentation
d. breech presentation and postpartum hemorrhage

65. A patient suspected of showing early signs of shock should usually be placed supine with his or her feet elevated. When is this position contraindicated?
a. when a head injury is suspected
b. if shock is due to hypovolemia
c. if you suspect respiratory alkalosis
d. if respirations are inadequate

66. Which statement about deflation of the PASG/MAST in the field setting is correct?
a. Deflation should be accomplished rapidly in the field.
b. Deflate the legs first and then the abdominal compartment.
c. Deflate the garment if the patient begins to experience dyspnea.
d. Deflation should not be attempted in the field without medical direction.

67. Which of the following statements is true regarding a single limb presentation during an emergency delivery?
a. Grasp the presenting part of the baby and gently rotate it so the baby will deliver.
b. This is a nondeliverable presentation and requires immediate transport to an appropriate receiving facility.
c. Assist the mother in delivering the baby by applying gentle traction to the limb.
d. Apply firm pressure to the presenting part to delay birth until the patient is transferred to the emergency department staff.

68. When responding to the scene of a hazardous material incident, the EMS crew should approach from
a. downhill and downwind.
b. downhill and upwind.
c. uphill and downwind.
d. uphill and upwind.

69. How should you position a patient with a suspected CVA and no other pertinent history?
   a. supine with the head raised 15 degrees
   b. in the left-lateral recumbent position
   c. supine with the feet raised 15 degrees
   d. in the right-lateral recumbent position

70. The vital signs of a patient experiencing the later stages of increased intracranial pressure will be characterized by which of the following?
   a. increased blood pressure, decreased pulse and respiratory rate
   b. increased blood pressure, pulse, and respiratory rate
   c. decreased blood pressure, increased pulse and respiratory rate
   d. decreased blood pressure, pulse, and respiratory rate

71. The T wave on an ECG tracing represents which of the following events?
   a. repolarization of the ventricles
   b. depolarization of the atria
   c. depolarization of the ventricles
   d. repolarization of the atria

72. You are analyzing a patient's heart rate on an ECG strip. You note that there are 13 complexes within one 6-second interval. You would record the heart rate as which of the following?
   a. 6
   b. 13
   c. 78
   d. 130

73. Normal atrial depolarization is seen on the Lead II ECG strip as which of the following waveforms?
   a. a negative rounded P wave
   b. a positive rounded P wave
   c. a flattened P wave
   d. a biphasic P wave

74. Which of the following is an abnormal finding on an ECG strip?
   a. a P-R interval of 0.16 sec
   b. a P-R interval of 0.10 sec
   c. a QRS complex of 0.10 sec
   d. a QRS complex of 0.08 sec

75. An EMS crew attempts to resuscitate a 50-year-old male in cardiac arrest, and is not successful. The family sues the EMS organization for negligence. The crew will need to prove that its actions during the resuscitation
   a. were extraordinary and heroic.
   b. were not within their duty to act.
   c. exceeded the standards set forth by the American Heart Association.
   d. were similar to the actions a reasonably prudent person would do under similar circumstances.

76. How does the Valsalva maneuver improve a too-rapid heart beat?
   a. It forces the patient to slow down his or her respirations.
   b. It stimulates the vagus nerve to slow the heart rate.
   c. It inhibits the release of acetylcholine, slowing the heart.
   d. It stimulates the carotid artery, slowing blood return.

77. Which dysrhythmia may be a sign of digitalis toxicity?
   a. atrial fibrillation with a ventricular rate of less than 60
   b. premature junctional contractions leading to tachycardia
   c. acute onset paroxysmal supraventricular tachycardia
   d. atrial flutter with a ventricular rate greater than 120

78. Your patient is a 67-year-old man who has a pulse and whose ECG strip shows ventricular tachycardia. What should you do after administering oxygen and placing an IV line?
   a. Administer 6 mg of adenosine via rapid IV push.
   b. Administer 2.5–5.0 mg of verapamil via IV.
   c. Sedate and perform synchronized cardioversion.
   d. Administer 1.0–1.5 mg/kg lidocaine via IV.

79. Which of the following is a risk factor for the formation of atherosclerosis?
   a. alcoholism
   b. excessive exercise
   c. diabetes mellitus
   d. cancer

80. The pain caused by myocardial infarction is usually relieved only by the use of which of the following medications?
   a. nitroglycerin
   b. acetaminophen
   c. oxygen
   d. morphine

81. During a multicasualty incident, the first two arriving paramedics should assume which roles?
   a. triage and treatment officers
   b. medical group supervisor and communications officer
   c. medical group supervisor and triage officer
   d. triage and transport officers

82. Which of the following statements best describes the function of the treatment area at a multicasualty incident?
   a. All red, yellow, and green patients are kept together in one treatment area.
   b. Full medical care should be delivered in the treatment area.
   c. The treatment officer personally treats each patient in the treatment area.
   d. The treatment officer works closely with the transport officer to get transport immediate/red patients as soon as possible.

83. Why are patients who present with pulmonary edema usually assumed to have had a myocardial infarction?
   a. An AMI is often the underlying cause of right heart failure.
   b. An AMI is frequently a common cause of left ventricle failure.
   c. An AMI decreases the oxygen-carrying capacity of the blood.
   d. An AMI can result in the formation of a pulmonary embolism.

84. What is the primary goal of management for a patient with left ventricle failure and pulmonary edema?
   a. decrease cardiac output
   b. initiate thrombolytic therapy
   c. decrease venous return
   d. prevent serious dysrhythmias

85. Your patient is a 68-year-old male with a history of two prior AMIs. Your assessment findings include a pulse rate of 124, peripheral edema, and jugular vein distention. The patient denies any chest pain or breathing difficulty. What condition should you suspect?
   a. left ventricular failure
   b. right ventricular failure
   c. pulmonary embolism
   d. myocardial infarction

86. Your patient is an 82-year-old female with a suspected MI. While en route to the hospital, you note that her systolic blood pressure, which had been stable, has started to drop, and that she is becoming confused. At the same time, her heart rhythm converts to sinus tachycardia. What should you should suspect is happening?
   a. She is developing cardiogenic shock.
   b. She is going into sudden cardiac arrest.
   c. Pulmonary edema is causing heart failure.
   d. She has thrown a pulmonary embolus.

87. Your patient is a 65-year-old male who is complaining of pain in his abdomen, back, and flanks. His blood pressure is 90/60. On examination, you note that the femoral pulses are markedly weaker than the radial pulses. What should you do next?
   a. Palpate the abdomen gently for a pulsatile mass.
   b. Administer dopamine to increase cardiac output.
   c. Treat for hypovolemia and transport rapidly.
   d. Administer lasix, morphine, nitroglycerine, and oxygen.

88. Which of the following are signs and symptoms of acute pulmonary embolism?
   a. rapid labored breathing and tachycardia
   b. slow labored breathing and cyanosis
   c. acute abdominal pain and anxiety
   d. pallor, chest pain, and tachycardia

89. Your patient is a 67-year-old female who complains of increasing leg pain and tenderness. The skin over the affected area is warm and red, and Homan's sign is positive. Vital signs are unremarkable. How should you treat this patient?
   a. Massage the affected area to relieve the pain and restore circulation.
   b. Elevate the leg and transport the patient for further evaluation.
   c. Give IV fluid boluses to treat the signs and symptoms of shock.
   d. Have the patient walk to the ambulance to promote blood flow.

90. In general, the court deems an emancipated minor to be one who
   1. is married.
   2. is economically independent.
   3. maintains a separate home.
   4. is in the military.
   a. 1, 2
   b. 1, 4
   c. 2, 3, 4
   d. 1, 2, 3, 4

91. What is the initial energy setting for defibrillation in an adult cardiac arrest patient?
   a. 100 joules
   b. 200 joules
   c. 300 joules
   d. 360 joules

92. Carotid sinus massage is used for patients with which dysrhythmia?
   a. nonperfusing ventricular tachycardia
   b. refractory ventricular fibrillation
   c. paroxysmal supraventricular tachycardia
   d. second-degree AB block (Mobitz II)

93. External cardiac pacing is used for which of the following rhythms?
   a. ventricular fibrillation
   b. symptomatic bradycardia
   c. PVCs occuring from irritability
   d. PVCs occuring as escape beats

94. What is the usual dosage and route of administration of diazepam given before synchronized cardioversion?
   a. 2–5 mg given intramuscularly
   b. 5–10 mg directly into the vein
   c. 5–15 mg by slow IV push
   d. 15–10 mg administered rectally

95. Which drug is used in management of congestive heart failure?
   a. dobutamine
   b. isoproterenol
   c. bretylium
   d. verapamil

96. Which heart sounds are normal findings on auscultation?
   a. S1 and S2
   b. S2 and S3
   c. S3 and S4
   d. S2 and S4

97. Which set of vital signs is suggestive of left ventricular heart failure with pulmonary edema?
   a. BP elevated, pulse slow and irregular, respirations slow and labored
   b. BP diminished, pulse slow and irregular, respirations rapid but easy
   c. BP diminished, pulse fast and regular, respirations rapid and labored
   d. BP elevated, pulse fast and irregular, respirations rapid and labored

Answer questions 98–103 on the basis of the following information.

You respond for a 44-year-old diabetic who is complaining of a general feeling of weakness. During your questioning, you learn that he has been "constantly thirsty and hungry." His breath has a fruity odor, and his level of consciousness appears to be diminishing.

98. Which diabetic emergency is this patient most likely suffering from?
   a. diabetic ketoacidosis
   b. diabetes mellitus
   c. hypoglycemia
   d. hyperosmolar hyperglycemic nonketotic coma (HHNK)

99. Which vital signs would you expect from this patient?
   a. cool clammy skin, bradycardia, increased respirations
   b. warm dry skin, tachycardia, increased respirations
   c. warm dry skin, bradycardia, decreased respirations
   d. cool clammy skin, tachycardia, decreased respirations

100. This patient's symptoms are most likely due to which condition?
   a. high levels of insulin
   b. low levels of insulin
   c. low levels of glucose
   d. dehydration

101. Which of the following statements is the most accurate with regard to this patient?
   a. He has not eaten in a while, resulting in hypoglycemia.
   b. He has taken too much insulin, resulting in hyperglycemia.
   c. He has not taken his correct dose of insulin or is ill.
   d. He has taken his insulin but did not regulate his fluid intake.

102. During transport, this patient slips into unconsciousness, and his breathing becomes very deep and rapid. What is this pattern called?
   a. Kussmaul's respirations
   b. HHNK respirations
   c. Cheyne-Stokes respirations
   d. Christianson's respirations

103. What does appropriate treatment for this patient include?
   a. an IV of D5W or Ringer's lactate, oxygen, and IM glucagon
   b. a blood glucose test, IV normal saline, and a fluid bolus
   c. a blood glucose test, 25 gm of dextrose 50%, and limited fluids
   d. hyperventilation, limited fluids, and sodium bicarbonate

104. After a critical incident, a "defusing" should be done
   a. 1–2 hours after the event.
   b. 8–10 hours after the event.
   c. 24–48 hours after the event.
   d. 60–72 hours after the event.

105. Asymmetrical movement during respiration typically suggests which condition?
   a. COPD
   b. flail chest
   c. brain damage
   d. hemothorax

106. Your patient suffers a head trauma that results in a transient loss of consciousness followed by a complete return of function. What is the term for this condition?
   a. cerebral contusion
   b. epidural hematoma
   c. contrecoup injury
   d. cerebral concussion

107. What is the proper procedure for aligning a fractured long bone?
   a. Stabilize the entire limb in the position in which it is found, and then immobilize.
   b. Immobilize the limb with all the joints in the position of function.
   c. Immobilize the distal portion of the limb, and then move the proximal portion.
   d. Stabilize the proximal portion, and then bring the distal portion into alignment.

108. When would you bandage and splint limb injuries on scene?
   a. only if the patient does not need rapid transport
   b. if the transport time will be longer than one hour
   c. after treating any life-threatening injuries first
   d. if the fracture has neurovascular compromise

109. What should you always do if your examination of a limb suggests that it is fractured?
   a. Apply traction to align the ends of long bones and position the joints.
   b. Treat it as if a fracture exists and immobilize it to prevent further injury.
   c. Check the proximal pulse, motor, and sensation, and adjust the position.
   d. Transport the patient as quickly as possible to preserve function of the limb.

110. Which type of wound would most likely require a tourniquet?
   a. amputation of the hand at the forearm
   b. bilateral open fractures of the femurs
   c. below the knee amputation by a machine
   d. tearing injury of the upper arm

111. A patient with hypoglycemia may present with which of the following signs or symptoms?
   a. bizarre behavior
   b. blurred vision
   c. gradual onset
   d. bradycardia

112. What is the primary reason that diazepam is given to a seizure patient?
   a. to help relieve any anxiety that may be caused from having a seizure
   b. to suppress the spread of electrical activity in the brain and relax muscles
   c. to prevent hypoglycemia by allowing the brain to effectively use insulin
   d. to help increase the blood pressure by lowering the seizure threshold

113. What is the correct dosage and route of administration of epinephrine for a patient in anaphylaxis?
   a. 0.3–0.5 mg epinephrine 1:10,000, administered intravenously
   b. 0.1–0.3 mg epinephrine 1:10,000, administered intravenously
   c. 0.3–0.5 mg epinephrine 1:1,000, administered subcutaneously
   d. 0.1–0.3 mg epinephrine 1:1,000, administered subcutaneously

114. What is the role of beta agonists like albuterol in the treatment of anaphylaxis?
   a. to relieve anxiety
   b. to prevent shock
   c. to raise blood pressure
   d. to reverse bronchospasm

115. During a multicasualty incident, a conscious patient presents with a fractured femur, a palpable radial pulse, and a respiratory rate of 24/min. According to START, this patient would be placed into what triage category?
   a. minor/green
   b. delayed/yellow
   c. immediate/red
   d. deceased/black

116. What do the symptoms of acetaminophen overdose include?
  a. nausea, vomiting, malaise, diaphoresis, and right upper quadrant pain
  b. nausea, vomiting, confusion, lethargy, seizures, and dysrhythmias
  c. altered mental status, hypotension, slurred speech, and bradycardia
  d. nausea, dilated pupils, rambling speech, lethargy, headache, and dizziness

117. Prehospital administration of sodium bicarbonate may be ordered for a patient who has overdosed on which of the following drugs?
  a. acetaminophen
  b. benzodiazepines
  c. narcotics
  d. antidepressants

118. Your patient is a 19-year-old female who has been stung by a stingray while swimming. What should you do after ensuring airway breathing and circulation are intact?
  a. Apply a tight constricting band between the wound and the heart.
  b. Apply heat or warm water to reduce pain and detoxify the poison.
  c. Use an icepack wrapped in a towel to relieve pain and swelling.
  d. Administer morphine sulfate IM or IM titrated to relieve pain.

119. Which drug can cause users to behave violently and aggressively?
  a. Elavil
  b. phenobarbital
  c. PCP
  d. LSD

120. Which of the following patients shows signs and symptoms of heat exhaustion?
  a. male, age 34: severe muscle cramps in legs and abdomen, fatigue, and dizziness
  b. female, age 45: rapid, shallow respirations, weak pulse, cold, clammy skin, dizziness
  c. male, age 42: deep respirations, rapid strong pulse, dry, hot skin, loss of consciousness
  d. female, age 70: shallow respirations, weak, rapid pulse, dilated pupils, seizures

121. Which of the following activities are performed by the EMT-Paramedic in the field?
  1. maintaining and preparing of emergency care equipment and supplies
  2. directing and coordinating patient transport by selecting the best methods
  3. assigning priorities of emergency treatment
  4. initiating and continuing emergency treatment
  a. 1, 2
  b. 2, 3
  c. 1, 3, 4
  d. 1, 2, 3, 4

122. Which of the following statements about care of a near-drowning victim is correct?
  a. The Heimlich maneuver should be used to clear the airway.
  b. Ventilation should not be provided until the patient is clear of the water.
  c. The patient should be admitted to the hospital for observation.
  d. Near-drowning victims seldom experience head or neck injury.

123. Which of the following are the signs and symptoms of air embolism?
- **a.** pruritus, skin pallor and cyanosis, pitting edema in the ankles
- **b.** sharp chest pain with sudden onset, dyspnea with coughing
- **c.** dizziness, auditory and vestibular disturbances, headache
- **d.** fatigue, pain in chest and lower abdomen, nausea, and vomiting

124. You are interviewing a 43-year-old woman with a long history of schizophrenia. She appears to try to cooperate, but there are long periods of silence in your conversation while she listens to her "voices." How should you respond during her silence?
- **a.** Repeat your last question.
- **b.** Restate her last response.
- **c.** Remain quietly attentive.
- **d.** Tell an interesting story.

125. Which of the following may be a sign of an anxiety disorder?
- **a.** loss of use of an extremity without apparent cause
- **b.** the onset of an elevated and expansive mood
- **c.** feelings of depression following the loss of a loved one
- **d.** hallucinations, delusions, or an inappropriate affect

Answer questions 126–128 on the basis of the following information.

You respond to a 12-year-old male patient who is wheezing and having difficulty breathing. The patient has a long history of asthma, and states that he used his inhaler but that it didn't help much. Upon examination, you discover that the patient is tachycardic and tachypneic with a nonproductive cough.

126. What is the primary goal in treating this patient?
- **a.** correct hypoxia, reverse bronchospasms, and decrease inflammation
- **b.** decrease respiratory drive, decrease heart rate, and increase blood pressure
- **c.** increase heart rate, decrease respiratory rate, and correct carbon dioxide levels
- **d.** correct carbon dioxide levels, decrease inflammation, and increase heart rate

127. This patient's condition might have been triggered by any of the following EXCEPT
- **a.** warm air.
- **b.** allergens.
- **c.** exercise.
- **d.** medications.

128. Treatment for this patient includes which of the following medications?
- **a.** versed, epinephrine, and valium
- **b.** albuterol, aminophylline, and atropine
- **c.** albuterol, terbutaline, and steroids
- **d.** terbutaline, steroids, and verapamil

129. You are about to start an IV in a 5-year-old female. Which of the following statements would be appropriate in this situation?
- **a.** "There will be some pain as I insert the catheter, but it's necessary for me to begin fluid therapy."
- **b.** "The needle will hurt for a second. Try to hold still. The medicine will help you get better."
- **c.** "Hold still, or the pain will be much worse. I'm sorry I have to do this to you and I hope you understand."
- **d.** "If you don't stop crying, I won't let your mom stay with you or let her go with us to the hospital."

130. Written procedures for the management of prehospital emergencies that are approved by representatives of the medical community are known as
a. online medical control.
b. protocols.
c. DOT standards.
d. conditions of employment.

131. Your 5-year-old patient has multiple injuries in various stages of healing, including raccoon eyes and a new suspected broken leg. On questioning, his mother states that he fell out of his bunk bed, but his sister, age 9, says that "Daddy beat him." The mother insists that her husband will take the child to the hospital when he gets home from work. How should you proceed?
a. Document your findings, convince the mother that transport to the hospital is necessary, and report your suspicions of child abuse.
b. Make sure his condition is stable, grant the mother's request for delayed transport, and follow-up that evening to confirm that treatment was sought.
c. Confront the mother with your suspicions, transport the child immediately, call the police, and have both parents arrested.
d. Remove both children from the home immediately and transport both of them to the hospital for a complete evaluation.

132. Until ruled out by a physician, documented fever in an infant younger than three months old is always considered to result from which of the following?
a. epilepsy
b. Reye's syndrome
c. epiglottitis
d. meningitis

133. What does appropriate management of a child with epiglottitis consist of?
a. visualization of the airway and insertion of an endotracheal tube
b. administration of racemic epinephrine and nebulized albuterol
c. airway maintenance and administration of humidified oxygen
d. administration of bronchodilators and corticosteroids

Answer questions 134–138 on the basis of the following information.

You respond to the residence of a 4-year-old male who was found in his backyard, head down in a 5-gallon bucket of water. The child, according to the mother, was in the water for approximately four minutes. The child is cyanotic, pulseless, and apneic. The ECG shows he is in asystole. The child weighs approximately 40 pounds.

134. While at a private clinic, the on-scene physician instructs you to provide care for a patient that you know to be inappropriate given the patient's present condition. Your best course of action will be to
a. contact the medical control physician and ask him to speak with the on-scene physician.
b. inform the on-scene physician that you disagree with his instructions and ask him to perform the procedures himself.
c. politely inform the physician that his instructions are inappropriate and ask him to leave the room.
d. ignore the on-scene physician's order, load the patient in the ambulance as quickly as possible, and transport rapidly to the hospital.

135. Which of the following would be the most reliable method for determining the proper medication dosing for this pediatric patient?
a. Give no more than $\frac{1}{2}$ the adult dose for all medications.
b. Give $\frac{1}{3}$ the adult dose for all medications except atropine.
c. Use the Broselow Tape or another length/weight measuring system.
d. Estimate the patient's kilogram weight by dividing by 2.2.

136. All of the following medications can be given through the endotracheal tube to pediatric patients EXCEPT
a. lidocaine.
b. epinephrine.
c. atropine.
d. Valium.

137. After endotracheal intubation of this patient, which of the following steps should be followed?
a. confirmation of ETT placement
b. inflation of the cuff to prevent air leakage
c. dilution of all ETT medication to 10 cc
d. tape the tube to the patient's maxilla

138. After the first round of ACLS drugs, the patient converts to a sinus bradycardia at a rate of 40 beats per minute. What is the drug of choice for managing this patient's bradycardia?
a. epinephrine
b. atropine
c. isoproterenol
d. dobutamine

139. Knee injuries and hip dislocations that occur during a motor vehicle crash are often the result of which pathway of energy transfer?
a. "down and under"
b. "down and back"
c. "up and over"
d. "up and back"

140. A high-velocity bullet passes through the body. Besides the direct damage caused by the bullet, what other related condition could cause harm to the patient?
a. the type of metal used to make the bullet
b. the internal opening created by cavitation
c. the gunpowder residue
d. the length of the bullet

141. Your patient is a 5-year-old girl who presents with breathing difficulty of rapid onset. She is sitting upright and drooling. Her temperature is 104.6° F. What should you suspect?
a. bronchiolitis
b. asthma
c. croup
d. epiglottitis

142. An injury to the brain opposite the site of a blunt force impact is called
a. contralateral.
b. concussion.
c. contrecoup.
d. coup force.

143. One way to determine the size of the endo-tracheal tube to use in a child is to use the following equation: 16 + the child's age divided by 4. Another consideration is the size of the child's
   a. glottic opening.
   b. pleural space.
   c. pharynx.
   d. cricoid ring.

144. What should you do in order to preserve physical evidence in cases of suspected sexual assault?
   a. Examine the patient's perineal area carefully.
   b. Bag all soiled articles of clothing together.
   c. Avoid cleaning wounds and handling clothing.
   d. Have the patient change clothes and bathe before transport.

145. A 17-year-old male complains of a steadily worsening headache several days after being struck in the head during football practice. Which of the following injuries best describes this patient's presentation?
   a. intervertebral bleed
   b. subdural hematoma
   c. epidural hematoma
   d. subarachnoid bleed

146. When should you examine a woman who is about to give birth for crowning?
   a. during a contraction
   b. between contractions
   c. during an internal pelvic exam
   d. only when time permits

147. Your patient is a 32-year-old woman who reports that she is 14 weeks pregnant. She complains of abdominal cramping and vaginal bleeding. How should you proceed?
   a. Perform an internal vaginal exam and treat her for any signs of ectopic pregnancy.
   b. Administer high-flow oxygen, monitor fetal heart tones, and transport immediately.
   c. Treat for signs and symptoms of hypovolemia, provide emotional support, and transport.
   d. Position the patient supine, open an OB kit, and prepare for emergency delivery in the field.

148. What is the cause of the supine-hypotensive syndrome in the pregnant patient?
   a. pressure of the uterus on the inferior vena cava
   b. normal volume depletion during pregnancy
   c. the occurance of abruptio placentae
   d. abnormal fetal presentation or positioning

149. Which of the following is a differential sign or symptom of spinal shock associated with trauma?
   a. an elevated heart rate
   b. decreasing blood pressure
   c. anxiety or sense of doom
   d. warm, dry skin distal to the injury site

150. During a normal delivery, you would tell the mother to stop pushing when what occurs?
   a. crowning begins
   b. the head is delivered
   c. delivery of the infant is complete
   d. the placenta is delivered

151. What is the appropriate treatment for a prolapsed cord?
a. Attempt to push the cord back into the vagina and deliver the infant normally.
b. Place two fingers on either side of the baby's nose and mouth and lift the head until it is delivered.
c. Place two fingers to raise the presenting part of the fetus off the cord, place the mother in knee-chest position, administer oxygen, and transport.
d. Assist and support the mother for a normal vaginal delivery.

152. Immediately after delivery, how should you position the neonate?
a. higher than the mother's vagina, with its head slightly elevated
b. at the level of the mother's vagina, with its head slightly lower than the body
c. lower than the mother's vagina, with the head at the same level as the body
d. at the level of the mother's vagina, with the head slightly elevated

153. A patient who complains of a sudden and painless loss of vision in one eye is most likely suffering from
a. acute retinal artery occlusion.
b. retinal detachment.
c. conjunctival hemorrhage.
d. hyphema.

154. The first step in the resuscitation of a distressed neonate is to
a. ventilate with 100% oxygen for 15–30 seconds.
b. evaluate the heart rate for a minimum of 30 seconds.
c. evaluate the respiratory rate and breath sounds.
d. initiate chest compressions.

155. Which statement about supplying supplemental oxygen to a neonate is incorrect?
a. Do not withhold oxygen from a neonate in the prehospital setting.
b. Oxygen toxicity in the prehospital setting is a serious concern.
c. Administer supplemental oxygen by blowing it across the neonate's face.
d. Oxygen should be warmed if possible prior to administration.

156. How much intravenous fluid should you administer to a distressed neonate who weighs 2 kg?
a. 10 mL
b. 20 mL
c. 30 mL
d. 40 mL

157. A patient was hit several times in the left chest with the large end of a pool cue. The patient is in severe respiratory distress with tachycardia and tachypnea. Crepitus can be felt over the left anterior fourth, fifth, sixth, and seventh rib area. Lung sounds are clear and equal, but diminished. Which of the following conditions best describes the patient's presentation?
a. flail chest segment
b. tension pneumothorax
c. pericardial tamponade
d. pulmonary contusion

158. Which statement describes a tiered EMS system?
a. Paramedics are the prehospital team leaders and they supervise lower level BLS providers.
b. Physicians directly supervise all aspects of care provided by prehospital personnel.
c. Varying levels of resources are dispatched to calls, depending on the nature of the incident.
d. After they arrive at the hospital, patients are assigned a priority for care by a triage nurse.

159. A patient is found lying supine on the floor with a stab wound to her right anterior chest, just below the breast. The patient is having difficulty breathing, with cool, clammy skin signs. No JVD is noted. Breath sounds are absent over the right side. This patient most likely is experiencing a

   a. pneumothorax.

   b. pericardial tamponade.

   c. tension pneumothorax.

   d. hemothorax.

160. Which activity is an example of indirect medical control?

   a. A licensed physician who does not work in the EMS system assumes control at an accident scene.

   b. A paramedic administers nitroglycerin to a patient with chest pain under standing medical orders.

   c. A mobile intensive care nurse communicates orders to paramedics while en route to the hospital.

   d. An EMS physician tells a paramedic on the radio to administer morphine sulfate to a patient.

Answer questions 161–165 on the basis of the following information.

You respond to reports of a bus collision. Upon arrival, it appears that you have approximately 35 patients.

161. What is your first priority?

   a. Set up the triage area close to the treament and transport areas.

   b. Establish the morgue area away from the view of the patients.

   c. Begin rapid treatment of the most seriously injured patients.

   d. Separate the walking wounded from the more severely injured.

162. The first parameter to assess when using the START triage algorithm should be

   a. blood pressure.

   b. breathing/airway.

   c. circulation.

   d. level of consciousness.

163. A male patient is found to have a respiratory rate of 38. This would place him in which of the following categories?

   a. delayed

   b. immediate

   c. nonsalvageable

   d. critical

164. Another male patient is found to have a respiratory rate of 28 and a radial pulse of 84. He is confused about the incident. This patient would be placed in which of the following categories?

   a. delayed

   b. immediate

   c. nonsalvageable

   d. critical

165. A female patient is found to have no spontaneous respirations. What should you do next?

   a. Use a bag-valve mask and ventilate with 100% oxygen.

   b. Classify the patient as immediate and move her to a treatment area.

   c. Reposition the airway and check her again for respirations.

   d. Start CPR and call for immediate removal to the treatment area.

166. A person with a serious illness can delegate the right to make medical decisions to someone else by enacting which of the following legal documents?
  a. living will
  b. durable power of attorney for healthcare
  c. Do Not Resuscitate order
  d. right to die order

167. What is the legal term for an intentional deviation from the accepted standard of care that results in harm to a patient?
  a. negligence
  b. liability
  c. res ipsa loquitur
  d. abandonment

168. You are acting under the doctrine of implied consent when you treat which of the following patients?
  a. a person who is drunk and refuses treatment
  b. a confused elderly man whose adult child is with him
  c. a small child whose parent is not present
  d. a person who is upset and mentally distraught

169. Your patient is a 28-year-old man who is suffering a seizure. You monitor his condition during the seizure and throughout the postictal period, but when the patient recovers, he refuses transport or further treatment. What should you do next?
  a. Explain the risks of refusing care and then restrain the patient before you begin treatment.
  b. Call for police assistance to help you convince the patient to go to the hospital.
  c. Sedate the patient and transport him to the hospital while he is unconscious.
  d. Consult with medical control, explain the risks of refusing care, and document the patient's refusal.

170. A wrestler feels his shoulder "pop" when his opponent twists his arm during a hold. There is immediate pain and loss of range of motion in the shoulder. What is the patient's likely injury?
  a. subluxation
  b. muscle strain
  c. ligament sprain
  d. glenoid contusion

171. Which statement about the care of patients who are contaminated by hazardous material is incorrect?
  a. Trained personnel should immediately remove nonambulatory patients from the "hot zone."
  b. Decontamination activities should be carried out while the patient is in the "warm zone."
  c. Intravenous therapy and invasive procedures should begin only under specific physician direction.
  d. A detailed physical exam should be done while the patient is located within the "hot zone."

172. Your unit is the first to arrive at the scene of a bombing at a large office building. The purpose of your initial size-up of the incident is to
  a. determine what additional resources will be needed.
  b. decide how seriously injured each patient is.
  c. assess whether the building can be salvaged.
  d. help the police look for clues about who placed the bomb.

173. At a major incident response, which of the following is the responsibility of the staging officer?
  a. Establish the triage, treatment, and transportation sectors in the most appropriate sites.
  b. Evaluate what resources are needed for treatment and report this to incident command.
  c. Collect and assess patients with minor injuries and remove them from the treatment areas.
  d. Maintain a log of units available and an inventory of special equipment.

174. Which statement about the triage operation at a mass-casualty incident is correct?
  a. Each patient's triage and initial assessment should take less than 60 seconds.
  b. A detailed physical exam of the walking wounded is part of the basic triage operation.
  c. Triage assessment of each individual patient takes approximately one to two minutes.
  d. Triage personnel at a mass-casualty incident should have extensive medical training.

175. Using the START triage method at a multiple-casualty accident scene, you encounter a patient who is making no spontaneous respiratory effort despite attempts at repositioning. What should you do next?
  a. Tag the patient as unsalvageable and move on.
  b. Request medical backup from the treatment area.
  c. Begin mouth to mask or bag-valve mask ventilation.
  d. Move the patient to the care area and intubate.

176. You have responded to a home for an unknown emergency. Your patient, a 74-year-old male named George Evans, has been found at home in rigor mortis with dependent lividity. The best thing to tell his family initially is
  a. "Mr. Evans is no longer with us."
  b. "I'm sorry to tell you that Mr. Evans has died."
  c. "It's obvious that Mr. Evans is long gone."
  d. "I think it's possible that Mr. Evans passed in his sleep."

177. Which statement about use of disposable gloves and infection control is incorrect?
  a. Gloves should be worn for every patient contact.
  b. Gloves should be changed for each new patient contact.
  c. Gloves cannot protect healthcare workers from needle sticks.
  d. Gloves should be worn while eating or drinking in the ambulance.

178. A 72-year-old man trips and falls while walking to his bathroom. Physical findings include a lateral rotation of the left foot and knee. The patient has tenderness and a protrusion in the left groin area. You suspect
   a. distal femur fracture.
   b. anterior dislocation of the hip.
   c. ischeal tuberosity fracture.
   d. posterior dislocation of the hip.

179. When is use of "reasonable" force or use of restraints permissible for a patient?
   a. The patient is alert, cooperative but anxious.
   b. The patient has altered level of conscious caused by injury, substance abuse, or illness.
   c. It is never appropriate to use any force on a patient.
   d. This is at the discretion of the paramedic or the crew's officer.

180. EMS providers often have to communicate incident and patient information to other personnel using radio telecommunications. Which of the following aids in achieving this goal?
   a. using technical terms as often as possible
   b. using radio codes to shorten communication time
   c. always using a set format when communicating with medical control
   d. using clear English in transmitting information

► Answers

1. **b.** This choice lists the organs that can be palpated in the right upper quadrant (liver, gall bladder, head of pancreas, part of duodenum, and part of the colon).

2. **a.** Stable angina is caused by a temporary low flow state in the coronary arteries that does not lead to cell injury or death (infarction). During hypoperfusion, lactic acid and excessive carbon dioxide are not carried away, causing irritation and pain.

3. **b.** Due to the low blood pressure, this patient would be classified as unstable. Immediate intervention will be needed to correct this condition. Delivering medications may take too long to administer. Defibrillation may invoke ventricular fibrillation.

4. **a.** In the AVPU algorithm, used to assess level of consciousness, the *P* stands for the patient's response to painful stimuli.

5. **b.** The focused history and physical exam, undertaken only after immediate threats to life have been corrected, consists of ascertaining the nature of illness or injury, previous history (via SAMPLE), vital signs, and focused exam.

6. **c.** Pulse pressure refers to the difference between the diastolic and systolic blood pressure readings. A narrowing pulse pressure indicates increasing diastolic pressure and decreasing systolic pressure. Perfusion will stop once both pressures come together.

7. **b.** The patient's heart is not pumping efficiently, possibly due to an MI. This would result in a loss of blood pressure throughout the cardiovascular system, including the pulmonary vessels. The lack of pressure causes plasma to leak into the interstitial space of the lungs, causing the adventitious breath sounds.

8. **b.** A sudden loss of blood flow to the leg within the arterial bed would account for the sudden change in skin color and temperature.

9. **b.** This set of vitals, known as Cushing's triad (respiratory rate increased, heart rate decreased, blood pressure increased), is common in closed head injuries.

10. **d.** Placing the victim in the sniffing position manipulates the head and neck, facilitating airflow.

11. **d.** Choices **a**, **b**, and **c** are all common in closed head injuries; **d** (hemopneumothorax) is not.

12. **b.** A patient with a detached retina will often complain of seeing a dark curtain in front of part of the field of vision.

13. **c.** While the patient may be complaining of chest discomfort, administering nitroglycerin would only worsen an already low blood pressure. Even with fluid leaking into the interstitial lung tissue secondary to the low blood pressure in the pulmonary circulation, a diuretic would also carry the same risk of reducing pressure even more. This patient requires a vasoactive medication such as dopamine to increase blood pressure.

14. **b.** Traumatic asphyxia occurs when serious rib injury pushes the chest wall inward, resulting in severe hypoventilation and backflow of venous blood. Important signs and symptoms of this include dyspnea, bloodshot eyes, distended neck veins, and a cyanotic upper body.

15. **b.** The head and upper back are each equal to 9% of body surface area.

16. **c.** This is often the appearance of a third-degree burn, which is painless because of destruction of nerve cells.

17. **d.** The vital signs listed in choice **d** indicate the presence of shock. An isolated injury of penetrating trauma to the upper arm is not generally life threatening. A 10-mile-per-hour impact to a pedestrian is not generally a significant MOI. Burns to the entire chest cover a body surface area of approximately 9%; this would not in itself require rapid transport unless other problems existed.

18. **c.** Eye opening = 2; verbal response = 2; motor response = 4.

19. **d.** The classic signs and symptoms of appendicitis are given.

20. **b.** The abdominal aorta is located in the retroperitoneal space. A sudden loss of pressure due to an aortic aneurysm will result in loss of perfusion below the site of injury.

21. **b.** Esophageal varices, or enlarged blood vessels in the esophagus, present as painless vomiting of blood (i.e., as painless hematemesis).

22. **a.** Although symptoms of full-blown AIDS include Kaposi's sarcoma and opportunistic infections, initial symptoms of infection with the AIDS virus often consist only of mild fatigue and fever.

23. **d.** The patient's heart rate is not fast enough to be the primary source of the chest pain. Therefore, administration of nitroglycerin may resolve the chief complaint, which in turn may slow the heart rate down.

24. **a.** The patient is displaying signs and symptoms of bowel obstruction.

25. **c.** There are many atypical signs and symptoms of MI in elderly patients; choices **a**, **b**, and **d** list three of them. A tearing sensation in the chest generally indicates a dissecting aneurysm is occuring.

26. **d.** Kussmaul breathing is characteristic of diabetic ketoacidosis.

27. **c.** The correct description of normal vesicular breath sounds (low in pitch, soft, with a long inspiratory phase and a short expiratory phase) is given.

28. **d.** The OPQRST mnemonic is used to define the chief complaint associated with medical conditions such as pain, dyspnea, dizziness, and vague sensations. It is not usually used in trauma or actual unconsciousness.

29. **a.** The pain of stable angina is brought on by exertion and relieved by rest, oxygen, and nitroglycerin.

30. **a.** PID causes lower abdominal discomfort that is difficult to localize and often has an associated fever. Pain associated with an ectopic pregnancy is more localized, as is the pain associated with solid organ involvement.

31. **d.** The most common signs and symptoms of hypertensive emergency (restlessness, confusion, blurred vision, nausea, and vomiting) are given.

32. **c.** The body's physiological mechanisms compensate for the insult that causes shock. Therefore, while changes in vital signs are ominous late signs in patients with poor tissue perfusion, they are unlikely to occur in a young healthy adult who has just entered a state of shock.

33. **c.** The head will tend to drop down as the shoulders begin to pass through the birth canal. The paramedic can gently guide the head to help with the process.

34. **a.** The release of catecholamines that results from the initial drop in blood pressure causes the feelings of anxiety and restlessness.

35. **d.** This patient is exhibiting the classic signs and symptoms of emphysema.

36. **b.** Epinephrine 1:1,000 is not indicated for this patient.

37. a. Breathing through pursed lips is a common compensatory mechanism COPD patients use to provide positive end-expiratory pressure, which forces more alveoli to inflate.

38. b. Carbon monoxide poisoning can cause a falsely high pulse oximetry reading.

39. d. Blockage of the airway by the tongue can occur when the patient is in any position.

40. b. The jaw thrust is used to open the airway of patients with suspected cervical spine injury. Any trauma patient with questionable or unknown mechanism of injury should be assumed to have a cervical spine unjury until it is ruled out.

41. c. The respiratory syncytial virus, which causes only mild upper-respiratory infections in older persons, causes bronchiolitis, a serious respiratory infection, in infants and young children.

42. a. This patient's blood pressure is still compensating for the allergic reaction; therefore, the patient is not in anaphylactic shock.

43. c. Isuprel, haldol, and dopamine are not indicated for this patient. Hydroxyzine is an antihistamine that can be used to treat the puritis (itchy red welts).

44. c. This patient needs to be monitored for possible anaphylactic shock.

45. a. If breath sounds are stronger on one side than on the other, or absent on one side, this suggests that the tube has been inserted too far and is resting in one bronchus.

46. c. With the exception of the blue extremities, the infant scores a "2" on Activity, Pulse, Grimace, and Respirations. Her "Appearance" scores as a 1.

47. d. A ruptured ectopic pregnancy usually occurs within the first trimester. Eclampsia and PID are not associated with bleeding.

48. c. Pulsus paradoxus, or a drop in blood pressure with each respiratory cycle, is associated with chronic obstructive pulmonary disease (COPD).

49. d. *Tracheal tugging* refers to retraction of neck tissues during respiratory effort.

50. c. A dull sound on chest percussion may be associated with pneumonia, hemothorax, or pulmonary edema.

51. a. Once it is attached to the patient's finger, the pulse oximeter will continuously record the pulse rate and oxygen saturation level.

52. b. The patient is showing signs and symptoms of emphysema. Administer low-flow oxygen to preserve his hypoxic drive.

53. b. A sudden rupture of an ectopic pregnancy would result in a loss of blood that would place the patient in compensatory shock.

54. a. Kussmaul's respirations, which are associated with diabetic ketoacidosis, are characterized by increased rate and depth of respirations.

55. a. Loss of pulmonary surfactant, which can occur in pneumonia and other conditions, increases the tendency of the alveoli to collapse and, thus, increases the work necessary for respiration.

56. b. Hydrogen ion concentration, or pH, is measured on a scale of 1 (highly acidic) to 14 (highly alkaline), with 7 being neutral. For each unit on the scale, the solution is ten times more acidic or alkaline. These measurements are very important in the consideration of the oxygen-diffusing capacity of the blood, where very small changes in pH are highly significant.

57. c. The first step in treating a conscious child of this age with a complete airway obstruction is to perform the Heimlich maneuver (i.e., subdiaphragmatic abdominal thrusts). Continue until the obstruction is relieved or the child becomes unconscious.

58. d. To prevent tissue damage, you should attempt to physically remove foreign material only if you can actually see the obstruction with a laryngoscope.

59. d. This patient has symptoms of a pulmonary embolism.

60. b. You would expect to see this patient in tachycardia rather than bradycardia due to the increasing dyspnea and hypoxia resulting from the pulmonary embolism.

61. a. The pulmonary embolism has caused the right side of the heart to have to pump harder against a resistance caused by the partial blockage. This results in the severe shortness of breath and hypoxia.

62. d. This patient should be transported in the position in which it is easiest for her to breathe (i.e., the shock position).

63. a. Myocardial infarction, ruptured aneurism, and anticoagulant use are not common causes of pulmonary embolism.

64. b. In both of these cases, relieving pressure off the trapped umbilical cord (prolapsed) or the face and airway passages (trapped breech) may be the life-saving measure provided by the paramedic.

65. a. The shock position is used only if head injury is not suspected.

66. d. Because the PASG corrects a symptom and not the underlying problem, deflation should be attempted only in the hospital after the underlying hypovolemia is corrected.

67. b. A limb presentation during delivery requires a cesarean section to complete the delivery. Provide high-flow oxygen and care to the mother during transport.

68. d. The rule of thumb when approaching a hazardous-materials situation can be remembered as being "up, up, and away." This will help minimize risk exposure to the crew.

69. a. The patient should be supine with the head elevated to enhance venous return. If congestive heart failure is present, the patient should be positioned at least semi-Fowler's (sitting up at least 45 degrees).

70. a. These changes (increased blood pressure, decreased pulse and respiratory rate) are characteristic of patients with increased intercranial pressure.

71. a. The T wave on the ECG reflects the repolarization of the ventricles.

72. d. Calculate the rate by multiplying the number of complexes in a 6-second interval by 10. The heart rate is 130.

73. b. Normal atrial depolarization is represented in Lead II as a positive rounded P wave.

74. b. A normal P-R interval is 0.12–0.20 seconds; a normal QRS complex lasts 0.04–0.12 seconds.

75. d. The "reasonable person" standard sets a minimum guideline for what similarly trained personnel would do under similar circumstances, in this case, a cardiac arrest. As long as the crew could demonstrate that its actions were reasonable and expected to be done by other prehospital care providers in a similar situation, this would avoid a negligence allegation.

76. b. The valsalva maneuver (bearing down against a closed glottis) stimulates the vagus nerve, which innervates the heart.

77. a. Atrial fibrillation with a low ventricular rate is suggestive of digitalis toxicity.

78. d. Lidocaine is the first-choice drug for perfusing ventricular tachycardia.

79. c. Risk factors for atherosclerosis include diabetes, advanced age, obesity, lack of exercise, hypertension, and smoking.

80. d. The pain of myocardial infarction is not relieved by nitroglycerin, acetaminophen, or oxygen; morphine is usually needed.

81. c. The medical group supervisor will need to establish overall responsibility for the medical section, interacting with other lead officers such as police, fire, and public works. The triage officer will need to establish the number of severity of victims as early as possible.

82. d. Patients are generally sorted into different areas according to the severity of their injuries. Austere medical care is typically provided at a treatment area. The treatment officer oversees the care provided by other medical personnel.

83. b. Myocardial infarction is a common cause of left ventricular failure, which is closely associated with pulmonary edema.

84. c. The primary goal for patients with left ventricular failure and pulmonary edema is to reduce venous return to the heart, or preload, and thus reduce pressure on the pulmonary circulation.

85. b. The patient's history, signs, and symptoms suggest right ventricular failure.

86. a. Signs of cardiogenic shock include a sudden drop in systolic blood pressure and increasing confusion.

87. c. The patient is showing signs and symptoms of abdominal aortic aneurysm. Do not palpate the abdomen unnecessarily; treat decreased tissue perfusion and transport.

88. a. The most common signs (rapid labored breathing and tachycardia) are given; onset is usually sudden, and there may or may not be chest pain.

89. b. The clinical picture suggests deep venous thrombosis. The correct action is to elevate the leg and transport the patient for further evaluation. Do not massage the area or allow the patient to walk, since pulmonary emboli may be provoked.

90. d. Each of the answers defines an emancipated minor.

91. b. Initial attempts in an adult patient typically use 200 joules; this is gradually increased to 360 joules.

92. c. Carotid sinus massage can convert PSVTs by increasing vagal tone and decreasing heart rate.

93. b. External cardiac pacing is used to correct symptomatic bradycardias by directing the heart's electrical system.

94. c. Five to fifteen mg by slow IV push is the correct dosage and route when diazepam is used to relax the patient and cause amnesia before cardioversion.

95. a. Dobutamine is used in patients with congestive heart failure to increase stroke volume and in that way increase cardiac output.

96. a. S1 and S2 are normal sounds; extra sounds are abnormal findings.

97. d. These vital signs (BP elevated, pulse fast and irregular, respirations rapid and labored) are consistent with left ventricular failure with pulmonary edema.

98. a. These are symptoms of diabetic ketoacidosis.

99. b. Warm, dry skin, tachycardia, and increased respirations are common vitals seen in keto-acidotic patients.

100. b. Ketoacidotic patients have low levels of insulin.

101. c. Most likely, this patient has not taken his insulin or has an infection that upset the glucose-insulin balance.

102. a. Kussmaul's respirations are very deep and rapid and represent the body's attempt to compensate for the metabolic acidosis produced by the ketones and organic acids in the blood.

103. b. The appropriate treatment for this patient would be a blood glucose test; an IV of isotonic crystalloid solution like normal saline, Ringer's lactate, or D5W; and an initial fluid bolus of 500 ml.

104. b. A defusing is different from a debriefing in that they are held 8–10 hours after the event, rather than 24–48 hours. Defusings are more informal than a debriefing as well.

105. b. Asymmetrical movements during respiration suggest injury to the chest wall.

106. d. A concussion is a brief loss of consciousness in response to head trauma.

107. d. Use gentle traction to bring the distal part of the limb into alignment with the proximal part.

108. a. If the patient's condition is such that rapid transport is necessary, you would care for limb injuries while en route, rather than completing a detailed physical exam and bandaging and splinting on scene.

109. b. You cannot harm a patient by immobilizing a limb properly, but you may possibly cause further injury by failing to immobilize a fracture.

110. d. Because a tearing wound can tear multiple large blood vessels, bleeding may be particularly difficult to control, and a tourniquet may be necessary.

111. a. Changes in behavior are the most common signs of hypoglycemia. Other signs and symptoms include diaphoresis, tachycardia, and headache.

112. b. Although diazepam (Valium) does reduce anxiety, it is given to seizure patients to suppress the spread of electrical activity through the brain, as well as to relax the muscles.

113. a. The correct dosage and route of administration (0.3–0.5 mg epinephrine 1:10,000, administered intravenously) is given.

114. d. Beta agonists such as albuterol are most frequently used in the treatment of reactive airway disease (asthma). They are also used to prevent or relieve bronchospasm and laryngeal edema in patients with anaphylaxis. Beta blockers are often used to control hypertension, but beta agonists are not given to raise blood pressure, making choice **c** incorrect.

115. b. According to START triage principles, transport of this patient to definitive care can be delayed. He is breathing spontaneously, has a radial pulse, and is conscious. The fractured femur is not factored into the evaluation of transport status.

116. a. The most common symptoms of acetaminophen overdose (nausea and vomiting, malaise, diaphoresis, right upper quadrant pain) are listed.

117. d. Sodium bicarbonate is sometimes ordered in the field for ingestions of tricyclic antidepressants with cardiac symptoms (wide-complex tachycardias).

118. b. Heat will cause the poison to break down and lessen the harm to the patient.

119. c. PCP can cause bizarre delusions as well as violent and uncontrollable behavior.

120. b. Rapid, shallow respirations, weak pulse, cold, clammy skin, and dizziness are signs and symptoms of heat exhaustion. Patients **c** and **d** show signs and symptoms of heat stroke and patient **a** shows signs of heat cramps.

121. d. All of the activities are related to the practice of the paramedic.

122. c. Due to the chance of post-event pulmonary edema, all near-drowning victims should be admitted to the hospital for observation.

123. b. All other options list signs and symptoms of decompression sickness; only **b** includes signs of air embolism (sharp chest pain with sudden onset; dyspnea with coughing).

124. c. During silences, remain relaxed and attentive and wait to hear what the patient has to say. This will encourage the patient to talk.

125. a. Physical complaints, such as loss of use of a body part, may be manifestations of anxiety disorders. Other manifestations include rapid breathing, unrealistic fears, trembling, and sweating. Most physical manifestations can be attributed to anxiety only after ruling out all other possible causes.

126. a. The goal with this asthma patient would be to correct hypoxia, reverse bronchospasms, and decrease inflammation.

127. a. Cold air, not warm air, is a common trigger for asthma. Choices **b**, **c**, and **d** are also triggers.

128. c. Albuterol, terbutaline, and/or steroids are commonly used in the treatment of asthma.

129. b. Tell the child realistically, in language she can understand, what you are doing and why.

130. b. Protocols are generally crafted by members of the local or regional medical community and guide the actions of the paramedic in the field.

131. a. In cases of suspected child abuse, your responsibility is to ensure that the patient receives necessary care immediately and report your findings.

132. d. Fever in a child younger than three months old is considered to be meningitis unless proven otherwise; transport all infants with fever promptly.

133. c. Management of epiglottitis consists of airway maintenance, oxygen, and prompt transport.

134. a. The medical control physician should be able to engage with the on-scene physician in discussion with the patient's condition, the level of care that will be provided by the EMS personnel, and the transportation destination decision.

135. c. Using the Broselow Tape or another length/weight measuring system is the most appropriate way to determine proper medication for a pediatric patient.

136. d. Valium is usually given orally or rectally.

137. a. Your first step following placement of the ET tube is to confirm its placement in the trachea. After confirmation of placement, secure the tube with tape or using a commercial device to help prevent dislodging of the tube. Pay especially close attention to these tubes as they are easily displaced, even when secured. Depending upon which size tube you use, it may or may not be a cuffed tube. Medication administration will follow after confirmation of placement and securing the tube.

138. a. Epinephrine is indicated for pediatric bradycardia in this situation.

139. a. During a frontal crash, the "down and under" pathway causes the knees to strike the lower dashboard violently, causing the described injury pattern.

140. b. Cavitation caused by the pressure wave of the bullet's forces creates both temporary and permanent openings within the tissues. Tremendous forces are transferred from the velocity of the bullet to the tissues, causing damage.

141. d. The signs and symptoms of epiglottitis are given.

142. c. During significant force to the head, the brain can shift and strike the opposite side of the skull away from the original force. This mechanism can cause a contracoup injury.

143. d. In addition to the child's age, the size of the endotracheal tube should be based on the size of the cricoid ring, which is the narrowest part of a child's airway.

144. c. To preserve physical evidence, avoid handling clothing and cleaning or bandaging wounds, unless there is hemorrhage. Do not allow the victim to bathe, comb her hair, or change her clothing. Do not subject the patient to any unnecessary physical examinations.

145. b. A subdural bleed occurs when a small vein bleeds into the area below the dura mater. It may take some time before pressure from the bleeding is high enough to cause clinical signs and symptoms.

146. a. Look for crowning, or the appearance of the baby's head at the opening of the vagina, only during a contraction.

147. c. The patient is most likely suffering a miscarriage. Treat her for signs and symptoms of shock due to blood loss, provide emotional support, retain any clumps of tissue she passes, and transport.

148. a. Supine-hypotensive syndrome, a normal occurrence during late pregnancy, is caused by the pressure of the pregnant uterus on the inferior vena cava when the patient is supine.

149. d. While the other answers are signs and symptoms of shock, only **d** reflects a specific sign that points directly to the underlying cause of hypoperfusion.

150. b. To avoid a precipitous delivery, tell the mother to stop pushing after the head is delivered.

151. c. A prolapsed cord should be treated by placing two fingers of a gloved hand to raise the presenting part of the fetus off the cord; then place the mother in Trendelenburg or knee-chest position, administer high-flow oxygen, and transport immediately.

152. b. Position the neonate at the level of the mother's vagina, with its head slightly lower than the body to facilitate drainage of secretions.

153. b. The retina captures the image that is projected by the lens of the eye. It can spontaneously separate from the inner surface of the eye, causing sudden and painless loss of vision.

154. a. Ventilate with 100% oxygen, and then evaluate the heart rate and initiate chest compressions if necessary.

155. b. Oxygen toxicity occurs only if oxygen is administered for several days; do not withhold oxygen in the prehospital setting.

156. b. Fluid therapy for a neonate consists of 10 mL/kg (= 20 mL for a 2-kg neonate), administered via syringe over a 5- to 10-minute period.

157. a. Flail segment is very possible in this case, due to the mechanism of injury. The lack of other signs or symptoms such as jugular venous distension or unequal or absent breath sounds minimizes the possibilities of a pneumothorax or tamponade.

158. c. A tiered EMS system is one in which varying levels of resources are dispatched to calls depending upon the nature of the incident as determined by the 911 dispatcher.

159. d. The lack of jugular venous distension in the supine position is very telling; it suggests a large loss of volume from the circulatory system.

160. b. Indirect (or offline) medical control is any EMS activity that involves medical (physician) input either before or after (but not during) the care of the patient (e.g., standing orders, run critiques, quality improvement).

161. d. Using START triage, separating out the walking wounded from the more severely injured patients is the first step in triaging large numbers of patients.

162. b. Breathing/airway is the first parameter that should be assessed, followed by pulse and mental status.

163. b. The START triage algorithm dictates that patients with respiratory rates above 30 be classified as immediate.

164. b. The decreased level of consciousness places the patient in the immediate category. Once he is moved to the treatment area, he may be monitored for a while or transported quickly.

165. c. Reposition the head and examine for spontaneous respirations. If they are immediately present, categorize the patient as immediate. If they are absent, categorize the patient as dead/unsalvageable and move on to the next patient.

166. b. A durable power of attorney for healthcare delegates the right to make medical decisions to someone else in the event that the patient becomes disabled or incompetent. Choices **a**, **b**, and **c** are all examples of advanced directives.

167. a. Negligence refers to an intentional deviation from the accepted standard of care that results in harm to a patient.

168. c. Implied consent covers situations in which the patient is not capable of consenting to treatment but a reasonable person would do so.

169. d. If a competent adult patient refuses treatment and transport, you should consult with medical control, explain to the patient the risks of refusal in detail, document the informed refusal, and, if possible, have the refusal witnessed by someone who is not an EMS employee.

170. a. A subluxation of the shoulder is a partial dislocation of the joint, due to injuries sustained by the rotator cuff during a severe twisting force to the joint.

171. d. Only absolutely essential care, such as ABCs and spinal immobilization, should be done in the "hot zone."

172. a. The purpose of the initial scene size-up at a mass-casualty incident is to determine what additional resources will be needed.

173. d. The staging officer is primarily responsible for assembling all available vehicles to make sure they are ready for deployment as needed.

174. a. START and METTAG, systems used at mass-casualty incidents, are designed to be carried out very quickly by minimally trained personnel.

175. a. If a patient continues to remain apneic following a second attempt to open the airway, he or she is considered unsalvageable.

176. b. Inform the family that the patient has died in plain, simple language. This avoids any misunderstanding and prevents any false hopes that may arise from a misunderstanding. Always deliver this news with compassion and respect.

177. d. Gloves cannot protect you from food- or airborne-infectious agents (and personnel should not eat or drink inside the ambulance).

178. b. The outward rotation of the left extremity along with the deformity in the groin area points to an anterior dislocation injury.

179. b. If the patient is altered and is placing himself or others in harm's way, the EMS provider should use any method within reason to control the patient's actions.

180. d. Using plain English will help reduce confusion in radio traffic, especially if the other agencies involved are not familiar with radio codes.

6 ▶ Paramedic Practice Exam 4

CHAPTER SUMMARY

This is the last of four practice exams in this book based on the National Registry EMT-Paramedic written exam. Using all of your experience and strategy that you gained from the other three, take this exam to see how far you have come since your first one.

 LTHOUGH THIS IS the last practice exam in this book, it is not designed to be any harder or trickier than the other three. It is simply another representation of what you might find on the real test. There shouldn't be anything here to surprise you. Because you have worked hard taking practice tests, that should be true of the real test, too—you **will** be prepared and you **won't** be surprised.

For this last test, pull together all the tips you've been practicing since the first test. Give yourself the time and the space to work. Select an unfamiliar location to take the test since you won't be taking the real test in your living room—the public library would be a good choice, as long as your branch is not excessively noisy. You should draw on what you have learned from reading the answer explanations. If you come across a question that you find puzzling, think back to those explanations and see if they can help you zero in on the correct answer.

Most of all, relax. You have worked hard and have every right to be confident!

Exam 4

1.	ⓐ	ⓑ	ⓒ	ⓓ	46.	ⓐ	ⓑ	ⓒ	ⓓ	91.	ⓐ	ⓑ	ⓒ	ⓓ
2.	ⓐ	ⓑ	ⓒ	ⓓ	47.	ⓐ	ⓑ	ⓒ	ⓓ	92.	ⓐ	ⓑ	ⓒ	ⓓ
3.	ⓐ	ⓑ	ⓒ	ⓓ	48.	ⓐ	ⓑ	ⓒ	ⓓ	93.	ⓐ	ⓑ	ⓒ	ⓓ
4.	ⓐ	ⓑ	ⓒ	ⓓ	49.	ⓐ	ⓑ	ⓒ	ⓓ	94.	ⓐ	ⓑ	ⓒ	ⓓ
5.	ⓐ	ⓑ	ⓒ	ⓓ	50.	ⓐ	ⓑ	ⓒ	ⓓ	95.	ⓐ	ⓑ	ⓒ	ⓓ
6.	ⓐ	ⓑ	ⓒ	ⓓ	51.	ⓐ	ⓑ	ⓒ	ⓓ	96.	ⓐ	ⓑ	ⓒ	ⓓ
7.	ⓐ	ⓑ	ⓒ	ⓓ	52.	ⓐ	ⓑ	ⓒ	ⓓ	97.	ⓐ	ⓑ	ⓒ	ⓓ
8.	ⓐ	ⓑ	ⓒ	ⓓ	53.	ⓐ	ⓑ	ⓒ	ⓓ	98.	ⓐ	ⓑ	ⓒ	ⓓ
9.	ⓐ	ⓑ	ⓒ	ⓓ	54.	ⓐ	ⓑ	ⓒ	ⓓ	99.	ⓐ	ⓑ	ⓒ	ⓓ
10.	ⓐ	ⓑ	ⓒ	ⓓ	55.	ⓐ	ⓑ	ⓒ	ⓓ	100.	ⓐ	ⓑ	ⓒ	ⓓ
11.	ⓐ	ⓑ	ⓒ	ⓓ	56.	ⓐ	ⓑ	ⓒ	ⓓ	101.	ⓐ	ⓑ	ⓒ	ⓓ
12.	ⓐ	ⓑ	ⓒ	ⓓ	57.	ⓐ	ⓑ	ⓒ	ⓓ	102.	ⓐ	ⓑ	ⓒ	ⓓ
13.	ⓐ	ⓑ	ⓒ	ⓓ	58.	ⓐ	ⓑ	ⓒ	ⓓ	103.	ⓐ	ⓑ	ⓒ	ⓓ
14.	ⓐ	ⓑ	ⓒ	ⓓ	59.	ⓐ	ⓑ	ⓒ	ⓓ	104.	ⓐ	ⓑ	ⓒ	ⓓ
15.	ⓐ	ⓑ	ⓒ	ⓓ	60.	ⓐ	ⓑ	ⓒ	ⓓ	105.	ⓐ	ⓑ	ⓒ	ⓓ
16.	ⓐ	ⓑ	ⓒ	ⓓ	61.	ⓐ	ⓑ	ⓒ	ⓓ	106.	ⓐ	ⓑ	ⓒ	ⓓ
17.	ⓐ	ⓑ	ⓒ	ⓓ	62.	ⓐ	ⓑ	ⓒ	ⓓ	107.	ⓐ	ⓑ	ⓒ	ⓓ
18.	ⓐ	ⓑ	ⓒ	ⓓ	63.	ⓐ	ⓑ	ⓒ	ⓓ	108.	ⓐ	ⓑ	ⓒ	ⓓ
19.	ⓐ	ⓑ	ⓒ	ⓓ	64.	ⓐ	ⓑ	ⓒ	ⓓ	109.	ⓐ	ⓑ	ⓒ	ⓓ
20.	ⓐ	ⓑ	ⓒ	ⓓ	65.	ⓐ	ⓑ	ⓒ	ⓓ	110.	ⓐ	ⓑ	ⓒ	ⓓ
21.	ⓐ	ⓑ	ⓒ	ⓓ	66.	ⓐ	ⓑ	ⓒ	ⓓ	111.	ⓐ	ⓑ	ⓒ	ⓓ
22.	ⓐ	ⓑ	ⓒ	ⓓ	67.	ⓐ	ⓑ	ⓒ	ⓓ	112.	ⓐ	ⓑ	ⓒ	ⓓ
23.	ⓐ	ⓑ	ⓒ	ⓓ	68.	ⓐ	ⓑ	ⓒ	ⓓ	113.	ⓐ	ⓑ	ⓒ	ⓓ
24.	ⓐ	ⓑ	ⓒ	ⓓ	69.	ⓐ	ⓑ	ⓒ	ⓓ	114.	ⓐ	ⓑ	ⓒ	ⓓ
25.	ⓐ	ⓑ	ⓒ	ⓓ	70.	ⓐ	ⓑ	ⓒ	ⓓ	115.	ⓐ	ⓑ	ⓒ	ⓓ
26.	ⓐ	ⓑ	ⓒ	ⓓ	71.	ⓐ	ⓑ	ⓒ	ⓓ	116.	ⓐ	ⓑ	ⓒ	ⓓ
27.	ⓐ	ⓑ	ⓒ	ⓓ	72.	ⓐ	ⓑ	ⓒ	ⓓ	117.	ⓐ	ⓑ	ⓒ	ⓓ
28.	ⓐ	ⓑ	ⓒ	ⓓ	73.	ⓐ	ⓑ	ⓒ	ⓓ	118.	ⓐ	ⓑ	ⓒ	ⓓ
29.	ⓐ	ⓑ	ⓒ	ⓓ	74.	ⓐ	ⓑ	ⓒ	ⓓ	119.	ⓐ	ⓑ	ⓒ	ⓓ
30.	ⓐ	ⓑ	ⓒ	ⓓ	75.	ⓐ	ⓑ	ⓒ	ⓓ	120.	ⓐ	ⓑ	ⓒ	ⓓ
31.	ⓐ	ⓑ	ⓒ	ⓓ	76.	ⓐ	ⓑ	ⓒ	ⓓ	121.	ⓐ	ⓑ	ⓒ	ⓓ
32.	ⓐ	ⓑ	ⓒ	ⓓ	77.	ⓐ	ⓑ	ⓒ	ⓓ	122.	ⓐ	ⓑ	ⓒ	ⓓ
33.	ⓐ	ⓑ	ⓒ	ⓓ	78.	ⓐ	ⓑ	ⓒ	ⓓ	123.	ⓐ	ⓑ	ⓒ	ⓓ
34.	ⓐ	ⓑ	ⓒ	ⓓ	79.	ⓐ	ⓑ	ⓒ	ⓓ	124.	ⓐ	ⓑ	ⓒ	ⓓ
35.	ⓐ	ⓑ	ⓒ	ⓓ	80.	ⓐ	ⓑ	ⓒ	ⓓ	125.	ⓐ	ⓑ	ⓒ	ⓓ
36.	ⓐ	ⓑ	ⓒ	ⓓ	81.	ⓐ	ⓑ	ⓒ	ⓓ	126.	ⓐ	ⓑ	ⓒ	ⓓ
37.	ⓐ	ⓑ	ⓒ	ⓓ	82.	ⓐ	ⓑ	ⓒ	ⓓ	127.	ⓐ	ⓑ	ⓒ	ⓓ
38.	ⓐ	ⓑ	ⓒ	ⓓ	83.	ⓐ	ⓑ	ⓒ	ⓓ	128.	ⓐ	ⓑ	ⓒ	ⓓ
39.	ⓐ	ⓑ	ⓒ	ⓓ	84.	ⓐ	ⓑ	ⓒ	ⓓ	129.	ⓐ	ⓑ	ⓒ	ⓓ
40.	ⓐ	ⓑ	ⓒ	ⓓ	85.	ⓐ	ⓑ	ⓒ	ⓓ	130.	ⓐ	ⓑ	ⓒ	ⓓ
41.	ⓐ	ⓑ	ⓒ	ⓓ	86.	ⓐ	ⓑ	ⓒ	ⓓ	131.	ⓐ	ⓑ	ⓒ	ⓓ
42.	ⓐ	ⓑ	ⓒ	ⓓ	87.	ⓐ	ⓑ	ⓒ	ⓓ	132.	ⓐ	ⓑ	ⓒ	ⓓ
43.	ⓐ	ⓑ	ⓒ	ⓓ	88.	ⓐ	ⓑ	ⓒ	ⓓ	133.	ⓐ	ⓑ	ⓒ	ⓓ
44.	ⓐ	ⓑ	ⓒ	ⓓ	89.	ⓐ	ⓑ	ⓒ	ⓓ	134.	ⓐ	ⓑ	ⓒ	ⓓ
45.	ⓐ	ⓑ	ⓒ	ⓓ	90.	ⓐ	ⓑ	ⓒ	ⓓ	135.	ⓐ	ⓑ	ⓒ	ⓓ

	a	b	c	d			a	b	c	d			a	b	c	d
136.	a	b	c	d		151.	a	b	c	d		166.	a	b	c	d
137.	a	b	c	d		152.	a	b	c	d		167.	a	b	c	d
138.	a	b	c	d		153.	a	b	c	d		168.	a	b	c	d
139.	a	b	c	d		154.	a	b	c	d		169.	a	b	c	d
140.	a	b	c	d		155.	a	b	c	d		170.	a	b	c	d
141.	a	b	c	d		156.	a	b	c	d		171.	a	b	c	d
142.	a	b	c	d		157.	a	b	c	d		172.	a	b	c	d
143.	a	b	c	d		158.	a	b	c	d		173.	a	b	c	d
144.	a	b	c	d		159.	a	b	c	d		174.	a	b	c	d
145.	a	b	c	d		160.	a	b	c	d		175.	a	b	c	d
146.	a	b	c	d		161.	a	b	c	d		176.	a	b	c	d
147.	a	b	c	d		162.	a	b	c	d		177.	a	b	c	d
148.	a	b	c	d		163.	a	b	c	d		178.	a	b	c	d
149.	a	b	c	d		164.	a	b	c	d		179.	a	b	c	d
150.	a	b	c	d		165.	a	b	c	d		180.	a	b	c	d

▶ Paramedic Exam 4

Answer questions 1–4 on the basis of the following information.

You respond code 3 to a "shortness of breath" call. Upon arrival, you find the First Responders placing a 70-year-old male patient on a nonrebreather mask, running the oxygen flowmeter at 15 lpm. Family members state that the patient came back from the store approximately 45 minutes ago, complaining of moderate respiratory distress. He has a history of "some sort of lung disease," for which he uses an inhaler. The family does not know what type of medication the patient is taking. There is no history of fever or recent illness.

You observe that the patient is cyanotic. The oxygen reservoir on the mask does not appear to collapse, even though the liter flow is set correctly. Although he is sitting on the edge of the bed, his eyes are closed and he does not respond to verbal commands. There is accessory muscle use evident, with intercostal muscle retractions.

His breath sounds are diminished in all fields and absent in both bases. Faint expiratory wheezing is auscultated at only the apices. His heart rate is 140, respiratory rate 42, and BP 106/72. The pulse oximeter registers an SpO2 of 75%. The rest of his physical exam is unremarkable.

1. Based on the information given, what might be a suspected assessment?
   a. toxic inhalation
   b. emphysema
   c. foreign body obstruction
   d. pneumonia

2. What would be your initial priority in managing this patient's condition?
   a. Get additional medical history from the family.
   b. Instruct First Responders to reduce the liter flow from 15 to 10 lpm to allow the reservoir to collapse.
   c. Instruct First Responders to assist the patient's ventilations with a BVM and 100% oxygen.
   d. Begin an IV of normal saline.

3. What airway adjunct(s) might you consider first for this patient?
   a. bag-valve mask
   b. nasal tracheal intubation
   c. combitube or PTL airway
   d. oral pharyngeal airway

4. Which of the following medications may be used in the management of this patient's condition?
   a. morphine sulfate
   b. albuterol
   c. adenosine
   d. epinephrine

5. Which patient's vital signs are considered normal for the age and sex described?
   a. male, age 76: P 88, R 26, BP 160/100
   b. female, age 40: P 72, R 18, BP 130/80
   c. male, age 14: P 62, R 12, BP 90/60
   d. female, age 3: P 130, R 40, BP 110/70

6. When using the OPQRST mnemonic to assess a patient's pain, you would assess the *R* portion of the mnemonic by asking
   a. "When did it start hurting you?"
   b. "Does the pain move anywhere?"
   c. "What makes it feel better?"
   d. "Does the pain feel sharp or dull?"

7. Which set of signs and symptoms is characteristic of a patient in compensated shock?
   a. lethargy; confusion; pulse and blood pressure normal to slightly elevated; skin cool; and capillary refill delayed
   b. coma; pulse and blood pressure very low; skin pale, cold, and clammy with delayed capillary refill time
   c. lapsing into unconsciousness; pulse and blood pressure moderately elevated; mottling of extremities; and cyanosis around lips
   d. unconsciousness; bradycardia; blood pressure dropping; extremities cold; capillary refill delayed; and absent radial pulses

8. A driver who follows a "down and under" pathway of injury after a collision is most likely to have which type of injury?
   a. fractured ribs
   b. ruptured diaphragm
   c. fractured femur
   d. lacerated liver or spleen

9. The *paper bag effect* occurs when the occupant of a car takes a deep breath just before a collision, resulting in which of the following injuries?
   a. pneumothorax
   b. pulmonary embolism
   c. shearing of the aorta
   d. lung laceration

10. A conscious adult who falls a distance of 20 feet is most likely to land on his or her
   a. head.
   b. hands.
   c. back.
   d. feet.

11. Your patient, a middle-aged female, was a pedestrian struck by a car. She opens her eyes only in response to pain and makes no verbal response; her best motor response is withdrawal in response to pain. The Glasgow Coma Scale score for this patient is
   a. 3.
   b. 5.
   c. 7.
   d. 9.

12. Your patient, the victim of an assault, is experiencing malocclusion and numbness to the chin. There is also a suspected nasal fracture, and significant facial bleeding and bruising. What treatment is appropriate for this patient?
   a. Secure the airway with a nasopharyngeal airway, control bleeding, and transport with the patient sitting upright.
   b. Secure the cervical spine, control the airway but avoid the use of a nasopharyngeal airway, control bleeding, and transport.
   c. Treat for signs and symptoms of shock, control the airway with nasal intubation and suction, and transport.
   d. Secure the cervical spine, attach ECG monitor, apply PASG, and control the airway, but avoid the use of a nasopharyngeal airway.

13. The presence of marked purplish-red raccoon eyes on a patient in the prehospital environment should lead you to suspect which of the following?
   a. shock and respiratory distress
   b. recent cervical spine trauma
   c. a significant mechanism of injury
   d. significant previous head injury

14. The best way to prevent decompensated shock in trauma patients is routinely to
 a. monitor for a drop in blood pressure so you can quickly correct any arising problems.
 b. search for early signs and symptoms in patients with a significant mechanism of injury.
 c. transport all seriously injured patients rapidly without taking time to stabilize on scene.
 d. immobilize your patient to a long spine board before moving him or her.

15. Your patient is a middle-aged female who has been in a car accident. Because the initial assessment showed no immediate life threats, you are now treating her most serious injuries, which include a suspected broken femur and kneecap. After stabilizing the injured leg and rechecking the pulse, motor responses, and sensation, you should
 a. repeat the initial assessment.
 b. stabilize the cervical spine.
 c. check the proximal pulse.
 d. apply the PASG and transport.

16. Your patient is a 26-year-old construction worker who has fallen approximately 35 feet and suffered multiple injuries. The Glasgow Coma Scale score is 9, respiratory rate is 32, respiratory expansion is normal, the blood pressure is 100/70, and capillary refill is delayed. What score should this patient receive if you are using the Revised Trauma Score?
 a. 15
 b. 13
 c. 11
 d. 9

Answer questions 17–19 on the basis of the following information.

Your unit is dispatched to a single automobile crash. The patient's car hit a large tree head-on. The patient, a young adult woman, is found conscious and alert but trapped in the car. The air bag deployed and she denies any head or neck pain, although she does complain of hip and left leg pain. After a difficult 20-minute extrication, the patient is finally released from the car. Suddenly your patient's vital signs begin to collapse.

17. This patient is most likely transitioning from
 a. decompensated shock to hypovolemic shock.
 b. cardiogenic shock to hypovolemic shock.
 c. compensated shock to decompensated shock.
 d. decompensated shock to compensated shock.

18. The patient has a closed fracture of the left ankle and the pelvis is stable. There is no penetrating trauma noted in the chest or abdomen, and the patient denies pregnancy. Which of the following chambers of the PASG should be inflated?
 a. both legs and the abdominal compartment
 b. the right leg and the abdominal compartments
 c. the left leg and the abdominal compartments
 d. None. PASG is not indicated in this patient.

19. You start a large bore IV of normal saline. Which of the following medications should you administer?
 a. lidocaine
 b. morphine
 c. dopamine
 d. None. Medication is not indicated.

20. A patient who complains of pain in the left upper abdominal quadrant may be suffering from which of the following?
   a. pancreatitis
   b. appendicitis
   c. hepatitis
   d. diverticulitis

21. The signs of uremia resulting from chronic renal failure include which of the following?
   a. pale skin, diaphoresis, and edematous extremities
   b. pasty, yellow skin and wasting of the extremities
   c. anxiety, delirium, nausea, and hallucinations
   d. anorexia, watery diarrhea, nausea, and vomiting

22. Your patient is a 75-year-old man. His wife called EMS because he "has a terrible headache and is very confused." Vital signs: respirations, 26; pulse, 78; and blood pressure, 200/120. The primary problem you must address is most likely which of the following?
   a. hypertensive emergency
   b. senile dementia
   c. cardiac tamponade
   d. elder abuse by the wife

23. Which assessment findings are consistent with cardiogenic shock in a patient who is suffering a presumed AMI?
   a. respirations 26, BP 100/70, and cyanosis
   b. respirations 10, BP 160/100, and diaphoresis
   c. respirations 36, BP 90/60, and cyanosis
   d. respirations 18, BP 140/90, and cool, dry skin

24. Your patient is a 67-year-old male who smokes cigarettes and has a history of previous MI. He complains of sudden onset severe pain in his right leg. He also relates numbness and diminished motor function in the right leg. Other assessment findings are diminished pulse, pallor, and lowered skin temperature in the right leg. You should suspect which of the following?
   a. femoral artery aneurysm
   b. occlusion of the femoral artery
   c. deep venous thrombosis
   d. hypertensive encephalopathy

Answer questions 25–28 on the basis of the following information.

You respond to a 41-year-old male who has been injured in an explosion at an illegal chemistry (drug) laboratory. During your assessment, you notice a spinal deformity and a possible closed head injury. Your patient also has ruptured tympanic membranes and sinus injuries.

25. Which of the following is not a phase of blast injury?
   a. alpha
   b. primary
   c. secondary
   d. tertiary impact

26. This patient's sinus injuries most likely occurred during which blast phase?
   a. alpha
   b. primary
   c. secondary
   d. tertiary impact

27. Your victim has first- and second-degree burns to his face. These are flash burns from the explosion. Witnesses deny that the patient's clothes were on fire. You should suspect what injury?
   a. extensive lung tissue burns
   b. extensive airway burns
   c. aspiration pneumonia
   d. limited airway burns

28. During your assessment, you notice a rigid, very tender abdomen. If this injury occurred in the secondary phase, it would be due to which of the following?
   a. thermal burns to the stomach
   b. flying debris and propelled objects
   c. deceleration impact with a hard surface
   d. compression of air-containing organs

29. Your patient is a 27-year-old male who is found unconscious on a bathroom floor. He is not breathing, has pinpoint pupils, and has a fresh puncture wound to his right forearm. He has multiple scars that form a bluish streak over the veins on the backs of both hands. This patient is most likely suffering from which of the following?
   a. a seizure disorder
   b. multiple spider bites
   c. a narcotic overdose
   d. anaphylactic shock

30. Your patient is an 84-year-old man with extreme difficulty breathing, apprehension, cyanosis, and diaphoresis. Assessment findings include elevated pulse and blood pressure. Rales and rhonchi are heard on auscultation. There is no chest pain. What condition should you treat this patient for?
   a. right-side heart failure
   b. cardiogenic shock secondary to MI
   c. dissecting aortic aneurysm
   d. left-side failure secondary to MI

31. Which of the following patient presentations would best be managed by a nasal intubation?
   a. The patient is unconscious, and apneic with a pulse.
   b. The patient is unconscious, apneic, and pulseless.
   c. The patient is unconscious, is breathing slowly, and has a gag reflex.
   d. The patient is semiconscious, is breathing slowly, and has a pulse.

32. After you orally intubate the patient, your partner ventilates the patient with a bag-valve device. You auscultate the lung sounds to confirm placement. No sounds are heard over the epigastrium; breath sounds are present on the right side of chest and are decreased over the left. What should you do next?
   a. Hyperventilate the patient and prepare for a cricothyrotomy.
   b. Withdraw the tube after deflating the cuff, insert an oropharyngeal airway, and ventilate the patient with a bag-valve device.
   c. Withdraw the tube slightly after deflating the cuff, reinflate the cuff, and re-evaluate lung sounds.
   d. Insert a large diameter needle into the fourth or fifth intercostal space, midaxillary line.

33. Your patient has a partial airway obstruction but adequate air exchange. You should
  a. perform the Heimlich maneuver as though a complete airway obstruction exists.
  b. intubate the patient nasally in an attempt to bypass the area of obstruction in the lungs.
  c. monitor the patient closely while he or she continues trying to clear the airway him- or herself.
  d. intubate the patient orally, administer high-flow oxygen, and transport immediately.

34. Common causes of aspiration include reduced level of consciousness and
  a. acute myocardial infarction.
  b. attempts to control the airway.
  c. trauma patient management.
  d. diabetic coma and insulin shock.

35. An important disadvantage in using both nasal- and oropharyngeal airway adjuncts is that they
  a. are unable to protect the lower airway from aspiration.
  b. may become obstructed by aspirated material.
  c. can be used only in patients whose gag reflex is intact.
  d. are not made in a wide enough range of sizes to fit all patients.

36. After inserting a blind-insertion-airway device, what step should you take before inflating the balloon to ensure that the tube is properly positioned?
  a. Measure the amount of the device outside the mouth.
  b. Hyperventilate the patient with 100% oxygen.
  c. Look for chest rise and auscultate the lungs and abdomen.
  d. Auscultate in the midaxillary line only for bilateral breath sounds.

37. An endotracheal tube that has been advanced too far is prone to enter which of the following structures?
  a. esophagus
  b. trachea
  c. left main bronchus
  d. right main bronchus

Answer questions 38–43 on the basis of the following information.

You are called to a nursing home and find a bed-ridden 78-year-old male patient with insulin-dependent diabetes who is in acute respiratory distress. The staff reports that the patient has been ill for the last few days and has had a persistent productive cough with thick yellow sputum. His blood pressure is 168/72. His respiratory rate is 40 and labored with coarse rhonchi upon auscultation of lung sounds. Lung sounds are absent in the lower third of his lung fields. The patient is also febrile with hot, dry, flushed skin.

38. This patient is most likely suffering from which condition?
  a. chronic bronchitis
  b. right-side heart failure
  c. emphysema
  d. pneumonia

39. Treatment of this patient should include which of the following medications?
  a. albuterol
  b. methylprednisolone
  c. oxygen
  d. bronchodilators

40. What common infectious disease does this patient's clinical presentation mimic?
   a. meningitis
   b. HIV/AIDS
   c. tuberculosis
   d. hepatitis B

41. What is most likely the cause of his decreased lung sounds?
   a. complications from diabetes mellitus
   b. atelectasis from inactivity
   c. congestive heart failure
   d. pulmonary hypertension

42. If this patient required tracheal suctioning, which of the following steps should be followed?
   a. Suction upon insertion of the suction catheter.
   b. Sterile technique is required for suctioning this patient.
   c. Wearing gloves is the only BSI required.
   d. Hyperventilate the patient only after suctioning.

43. How should this patient be positioned for transport?
   a. high Fowler's position
   b. supine
   c. left-lateral recumbent
   d. prone

44. Which of the following drugs is administered only by inhalation?
   a. albuterol
   b. terbutaline sulfate
   c. aminophylline
   d. epinephrine 1:10,00

45. Prehospital care of an open pneumothorax includes
   a. high-flow oxygen, monitoring for signs of tension pneumothorax, and intubation.
   b. needle decompression, ventilatory support, and rapid transport.
   c. occlusive dressing, high-flow oxygen, and rapid transport.
   d. airway maintenance, creation of a one-way valve, and fluid boluses.

46. You are called for a 55-year-old man who "suddenly collapsed." He is apneic and pulseless. Initial management of this patient's airway should include
   a. assisted ventilation with a bag-valve mask at 6–10 L/min.
   b. immediate endotracheal intubation and ventilation with a bag-valve device.
   c. assisted ventilation with a nonrebreather mask at 10–15 L/min.
   d. insertion of an oropharyngeal airway and ventilation with bag-valve mask.

47. A whistling or musical sound heard on exhalation is referred to as what abnormal breath sound?
   a. snoring
   b. wheezing
   c. stridor
   d. friction rub

48. Your patient is an adult female whom you suspect is unconscious as a result of an upper-airway obstruction. You use the head-tilt/chin-lift method to open her airway and then attempt to give two ventilations, which are unsuccessful. What is the next thing you should do?
   a. give five thrusts on her abdomen
   b. give five chest thrusts on her sternum
   c. finger sweep from cheek to cheek
   d. reposition and attempt to ventilate again

49. Your patient is a 67-year-old male who reports a 45-pack-a-year smoking history, frequent respiratory infections, and a chronic cough. He is overweight and has peripheral cyanosis. Auscultation of the chest reveals rhonchi. There is also noticeable jugular vein distention. What disease process should you suspect?
- **a.** emphysema
- **b.** status asthmaticus
- **c.** chronic bronchitis
- **d.** lung cancer

50. When using a peak flow meter to measure peak expiratory flow, the correct procedure is to
- **a.** ask the patient to inhale deeply, then exhale once as quickly as possible, taking one reading.
- **b.** ask the patient to inhale normally and exhale twice, recording the lowest reading.
- **c.** ask the patient to inhale and exhale as hard and fast as possible, taking one reading only.
- **d.** ask the patient to inhale and exhale twice as hard as possible, recording the highest reading.

51. What is the correct dosage of methylprednisolone for a patient who is experiencing a severe asthma attack?
- **a.** 300–500 mg, given subcutaneously or intramuscularly
- **b.** 125–250 mg, given via IV or intramuscularly
- **c.** 275 mg, given intramuscularly, followed by 1 gram IM 2 hours later
- **d.** 200–300 mg, diluted in 2–3 mL normal saline, via nebulizer

52. Hyperventilation syndrome most often occurs in a patient who is
- **a.** anxious and upset.
- **b.** asthmatic.
- **c.** in shock from trauma.
- **d.** a heavy smoker.

53. Your patient is a 51-year-old male with a history of COPD. He states that he has called EMS because he "can hardly breathe." On initial assessment, you determine that the patient is in obvious respiratory distress but not too hypoxic. You should
- **a.** administer high-flow oxygen and prepare to intubate.
- **b.** withhold oxygen to avoid decreasing the hypoxic drive.
- **c.** administer oxygen at a rate of 10–15 L/min via nonrebreather mask.
- **d.** administer low-flow oxygen at a rate of 2–6 L/min via nasal cannula.

54. Your patient is an obese 77-year-old woman who has called EMS complaining of a sudden onset of dyspnea, coughing, hemoptysis, and diaphoresis. On examination, you note tachypnea and tachycardia, crackles and localized wheezing, and distended neck veins and varicose veins. You should suspect
- **a.** myocardial infarction.
- **b.** pulmonary embolism.
- **c.** aortic aneurysm.
- **d.** status asthmaticus.

55. How should you maintain respiratory isolation when transporting a patient suspected of having tuberculosis?
- **a.** Have the patient ride alone in the back of the ambulance.
- **b.** Have the patient wear an oxygen mask while in the unit.
- **c.** Have EMS personnel wear HEPA- or OSHA-approved particle masks.
- **d.** Have both patient and personnel wear the appropriate masks.

Answer questions 56–61 on the basis of the following information.

You are called to the home of a 26-year-old male who is having difficulty breathing. Your assessment reveals a pulse rate of 100 with a strong and regular radial pulse, a blood pressure of 132/78, and a respiratory rate of 36, labored with audible wheezes. The patient's skin is pale, moist, and at a normal temperature. He is having difficulty exhaling and says that he has experienced this before. He rates this event as a 9 on a 1–10 severity scale. He states that this event was unprovoked and that he has been having dyspnea for 20–30 minutes.

56. This patient is most likely suffering from which of the following conditions?
- **a.** pulmonary edema
- **b.** upper airway obstruction
- **c.** asthma
- **d.** simple pneumothorax

57. Treating this patient with nebulized steroids would
- **a.** provide no immediate relief of the bronchospasm.
- **b.** reverse the effects of the bronchospasm in the lungs.
- **c.** increase the severity of the bronchospasm.
- **d.** be potentially dangerous due to increased blood pressure.

58. Which of the following medications should be used for the treatment of this patient?
- **a.** terbutaline sulfate
- **b.** epinephrine 1:1,000 IM
- **c.** albuterol via nebulizer
- **d.** all of the above

59. This patient's respiratory distress is due to which of the following?
- **a.** increased cardiac preload and afterload
- **b.** decreased left ventricle stroke volume
- **c.** constriction of the trachea and bronchi
- **d.** constriction of the smaller airways

60. This patient's disease is regarded as a(n)
- **a.** chronic obstructive pulmonary disease.
- **b.** acute obstructive pulmonary disease.
- **c.** chronic inflammatory disease.
- **d.** acute inflammatory disease.

61. This patient's respiratory distress may have been caused by one of several triggers. These triggers include allergens, irritants, and which of the following?
- **a.** viral infections
- **b.** hot weather
- **c.** exercise
- **d.** bee stings

62. Blood enters the right atrium of the heart through which of the following structures?
 a. tricuspid valve
 b. right ventricle
 c. left pulmonary arteries
 d. superior and inferior vena cava

63. What is the systolic blood pressure is estimated to be if a patient's carotid pulse is palpable, but the radial and femoral pulse are not?
 a. 40 mmHg
 b. 60 mmHg
 c. 80 mmHg
 d. 100 mmHg

64. Simultaneous palpation of the apical impulse and the carotid pulse allows you to assess the relationship between the
 a. heart and lungs.
 b. central and peripheral circulation.
 c. pulse and blood pressure.
 d. ventricular contractions and pulse.

65. A patient presents with a sudden onset of sharp chest pain and respiratory distress. She has clear lung sounds, a pulse rate of 110 and regular, BP of 112/76, and respirations of 28. Which of the following conditions best describes this patient presentation?
 a. psychogenic hyperventilation
 b. acute exacerbation of asthma
 c. pulmonary embolism
 d. pulmonary edema

66. You are starting an IV, and your first cannulation attempt is unsuccessful. The second attempt should be made where?
 a. inferior to the first
 b. superior to the first
 c. on a different limb
 d. in a central vein

67. A 2-year-old female presents with lethargy and poor feeding. The parent states that the patient has had a moderate fever for the past seven days, with diarrhea, nausea, and vomiting for the past four days. She presents with pale, cool skin, a pulse rate of 180, and a respiratory rate of 40. She cries weakly when a painful stimulus is applied. The EKG shows a rapid narrow complex dysrhythmia. Based upon this information, what is the patient's primary problem?
 a. respiratory distress
 b. respiratory failure
 c. hypoperfusion
 d. dysrythmia

68. What vasopressor drug is most commonly used to treat cardiogenic shock in the prehospital environment?
 a. norepinephrine
 b. epinephrine
 c. dopamine
 d. dobutamine

69. Your patient has received penetrating trauma to the neck and is bleeding profusely from several large vessels. You should
 a. apply constant direct pressure over the clavicle.
 b. apply an occlusive dressing, then apply pressure.
 c. clamp the injured vessels and apply sterile plastic.
 d. tamponade the vessels with gauze and 4×4s.

70. The signs and symptoms of cerebral hemorrhage include which of the following?
a. disorientation and confusion, decreased pulse and blood pressure, and cyanosis
b. transient loss of consciousness, headache, drowsiness, nausea, and vomiting
c. leakage of cerebrospinal fluid, headache, and bleeding from the nose or ears
d. headache, Battle's sign, confusion, lethargy, and rapid loss of consciousness

71. A 2-year-old female presents with lethargy and poor feeding. The parent states that the patient began looking irritable a few hours ago and has become increasingly difficult to arouse. The patient had vomited once prior to your arrival. She presents with pale, cool skin, a pulse rate of 200, and a respiratory rate of 40. She cries weakly when a painful stimulus is applied. The EKG shows a rapid narrow complex tachydysrhythmia. What is the patient's primary problem?
a. respiratory distress
b. respiratory failure
c. hypoperfusion
d. dysrythmia

72. Which statement about hypoglycemia is correct?
a. Hypoglycemia may occur in nondiabetic patients, especially in chronic alcoholics.
b. In nondiabetics, hypoglycemia usually results from taking too much food or exercise.
c. Signs and symptoms of hypoglycemia are slow in onset and develop over several hours.
d. In late stages of hypoglycemia, the patient may complain of extreme hunger and thirst.

73. What are the predisposing factors for the development of hyperosmolar hyperglycemic nonketotic coma (HHNK)?
a. old age, Type II diabetes, coexisting cardiac or renal disease, and increased insulin requirements
b. young age, Type I diabetes, coexisting cardiac or respiratory disease, and decreased insulin requirements
c. obesity, Type II diabetes, viral infections, chronic alcoholism, and poor carbohydrate metabolism
d. coexisting kidney disease, Type I diabetes, narcotics use, and noncompliance with insulin regimen

74. Myocardial infarction may go unrecognized in elderly patients. Why is this true?
a. They tend to have abnormal ECGs even in the presence of an AMI.
b. They take prescription nitroglycerin to relieve their symptoms.
c. They are not able to describe their symptoms clearly to the doctor.
d. They lack typical symptoms such as frequent chest pain or discomfort.

75. Blood flows from the pulmonary veins into which structure?
a. left atrium of the heart
b. right atrium of the heart
c. capillaries of the lungs
d. right ventricle of the heart

76. A 12-year-old unconscious male is being drawn to the edge of the pool by two lifeguards. He is apneic. How would you establish his airway?

    a. manual cervical spine precautions, head-tilt/chin-lift

    b. manual cervical spine precautions, modified jaw thrust

    c. Either is appropriate.

    d. Neither is appropriate.

77. What is the effect of parasympathetic stimulation on the heart?

    a. an increased heart rate and increased stroke volume

    b. a decreased heart rate and increased stroke volume

    c. an increased heart rate and decreased stroke volume

    d. a decreased heart rate and decreased stroke volume

78. Unilateral wheezing in a 14-month-old child is suggestive of

    a. asthma.

    b. aspiration of a foreign body.

    c. heart failure.

    d. croup.

79. What does a normal P-R interval on an ECG recording indicate?

    a. The interventricular septum has been depolarized, and the impulse is now in the AV node.

    b. The right and left ventricles have depolarized, sending the impulse to the Purkinje fibers.

    c. The ventricular myocardial cells have repolarized during the last part of ventricular systole.

    d. The electrical impulse has been successfully conducted through the atria and the AV node.

80. What does a QRS complex that is longer than 0.12 seconds or bizarre in shape indicate?

    a. an artifact is present on the ECG tracing

    b. a conduction abnormality in the ventricles

    c. a pacemaker abnormality in the AV node

    d. a conduction abnormality in the atria

81. Which statement about the care of a patient with a cardiac problem is correct?

    a. The paramedic should always treat the dysrhythmia, not the patient.

    b. All intravenous cardiac medications are administered by rapid IV bolus.

    c. Administration of medications takes precedence over life-support measures.

    d. Epinephrine, lidocaine, and atropine can all be administered via the ET tube.

82. On the ECG tracing, dysrhythmias that originate in the SA node share which of the following features in Lead II?

    a. All P waves are similar in appearance.

    b. All QRS complexes are of normal duration.

    c. All P-R intervals are shortened and irregular.

    d. The rhythm is usually regularly irregular.

83. What is the first treatment for a symptomatic patient with atrial fibrillation with a sustained ventricular rate greater than 150 beats per minute?

    a. vagal or Valsalva maneuvers

    b. immediate cardioversion

    c. administration of adenosine

    d. administration of lidocaine

84. Which statement about ventricular fibrillation is correct?
   a. Fine ventricular fibrillation indicates the most recent onset of dysrhythmia.
   b. A single precordial thump should be attempted before BLS or defibrillation is begun.
   c. Ventricular fibrillation and nonperfusing ventricular tachycardia are treated alike.
   d. Patients can often tolerate ventricular fibrillation for up to 15 minutes.

85. A 110-pound child is apneic and pulseless. The monitor reveals ventricular fibrillation. CPR is in progress. Initial management of the child will include an initial defibrillation of
   a. 25 joules.
   b. 50 joules.
   c. 100 joules.
   d. 200 joules.

86. A 5-year-old patient weighing 40 pounds was struck by a car. He is hypotensive and tachycardic. You successfully start an IV in the patient's left antecubital vein. You should infuse which of the following?
   a. 260 ml of NS as a bolus
   b. 360 ml of D_5W as a drip
   c. 800 ml of NS as a bolus
   d. 360 ml of NS as a bolus

87. A patient with a suspected MI but without respiratory compromise should receive oxygen by what rate and delivery device?
   a. 3–4 L/min by nasal cannula
   b. 5–10 L/min by simple face mask
   c. 10–15 L/min by nonrebreather mask
   d. 15–20 L/min by bag-valve mask

88. Which of the following factors would exclude a patient from receiving thrombolytic therapy after an AMI?
   a. The patient is less than 75 years old.
   b. The chest pain persists after nitroglycerin.
   c. The chest pain lasts longer than 30 minutes.
   d. He or she has had recent ulcer or gastrointestinal bleeding.

89. If it is not treated, left ventricular failure results in which of the following conditions?
   a. ischemic heart disease
   b. pulmonary edema
   c. chronic hypertension
   d. cor pulmonale

90. Which of the following features distinguishes dissecting aortic aneurysm from acute myocardial infarction?
   a. The pain of dissecting aortic aneurysm is severe from the outset.
   b. The pain of dissecting aortic aneurysm usually migrates to the right arm.
   c. Patients with dissecting aortic aneurysm have equal peripheral pulses.
   d. Patients with dissecting aortic aneurysm show signs of pericardial tamponade.

91. What is the prehospital treatment for patients with suspected deep venous thrombosis?
   a. treatment for shock, including oxygen and PASG
   b. administration of nitroglycerin and heparin
   c. initiation of thrombolytic therapy to control the clot
   d. immobilization and elevation of the extremity

92. The presence of delta waves on an ECG is indicative of
  a. acute myocardial infarction.
  b. new bundle branch block.
  c. Wolff-Parkinson-White syndrome.
  d. paroxysmal junctional tachycardia.

93. Your patient is a 47-year-old male who is experiencing paroxysmal junctional tachycardia. He called EMS because of a sensation of palpitations and lightheadedness. There is no previous history of heart disease. The ventricular rate is approximately 130 per minute, BP is 100/70 and falling, and respirations are 32 and shallow. What should you do?
  a. Do nothing as this dysrhythmia is usually well tolerated.
  b. Attempt vagal maneuvers to slow the heart rate down.
  c. Administer 6 mg Adenosine by rapid IV bolus.
  d. Attempt synchronized cardioversion with 50 joules.

94. Which of the following features is common to all dysrhythmias that originate in the AV junction?
  a. inverted P waves, shortened P-R interval, normal duration of QRS complex
  b. absent P waves with no P-R interval and prolonged QRS complex
  c. upright P waves, normal P-R interval, normal duration of QRS complex
  d. P waves change from beat to beat or disappear entirely, normal QRS complex

95. A 3-year-old patient presents with a rapid narrow complex tachycardia with a rate of 260. He is alert, clings to his parent, and has a strong pulse. How should this patient be treated?
  a. Do nothing, since this is normal.
  b. Administer a 20 ml/kg fluid challenge, since this is a shock condition.
  c. Administer adenosine, since this is a stable SVT.
  d. Cardiovert the patient, since this is an unstable SVT.

96. A transmural myocardial infarction is associated with what kinds of changes on the ECG?
  a. Q wave changes
  b. P-R interval changes
  c. T wave changes
  d. P wave changes

97. Which of the following statements regarding airway management in the pediatric patient is correct?
  a. The curved blade is preferred in infants and children.
  b. The narrowest diameter of the airway in infants and children is just below the glottic opening.
  c. Cuffed endotracheal tubes should be used in children under the age of eight years.
  d. A 4.0 mm i.d. endotracheal tube is recommended for an 18-month-old child.

98. What is the purpose of the body's physiological response to a stressor?
  a. to signal the brain that danger is present
  b. to decrease normal physiological functions
  c. to shut down the autonomic nervous system
  d. to prepare for the most efficient reaction

99. Anxiety may be best defined as which of the following?
   a. a general feeling of uneasiness
   b. an unconscious reaction to a stressor
   c. a factor or event that causes stress
   d. regulation of involuntary movement

Answer questions 100–102 on the basis of the following information.

You respond to a 17-year-old female found unconscious in her backyard by her parents. She has a newly developing skin rash on her right arm, and is having difficulty breathing. You note that she is wheezing. Her parents state that she has no history of respiratory problems or other medical disorders.

100. Which of the following is a possible cause of her condition?
   a. anaphylaxis
   b. febrile seizures
   c. status asthmaticus
   d. epiglottitis

101. What is the first step in managing this patient?
   a. Administer IM diphenhydramine.
   b. Give 2 liters of oxygen via NC.
   c. Aggressively manage the airway.
   d. Administer morphine sulfate.

102. The next step in treating this patient is to start a normal saline or Ringer's lactate IV and to give which of the following medications?
   a. epinephrine
   b. diphenhydramine
   c. albuterol
   d. morphine sulfate

103. A 110-pound child has lost consciousness. The cardiac monitor displays a narrow QRS tachycardia at a rate of 200 beats/minute. A weak pulse is present and the blood pressure is 80/60. Capillary refill is delayed. Oxygen is being administered and an IV has been established. Initial management of this patient will include
   a. synchronized countershock with 25 joules.
   b. synchronized countershock with 50 joules.
   c. unsynchronized countershock with 100 joules.
   d. unsynchronized countershock with 200 joules.

104. A 72-year-old male is found unconscious in his front yard after working in the yard for five hours without a break. He is tachycardic, with hot dry skin and shallow respirations. Management should include which of the following procedures?
   a. Administer furosemide to increase the functioning of the kidneys.
   b. Administer high-flow oxygen.
   c. Establish an IV at TKO rate.
   d. Preserve body heat to reduce chances of a seizure.

105. Moving the outstretched forearm so that the anterior surface is facing downward is called
   a. rotation.
   b. supination.
   c. pronation.
   d. extension.

106. Before using nitrous oxide (Nitronox) for a chest-injury patient, you should exclude the possibility that the patient has which of the following injuries?
   a. cervical spine injury
   b. flail chest
   c. pericardial tamponade
   d. pneumothorax

107. Your patient is a 26-year-old male with a mid-shaft femur fracture and no other apparent injuries. The patient is alert and oriented, and all vital signs are normal. The best way to immobilize this fracture is to use which of the following devices?
   a. the PASG/MAST
   b. a long spine board
   c. a traction splint
   d. a softly padded board

108. In a patient with a thermal burn to the airway, it is critical to watch for signs and symptoms of the development of which of the following?
   a. laryngeal edema
   b. shock
   c. respiratory arrest
   d. bronchiolitis

109. An adult with burns over the front of both arms and the chest is burned over what percentage of her body surface area (BSA)?
   a. 9%
   b. 13%
   c. 18%
   d. 27%

110. How will the skin over a second-degree burn appear?
   a. bright red
   b. mottled red
   c. pearly white
   d. charred black

111. Which patient is most likely to need burn center care versus trauma center care?
   a. female, age 34, second-degree burn over 10% of BSA
   b. male, age 46, third-degree burn over a small area of the back
   c. female, age 52, second-degree burns to face and right hand
   d. male, age 27, second-degree burn over entire left arm excluding hand

112. Prehospital care for a patient who has moderate to severe burns includes which of the following?
   a. wet dressings, one IV line held at a TKO rate, IV antibiotics
   b. wet dressings, two IV lines with large-bore catheters
   c. dry sterile dressings, one IV line held at a TKO rate, epinephrine 1:1,000
   d. dry sterile dressings, two IV lines with large-bore catheters held at a TKO rate

113. Your 16-year-old male patient complains of a fever, sore neck, nausea, vomiting, and headache. During transport, he begins to have a seizure. Which of the following would be your most likely field impression?
   a. brain abscess
   b. cerebral neoplasm
   c. meningitis
   d. sepsis

114. A patient who experienced a seizure, rather than a period of syncope, usually reports that the episode
   a. started when she was standing up.
   b. happened without any warning.
   c. was associated with bradycardia.
   d. lasted only two or three minutes.

115. What is included in the management of a patient in a postictal state?
   a. having the patient sit up, administering high-flow oxygen, and transporting immediately
   b. placing the patient in shock position and treating for signs and symptoms of shock
   c. moving obstacles away from the patient, or moving him or her to a safe location
   d. placing the patient in a recumbent position and administering supplemental oxygen

116. General management for a patient with altered mental status should include which of the following procedures?
   a. Provide low-flow oxygen.
   b. Apply a 12-lead EKG.
   c. Determine blood glucose levels.
   d. Administer dextrose routinely.

117. What are the two most common causes of severe anaphylaxis?
   a. shellfish and roasted peanuts
   b. aspirin and synthetic opiates
   c. egg whites and sesame seeds
   d. penicillin and insect bites/stings

118. A 72-year-old male is complaining of difficulty breathing. His ECG shows a rhythm of 44 with corresponding pulses, a P-R interval of 0.18, and normal R-R intervals. Vitals are blood pressure of 92/56 and respirations of 32. The patient also states that he feels very nauseated and dizzy. Treatment for this patient should include
   a. atropine 0.5 mg.
   b. epinephrine 1:1,000 0.3 mg.
   c. epinephrine 1:10,000 1 mg.
   d. isuprel 2–10 mcg/min.

119. A 52-year-old male patient is experiencing chest palpitations and shortness of breath. Vitals are blood pressure 116/64, pulse 180 and regular, and respirations 36. ECG shows a narrow complex rhythm at a rate of 200 and no discernible P waves. Which of the following regimens is indicated for this patient?
   a. IV, O2, adenosine 6 mg
   b. IV, O2, atropine 0.5 mg
   c. IV, O2, lidocaine 1.5 mg/kg
   d. IV, O2, verapamil 2.5 mg

120. A 58-year-old patient is experiencing shortness of breath. ECG shows a sinus tachycardia at 126; pulse is weak, and blood pressure is 82/52. Which medication and dose would be most appropriate for this patient?
   a. dopamine 5–10 mcg/kg/min
   b. lasix 40 mg
   c. morphine sulfate 5 mg
   d. nitrostat 0.4 mg SL

121. Which finding is helpful in distinguishing poisoning by spider venom from an acute abdominal condition?
   a. abdominal rigidity with no palpable tenderness
   b. right-lower-quadrant pain in the absence of fever
   c. diaphoresis accompanied by chills and fever
   d. the presence of multiple bite marks on the stomach

122. Early symptoms of overdose of tricyclic antidepressants include which of the following?
   a. tachycardia and a wide QRS complex
   b. nausea, vomiting, and severe diarrhea
   c. psychosis and bizarre behavioral changes
   d. altered mental status and slurred speech

123. Which of the following patient scenarios is the typical profile for a victim of classic heat stroke?
   a. a healthy young adult who has been exercising in hot, humid weather
   b. someone sweating profusely and drinking large amounts of water without salt
   c. an elderly person with chronic illness who is confined to a hot room
   d. an infant who is exposed to overly high ambient temperatures indoors

124. Your patient is a hypothermia victim whose body temperature has fallen to 93° F. A symptom of this temperature reading is likely to be
   a. severe shivering.
   b. impaired judgment.
   c. respiratory depression.
   d. bradycardia.

125. Which statement about suicide is correct?
   a. People who talk about suicide rarely attempt it by deadly means.
   b. Suicidal patients are mentally ill and require institutionalization.
   c. The suicide rate is lowest during holiday seasons or birthdays.
   d. There is a high correlation between suicide attempts and alcohol consumption.

Answer questions 126–128 on the basis of the following information.

You respond to a 4-year-old female who has taken an unknown quantity of children's aspirin. Upon arrival, you find the patient conscious, crying, and lethargic. Her mother states that she found the child playing in the bathroom. A flavored children's aspirin bottle was found nearby with only a few tablets in it.

126. In this situation, you should make the assumption that
   a. the aspirin bottle was full and treat accordingly.
   b. the child couldn't possibly have taken all the aspirin tablets.
   c. there is a reason to suspect child abuse due to neglect.
   d. because of the flavorings, the child is not in danger of overdosing.

127. Children's aspirin is in which of the following classes of medications?
   a. tricyclics
   b. acetaminophen
   c. salicylates
   d. benzodiazepines

128. Correct treatment for this patient may include
   a. IV, oxygen, naloxone, and NG tube insertion.
   b. IV, oxygen, ECG, ipecac, and activated charcoal.
   c. IV, ECG, sodium bicarbonate, and epinephrine.
   d. IV, naloxone, and activated charcoal.

129. A 52-year-old female is complaining of chest tightness with radiation to the back. Her EKG shows a sinus tachycardia with multifocal premature ventricular contractions occurring ten times per minute. Her blood pressure is 112/68, and her heart rate is 96 and irregular. Which of the following medications would be indicated for her condition?
   a. lidocaine
   b. adenosine
   c. magnesium sulfate
   d. glucagon

130. Children of which age group are in the greatest danger from airway obstruction caused by aspirated foreign objects?
   a. 1–12 months
   b. 1–3 years
   c. 3–5 years
   d. 6–12 years

131. What is the usual pediatric dose of naloxone for a child less than five years old?
   a. 0.01 mg/kg via IV bolus
   b. 0.1 mg/kg via IV bolus
   c. 1 mg via IV bolus
   d. 2 mg via IV bolus

132. You are called to the scene of a possible drowning at a local pool. Upon arrival, you discover that lifeguards have removed the patient from the pool and are performing rescue ventilations since the patient has a pulse. Upon placing the monitor, you discover a rapid rhythm at 200 beats per minute, no P waves, and a QRS complex of 0.16. Management should consist of
   a. amiodarone 150 mg.
   b. cardioversion 100 joules.
   c. defibrillation 200 joules.
   d. lidocaine 1.5 mg/kg.

133. You must perform chest compressions on a newborn infant if, after oxygenation and ventilation, the heart rate persists in being less than what number?
   a. 60/min
   b. 80/min
   c. 100/min
   d. 120/min

134. Your patient is age 7 and has a suspected broken arm and numerous bruises. The mother states that the child was hurt when he fell off his bike in the morning. What finding would lead you to suspect that the mother's account of the injuries is not true?
   a. multiple fresh bruises on the child's arm and leg
   b. the child cries from pain when you palpate
   c. the child clings to the mother during transport
   d. purplish, yellowish, and greenish bruises

Answer questions 135–137 on the basis of the following information.

You respond to a 25-year-old female who is complaining of vaginal bleeding and abdominal pain. The patient states that she is 33 weeks pregnant and that this is her first pregnancy. She says that when the pain started, it felt like "something was tearing." She denies vaginal bleeding during the pregnancy prior to this event. Upon assessment, you notice what appears to be approximately 500 cc of dark, almost black, blood.

135. Which condition is this patient most likely suffering from?
   a. abruptio placenta
   b. placenta previa
   c. uterine rupture
   d. eclampsia

136. This event is dangerous to
   a. the mother only.
   b. the baby only.
   c. neither patient.
   d. both patients.

137. In addition to high-flow oxygen and continuous monitoring of the mother's vital signs and the baby's fetal heart tones, you should treat this patient with
  a. one or two large bore IVs of normal saline or Ringer's lactate.
  b. one minidrip IV of normal saline and pitocin or terbutaline.
  c. one minidrip IV and PASG with all compartments inflated.
  d. basic life support treatments are all that are needed.

138. Patients with pelvic inflammatory disease often complain of which of the following?
  a. diffuse lower abdominal pain
  b. severe vaginal bleeding
  c. tearing pain in the uterus
  d. itching upon urination

139. The two primary goals of prehospital care of a sexual assault victim are to preserve the victim's privacy and dignity and to
  a. obtain a complete description of the assault.
  b. collect samples of body fluids from the patient.
  c. preserve all physical evidence for the police.
  d. help the victim bathe and change her clothing.

140. A 24-year-old female is complaining of chest pain and difficulty breathing. She has been up for three days studying for finals and has been taking ephedrine supplements to help her stay awake and alert. She also admits to drinking 12 caffeinated soft drinks in the past day. Vitals are BP 80/40, P 180 carotid, and R 42. She is very pale and lethargic. The ECG shows a narrow QRS complex with regular R-R intervals, with no discernable P or T waves at 200 beats per minute. The best treatment for this patient would include
  a. adenosine 6 mg rapid IVP.
  b. cardioversion at 100 joules.
  c. vagal maneuvers.
  d. verapamil 2.5 mg slow IVP.

141. What does it mean if a woman is described as *multipara*?
  a. She is pregnant and morbidly obese.
  b. She has delivered more than one baby.
  c. She has never delivered a viable infant.
  d. She is over 45 years old and pregnant.

142. Your patient is a 32-year-old woman who reports that she is nine weeks pregnant. She is complaining of severe abdominal pain, slight vaginal bleeding, and shoulder pain. Abdominal examination reveals significant tenderness in the lower right quadrant. The patient is somewhat agitated and tachycardic. You should suspect developing shock resulting from which of the following conditions?
  a. ruptured appendix
  b. abruptio placenta
  c. placenta previa
  d. ectopic pregnancy

143. What is the usual clinical presentation of placenta previa?
a. tearing pain and dark red bleeding
b. diffuse abdominal pain and slight bleeding
c. painless bright red bleeding
d. elevated blood pressure and diffuse pain

144. Which of the following findings or factors would make you opt for immediate transport of a pregnant woman rather than attempt delivery in the field?
a. the mother's urge to push
b. the presence of crowning
c. meconium-stained amniotic fluid
d. multiparity with explosive births

145. During a normal delivery, you would suction the infant's mouth and nose just after
a. the head is out of the vagina.
b. the entire infant is delivered.
c. the head and chest are delivered.
d. you clamp the cord.

146. You are managing a patient with symptomatic bradycardia and multifocal PVCs. Suddenly, your patient slumps unconscious and goes into ventricular fibrillation. You confirm that your patient is pulseless. Your next action would be to
a. administer lidocaine 1.5 mg/kg.
b. begin CPR.
c. cardiovert at 200 joules.
d. defibrillate at 200 joules.

147. What is the correct method to stimulate respirations in a neonate?
a. Hold it by the feet while you slap the buttocks.
b. Slap the soles of the feet and rub the back.
c. Let the cool air cause it to shiver a little.
d. Rub the head but avoid touching the fontanel.

148. What is the greatest concern when a person experiences blunt force trauma to the head?
a. It can interrupt the integrity of the blood brain barrier.
b. It can cause a significant increase in intracranial pressure.
c. It can cause significant ringing in the ears.
d. It can lacerate the scalp, causing bleeding.

149. Why must your assessment be especially diligent in an intoxicated patient?
a. Alcohol can decrease pain tolerance in the patient.
b. Alcohol can mask signs and symptoms of injury.
c. Alcohol can increase the patient's willingness to cooperate.
d. Alcohol can decrease an injury's effect on the patient's level of consciousness.

150. What are the blood vessels in the umbilical cord?
a. one artery and one vein
b. two arteries and two veins
c. one artery and two veins
d. two arteries and one vein

Answer questions 151–154 on the basis of the following information.

You respond to a 19-year-old female who is 25 weeks pregnant and is complaining of a severe headache and blurred vision. Upon initial assessment, you notice that she has substantial edema, especially in her feet and hands. She states that she has not been under the regular care of a physician during this pregnancy.

151. What abnormality would you expect to see in this patient's vital signs?
- **a.** tachycardia
- **b.** tachypnea
- **c.** hypertension
- **d.** hypotension

152. This patient is most likely suffering from the condition known as
- **a.** abruptio placenta.
- **b.** placenta previa.
- **c.** pre-eclampsia.
- **d.** supine-hypotensive disorder.

153. Treatment for this patient includes rapid transport without lights and sirens, an IV of normal saline or Ringer's lactate, and oxygen. It may also call for the administration of which of the following medications?
- **a.** magnesium sulfate
- **b.** pitocin
- **c.** terbutaline sulfate
- **d.** naloxone

154. If left untreated, this patient's condition may worsen and she may begin to experience which of the following?
- **a.** angina pectoris
- **b.** necrosis of tissues
- **c.** grand mal seizures
- **d.** labor pains

155. When should sensory, motor, and perfusion status of an injured extremity be assessed when splinting?
- **a.** only after the splinting device is *fully in place* to assure that adjustments do not cause further impairments
- **b.** before, during, and after the application of any immobilization device
- **c.** only in the conscious, adult patient who is able to understand and follow commands
- **d.** just prior to arrival at the hospital to ensure that your report is accurate and concise

156. You are caring for a 69-year-old AMI patient using online medical control. A bystander, who identifies herself as a physician, looks at the ECG, sees you beginning to administer epinephrine, and requests that you substitute atropine. What should you do?
- **a.** Have the online physician consult directly with the on-scene physician.
- **b.** Follow the directions of the on-scene physician who has assumed care.
- **c.** Ignore the on-scene physician and follow the directions of the online physician.
- **d.** Leave the scene and the patient in the care of the on-scene physician.

157. What is the purpose of offline medical protocols?
- **a.** to provide a standardized approach to common patient problems
- **b.** to give ultimate responsibility to the medical control physician
- **c.** to remove the possibility of malpractice from the EMS provider
- **d.** to allow the paramedic to train less experienced EMS providers

158. Which of the following statements regarding falls among the elderly is most accurate?
a. The elderly have the highest incidence of falls.
b. Fall-related injuries represent the leading cause of accidental death among the elderly.
c. Falls account for the highest percentage of emergency department visits among the elderly.
d. A majority of falls are primarily related to *infrapatellar bursitis.*

159. EMS providers are often the first to identify situations that pose a risk for illness or injury in homes, schools or businesses. Because of this, the EMS provider
a. should be teaching only in the wealthy areas of the cities.
b. should be teaching only in the high schools.
c. is a valuable resource in public education and a component of health promotion.
d. should not teach, since this could take away from the performance of patient care duties.

160. Which of the following situations constitutes abandonment?
a. A paramedic yields control of a patient's care to a physician who has just arrived on the scene.
b. A paramedic yields control of a patient's care to an EMT while the patient still needs ALS level care.
c. An EMT yields control of a patient's care to a paramedic even though the patient only needs BLS level care.
d. A patient refuses transport and the paramedic leaves after obtaining a signature on a refusal of treatment form.

161. In which of the following situations is an EMS provider required to make a report to law enforcement?
a. suspected sexual assault
b. alcohol-related trauma
c. MCV with entrapment
d. illegal drug possession

162. Which patient may be legally placed in protective custody by the police if he or she refuses treatment?
a. a competent 85-year-old man who has signed a DNR order at the nursing home
b. a patient who is drunk and disorderly and who refuses treatment for a head wound
c. an epileptic patient who has just recovered from a seizure but refuses transport
d. a diabetic who has just recovered from insulin shock and wants to go home

163. You are dispatched to the home of a dying patient who has signed a Do Not Resuscitate order. What should you do?
a. Contact medical control before providing any patient care.
b. Give only emotional support to the patient and family members.
c. Carry out all necessary care since such orders apply only to hospitals.
d. Leave immediately without providing any care for the patient.

164. What are the two basic goals of patient packaging?
a. thorough initial and rapid trauma assessments
b. secure the airway and stabilize the cervical spine
c. oxygenate and effective bleeding control
d. stabilize and prepare for transport

165. Which of the following situations is most likely to be declared a major incident?
   a. an accident involving a school bus and car with five patients
   b. a fire at a chemical plant during working hours
   c. a water accident on a state line with two people in the water
   d. a fire involving an isolated single-family residence

166. What is the major responsibility of the finance sector at a major incident?
   a. to document the number of personnel and hours worked
   b. to acquire resources needed to resolve the incident
   c. to predict future needs resulting from the incident and provide for them
   d. to define objectives for resolving the incident

167. You are conducting triage using the START system at a major incident. You encounter a patient who is not breathing. After you position the airway, the patient begins to breathe at a rate of six respirations per minute. Into which category would you now triage this patient?
   a. dead or dying
   b. immediate or critical
   c. delayed
   d. urgent or noncritical

168. The set of duties and skills that a paramedic is permitted to perform during a medical situation is called
   a. primary practice.
   b. consent to practice.
   c. scope of practice.
   d. regional practice.

169. Drawing a patient's blood without her permission may be an example of
   a. battery.
   b. slander.
   c. false imprisonment.
   d. assault.

170. For which of the following procedures is it necessary to wear gloves, gown, mask, and protective eyewear?
   a. starting an IV in a moving ambulance
   b. bleeding control with minimal bleeding
   c. assisting with an emergency childbirth
   d. administering an intramuscular injection

171. Which form of hepatitis poses the lowest risk to paramedics?
   a. hepatitis A
   b. hepatitis B
   c. hepatitis C
   d. hepatitis D

172. The use of alcohol-based handwash is encouraged in the field setting when hot water and soap are not readily available. To be most effective, you should also do which of the following?
   a. Allow the skin to stay wet with the alcohol for at least ten minutes.
   b. Remove gross matter from your hands, since alcohol cannot penetrate protein.
   c. Place your wet hands quickly into gloves to allow the alcohol to penetrate fully.
   d. Quickly dry the alcohol approximately 30 seconds after applying it.

173. When you are caring for more than one trauma patient at a time, you should change your gloves how often?
- **a.** whenever time permits
- **b.** for each new patient
- **c.** for each new procedure
- **d.** whenever they become soiled

174. You are interviewing Mrs. Rodriguez, age 87, who called EMS but seems reluctant to state her primary problem. Mrs. Rodriguez speaks English but is answering your questions slowly and haltingly. Her 20-year-old grandson is also present. In an attempt to obtain the necessary information, you should
- **a.** direct your questions to the grandson only, since Mrs. Rodriguez is probably senile.
- **b.** ask the grandson to translate for Mrs. Rodriguez since she does not understand you.
- **c.** ask questions slowly, clearly, and respectfully, giving Mrs. Rodriguez time to respond.
- **d.** stop the interview and ask the grandson to leave the room, then resume questioning.

175. Which of the following is NOT typically a characteristic of an abused elderly person?
- **a.** wealthy but refuses to give financial assistance to relatives
- **b.** multiple physical and mental impairments, such as dementia
- **c.** incontinent, mentally handicapped, and over the age of 65
- **d.** physically handicapped, over the age of 75, and frail

176. Which of the following is an example of acknowledging and labeling the patient's feelings?
- **a.** "Stop threatening me. I've never hurt you."
- **b.** "You seem angry. Do you want to tell me about it?"
- **c.** "I get angry myself sometimes."
- **d.** "Anger is a hostile emotion. Let's be more positive."

Answer questions 177–180 on the basis of the following information.

Your ambulance is the first on the scene of a suspected radiation emergency. Dispatch has stated that a box containing radioactive material was found unattended and open in a park. No patients have been identified yet and the police department is sealing off the area.

177. When you approach the park, the three principles of safety to keep in mind are
- **a.** time, distance, and shielding.
- **b.** distance, crowd control, and decontamination.
- **c.** decontamination, clothing, and eye protection.
- **d.** gloves, eye protection, and shielding.

178. If you are asked to set up a staging area for additional responding rescue crews, which of the following would be the best location?
- **a.** upwind, close visual range, in an open area
- **b.** downwind, close visual range, in an open area
- **c.** upwind, no visual range, in a building
- **d.** downwind, no visual range, in a building

179. In this situation, who has the responsibility for decontamination of patients?
- **a.** first responding ambulance
- **b.** first responding fire agency
- **c.** hazardous materials team
- **d.** triage and treatment officer

180. Which type of radiation is the most serious?
- **a.** alpha particles
- **b.** beta particles
- **c.** gamma rays
- **d.** delta rays

► Answers

1. **b.** The timing of the onset, medical history, and physical findings point to emphysema as the primary suspect.

2. **c.** This patient has begun to decompensate in terms of his ability to ventilate adequately, as evidenced by the decreased mental status and very poor skin signs. This patient will require aggressive airway management in order to be ventilated.

3. **a.** The most immediate piece of ventilation equipment to use would be a BVM. The patient will need preoxygenation before any attempt of intubation. In addition, as implied by the patient's presenting position, he will likely have an intact gag reflex, making insertion of an OPA difficult, if not impossible.

4. **b.** A beta agonist like albuterol is indicated in this situation. Morphine sulfate may worsen the patient's condition by potentially depressing respiratory dirve. Adenosine is a cardiac medication used to control supraventricular tachycardia. Epinephrine has significant cardiac side effects, especially in older patients.

5. **b.** Only this patient's vital signs are within normal limits for her age. Patient **a** has increased respirations and the systolic blood pressure is within the hypertensive range. Patient **c** has bradycardia (he is 14) and is at the lower end of normal for respirations and blood pressure. Patient **d** is dangerously hypertensive and the heart rate and respiratory rate are above normal limits for that age range.

6. **b.** In the OPQRST mnemonic, *R* stands for *radiation.* You should determine if the pain is radiating, referred, or causing any associated problems.

7. **a.** The signs and symptoms given (lethargy, confusion, pulse and blood pressure normal to slightly elevated, skin cool, and capillary refill delayed) are characteristic of early, or compensated, shock. The single characteristic signaling the change from compensated to uncompensated shock is a drop in blood pressure that remains below normal despite intervention and treatment. You should never wait to see a decrease in BP to decide if shock is present or not, since early in the shock process, sympathetic stimulation during compensation may result in a slight elevation of the diastolic blood pressure.

8. **c.** The down-and-under pathway results in injury to the pelvis and legs rather than to the abdominal and thoracic organs. These injuries are caused as the patient's knees strike the lower part of the dashboard and energy forces travel along the femur to the pelvis and maybe even into the lower spine.

9. **a.** The paper bag effect or paper bag syndrome is thought to be responsible for most pneumothoraces that result from car crashes. During this event, the closed glottis traps pressurized air in the chest. When compression occurs during the crash against the closed glottis, severe damage can occur to the hyperinflated alveoli and bronchioles, resulting in collapse.

10. **d.** Conscious adults who fall more than three times their height tend to land on their feet; this tends to cause bilateral calcaneus fractures, hip dislocations, and compression fractures of the spinal column.

11. c. Her score is 7 and is composed of 2 points for pain, 1 point for verbal response, and 4 points for motor response.

12. b. Patients with facial fractures also have suspected spinal trauma and should be immobilized appropriately. Avoid the use of any nasopharyngeal airway manipulations in a patient with facial fractures, as the device could be introduced directly into the brain by perforating through the area of the fracture. Cardiac (ECG) monitoring, pulse oximetry, and other monitoring devices are always appropriate when you have a seriously injured patient. PASG is not indicated in this patient.

13. d. Periorbital ecchymosis, or "raccoon eyes," presents as bruises circling around the eyes. It often indicates basal or other skull fracture, but when seen in the prehospital environment, it suggests significant previous injury because this condition takes time to develop after injury. The earliest finding you would note with a newly developing skull injury is extreme swelling of the soft tissues around each eye that may make it difficult even to open the eyes to check pupils.

14. b. The best way to prevent shock is to look actively for early signs and symptoms rather than to wait for late signs, such as a drop in blood pressure. Always evaluate the mechanism of injury as this can provide valuable clues to the cause of injuries. This information will also carry weight when you decide whether this patient is "load and go" or "stay and play." Any evidence or strong suspicion of shock means you have a high priority patient.

15. a. Quickly repeat the initial assessment after every significant intervention. You and your partner have had your attention on her lower extremity for a few minutes, and now you should refocus and repeat an ABC assessment. Cervical immobilization with a collar should be completed prior to treatment of the leg. PASG/MAST is not indicated for this patient. Proximal pulse check is part of the reassessment survey that occurs immediately after stabilizing and splinting the leg.

16. b. The score on the Glasgow Coma Scale translates into 4 points on the Revised Trauma Score; the patient receives 3 points for respiratory rate, 1 point for respiratory expansion, 4 points for blood pressure, and 1 point for delayed capillary refill.

17. c. This patient's body is showing signs that it can no longer compensate for the damage done by the traumatic event. In addition, toxic metabolic products may have been trapped in the injured tissues and now be circulating back toward the heart. These toxins may result in cardiac dysrhythmias or cardiac arrest.

18. d. PASG is no longer indicated for routine management of shock patients. If this patient has an unstable pelvis fracture in addition to the presence of shock, PASG could be used as an air splint to assist in stabilizing the fractured pelvis. Because the pelvis is intact, it would be better to rapidly transport her (after full-body and cervical spine immobilization) to a well-padded long spine board. Shock can be managed with oxygen, positioning (elevate lower end of long board), rapid transport, and careful fluid administration. Some services use pulmonary edema and penetrating chest trauma as the only contraindications to the use of PASG. If that is the case in your service area, then PASG could be used for this patient, but in that case, all compartments should be inflated. You would never inflate only one leg and then the abdominal section. Most likely, the garment would not help stabilize the ankle fracture and additional splinting would be required.

19. d. Although your assessment of the pelvis was negative, the mechanism of injury suggests this patient is most likely hemorrhaging internally, resulting in hypovolemic shock. Medications are rarely used in the prehospital management of hypovolemic shock. Dopamine is indicated for cardiogenic shock, and is never indicated with uncorrected hypovolemic shock. Morphine sulfate may help control pain, but its use for this patient is not advisable in the prehospital setting due to the unknown nature of all of her injuries. Your treatment centers around improving oxygenation and prompt transport to the appropriate definitive care facility.

20. a. Pain in the left upper quadrant is most often due to pancreatitis, gastritis, or diseases of the left kidney. Appendicitis often results in right lower quadrant pain, but the actual location of the area of the appendix that is inflamed may result in left lower quadrant or even flank pain. Hepatitis results in dull right upper quadrant pain that is independent of the presence of food in the GI tract. Diverticulitis presents much like an appendicitis, but it is generally localized to the left lower abdomen.

21. b. Signs of uremia are pasty, yellow skin and thin extremities; urea frost is a late sign. These signs result from jaundice, poor nutrition, and protein loss in the tissues. In extreme cases, the potassium level can be dangerously elevated. Pericardial tamponade and uremic encephalopathy may also be present. Coupled with kidney failure, you will see noncardiac pulmonary edema, severe dyspnea, ascites, neck vein distension, and rales in the bases.

22. a. Although the chief complaint was headache and confusion, it is likely that the primary problem to address is hypertensive crisis.

Senile dementia of new onset could have a variety of causes, but in this case, it may be connected to the hypertensive crisis. There is not enough information to determine if elder abuse or cardiac tamponade is present, but it is unlikely in this scenario. Another possibility for this patient is a stroke. If stroke is occurring, prompt management of the hypertensive crisis can reduce morbidity.

23. c. In a patient with acute MI, signs of cardiogenic shock result from cardiac insufficiency from decreased coronary artery perfusion due to inadequate pumping of the heart (mainly the left ventricle). The signs and symptoms include low blood pressure, cyanosis or cool, clammy skin, and rapid breathing. Most of these patients have adequate blood volume and vascular system but an ineffective "pump."

24. b. The patient is displaying signs and symptoms of acute occlusion of the femoral artery. Aneurysms generally do not occur in the femoral artery. If an aneurysm were present, the signs and symptoms would be different from those presented. Deep vein thrombosis would result in vascular pooling distal to the site of occlusion, and edema would be present or developing in the extremity, but arterial circulation would be unaffected.

25. a. Blast injury impact is divided into three phases: primary, secondary, and tertiary. The primary phase occurs during the initial air blast and pressure wave. The secondary phase occurs when the patient is hit by debris propelled by the overpressure of the blast wave. The tertiary phase occurs when the victim is thrown away from the blast into the ground or other hard objects.

26. **b.** During the primary blast, forces from the pressure wave and initial air blast result in compression of air-containing organs such as the sinuses, auditory canals, stomach, lungs, and intestines.

27. **d.** Often, burns are limited to the oro- and nasopharynx in the upper airway. Worsening stridor or hoarseness indicates that edema is developing, which may lead to airway compromise. Flash burns rarely result in extensive airway or lung tissue burns. Aspiration pneumonia is an infectious process that develops following the introduction of a foreign body into the lungs. It is unlikely in this scenario, and if it has occurred, there will be no signs of infection yet.

28. **b.** Compression of air-containing organs is common in the primary blast phase. Deceleration injuries occur during the tertiary phase and thermal burns can occur during any phase of the blast, depending upon whether the pressure wave is superheated, if flaming objects are striking the patient, or if the patient is thrown into a burning area. A rigid, tender abdomen indicates there are internal injuries under the skin, and not surface injuries to the dermis from burns. This injury was most likely caused by flying debris or propelled objects striking the patient.

29. **c.** Common signs of a narcotic overdose are described: Pinpoint pupils are characteristic of heroin and narcotic use, a fresh puncture wound over a vein indicates a recent injection site, and bluish scarring over the veins is consistent with the presence of track marks.

30. **d.** The patient is displaying signs and symptoms of left ventricular failure, which most often occurs secondary to MI. Hypertension and tachycardia is due in part to increased left atrial pressure that is transmitted to the pulmonary vessels. Rales and rhonchi indicate that pulmonary edema is present. Right-side failure can lead to left-side failure, but such a patient generally has dry lungs and dependent edema (usually pedal) as the presenting sign. A dissecting aneurysm will present with pain, syncope, stroke, absent or reduced pulses, heart failure, pericardial tamponade, and/or signs of AMI. If the ventricular failure worsens, cardiogenic shock may develop. You will see the systolic pressure drop dramatically (often to less than 80 mmHg) when this occurs.

31. **c.** There must be some spontaneous respiratory effort for the blind insertion to have a good chance of successful placement. The presentation in answer **d** can probably be managed by basic airway maneuvers.

32. **c.** The original breath sounds indicated that the tube was placed in the trachea, but perhaps too deep. Adjusting the depth of the tube so that the distal end is sitting just above the carina will likely resolve this situation.

33. **c.** If a patient has a partial airway obstruction but adequate air exchange, allow her to continue her spontaneous efforts to clear the airway (coughing), but monitor her carefully. Your interference may actually worsen the obstruction by making it complete. If air exchange becomes inadequate, treat her as if the obstruction is total by performing the Heimlich, intubation, suction, or other efforts to relieve the obstruction.

34. **b.** Attempts to control the upper airway through the insertion of tubes and devices is a common cause of aspiration, which carries a high mortality rate.

35. **a.** Neither the nasopharyngeal nor the oropharygneal airway is long enough to protect the lower airway from aspirated material. Generally, the presence of vomitus or blood in the airway does not affect their use, since suction is easily performed through and around these devices. The devices come in a wide variety of sizes and styles. Use of the oropharyngeal airway is limited to patients who do not have a gag reflex.

36. c. Regardless of which device you use, confirmation of placement is generally advisable prior to inflation of any balloons on the device by looking for chest rise and fall and listening for breath sounds in the chest and abdomen.

37. d. Because of anatomical appearance of the distal trachea, it is most common for an ET tube that has been inserted too far to enter the right main bronchus, resulting in atelectasis and insufficiency of the left lung.

38. d. This patient shows signs and symptoms of pneumonia. The fever is the symptom that provides the differential diagnosis between the various choices.

39. c. In addition to oxygen, this patient needs antibiotics.

40. c. Active tuberculosis presents with fever, flu-like symptoms, and productive cough. Meningitis presents with high fever and flu-like symptoms, but does not have respiratory involvement. HIV may not have any symptoms, although AIDS can present as a variety of diseases depending upon which opportunistic disease has caused infection. Hepatitis B will present primarily with GI problems (nausea, vomiting, pain) and upper right quadrant abdominal pain.

41. b. Diabetic patients heal more slowly from pneumonia when it occurs, but it is not a common disease for them. CHF and pulmonary hypertension would certainly contribute to worsening his signs and symptoms, but the most likely cause of absent or decreased lung sounds in the lower

lobes of a sick elderly patient is incomplete expansion and shallow respiration due to inactivity.

42. b. Because tracheal suctioning will be performed on this patient, sterile technique is required. Suction should only be performed upon withdrawal of the catheter. For protection of the rescuer, gloves, eye protection, and face mask should be worn during the procedure. If the patient is being ventilated you should hyperventilate before and after suctioning.

43. a. Position of comfort is always the optimal transport position for nontraumatic patients when the patient is conscious and oriented. To facilitate breathing and maximize efforts, the best position for this patient would be high Fowler's position.

44. a. Albuterol (Ventolin) is administered only by inhalation.

45. c. The steps involved in management of this injury are occlusive dressing, high-flow oxygen, and rapid transport. Intubation is not necessary for each patient. Needle decompression is not necessary if tension pneumothorax develops. If dyspnea worsens, open the dressing to relieve some of the pressure that is built up. An IV lifeline should be established but large volume fluid resuscitation should be withheld.

46. d. An apneic and pulseless patient is unlikely to have an intact gag reflex, necessitating an OPA to help control the upper airway. A BVM will need at least 10 lpm of oxygen flow in order to adequately oxygenate the patient during ventilations.

47. b. Wheezing, a whistling sound heard on expiration, is generally associated with asthma. Snoring and stridor are upper airway obstructions and a friction rub sounds like rubbing.

48. d. During the initial resuscitation attempt, the next step after two unsuccessful attempts at ventilation for an unconscious adult patient is to reposition the head and try again. Once you have confirmed obstruction, you do not need to repeat this step (repositioning) again. Perform the blind finger sweep following the abdominal thrusts before attempting ventilation each time. Chest thrusts for relieving airway obstruction are reserved for obese and very pregnant adults.

49. c. The patient's history, signs, and symptoms are consistent with chronic bronchitis. The "blue bloater" frequently has peripheral edema, cyanosis, and JVD due to right side heart failure in addition to the respiratory problems. Emphysema patients present with barrel chest and signs of wasting of the extremities.

50. a. The correct procedure is to have the patient inhale deeply and exhale quickly. Some meters ask you to repeat the procedure and average your findings, but you would still have the patient inhale deeply and quickly exhale with each reading.

51. b. The correct dosage and route is 125–250 mg, given via IV or intramuscularly.

52. a. Hyperventilation syndrome, which is characterized by rapid breathing, is most often caused by anxiety, though it is also associated with many organic diseases.

53. d. Administer low-flow oxygen to patients with exacerbation of COPD. Do not ever withhold oxygen from any patient in respiratory distress. Use a pulse oximeter to monitor their SAO$_2$ levels. If the patient becomes dizzy or sleepy, monitor him closely and encourage him to take normal breaths.

54. b. This patient displays many of the risk factors for pulmonary embolism; her signs and symptoms also fit. The rapid onset of the problem should lead you to hypothesize acute pulmonary embolism.

55. d. Both the patient and all personnel who come in contact with him or her should wear appropriate masks in order to maintain respiratory isolation. For your own legal protection and for the optimal patient care, you should never transport a patient unattended in your unit.

56. c. This patient shows the clinical symptoms of asthma. Due to the repeat nature of this episode, it is unlikely that this is pulmonary edema, upper airway obstruction, or simple pneumothorax. If he were suffering from pulmonary edema, you would also expect hemoptysis. A spontaneous (or simple) pneumothorax would also present with a sudden onset, but would most likely not also have wheezing or a history of recurrence.

57. a. Nebulized steroids would provide no immediate relief of this patient's bronchospasm as they will not prevent or lessen attacks in progress. Steroid therapy is useful as a long-term suppressive treatment.

58. d. Any of these medications can be used to treat this patient.

59. d. Constriction of the smaller airways is causing air to be trapped in the alveoli.

60. c. Asthma is regarded as a chronic inflammatory disease. Chronic obstructive pulmonary diseases commonly include emphysema and chronic bronchitis.

61. c. Allergens, exercise, and irritants are common triggers of asthma attacks. Cold weather, stress, and anxiety are lesser triggers.

62. d. Blood enters the right atrium through the superior and inferior vena cava and is pumped through the tricuspid valve into the right ventricle. From there, it passes through the pulmonic valve into the pulmonary arteries and into the lungs.

63. b. If, on initial assessment, the carotid pulse is palpable but the radial pulse is not, the patient's systolic blood pressure is 60–80 mmHg. (Cerebral blood flow stops below 60 mmHg, so it cannot be lower than that.) When the radial is absent but the femoral is present, the pulse is estimated to be around 70 mmHg. When the radial pulse is present the systolic pressure is considered to be at least 80 mmHg. In light of the complete description given, then, the best approximation of the patient's pulse is 60 mmHg.

64. d. Determining the relationship between the apical impulse and the carotid pulse may give you the first indication of a cardiac irregularity, such as a dysrhythmia. To assess central and peripheral circulation, you should assess carotid (central) and radial (peripheral) pulses. Remember that the cardiovascular system requires three factors to work effectively: intact and functioning pump, an adequate circulating blood volume, and a container (vascular vessels) of the appropriate size to circulate the blood effectively. An apical pulse indicated the pump is functioning and a carotid pulse shows you that the circulating blood volume is reaching target tissues.

65. c. The lack of findings is almost as important as the reported ones. For example, not having pedal edema, crackles or wheezes in the lung fields, or hypertension reduces the possibility of pulmonary edema. The lack of medical history or wheezes minimizes asthma as a possible cause.

66. b. A second puncture attempt should be made superior to the first because there is a chance of leakage from the first puncture site.

67. c. The history of diarrhea, nausea, and vomiting indicates a strong dehydration situation resulting in the tachycardia and dyspnea.

68. c. Dopamine is the preferred drug for raising blood pressure in patients in cardiogenic shock. Note that it should never be administered if you suspect the reason for low blood pressure is hypovolemia. Once hypovolemia is corrected, dopamine can be administered.

69. b. Apply an occlusive dressing (a gloved hand can be used in the interim until the occlusive dressing is applied), then attempt to stop the bleeding with constant, direct pressure, but do not clamp neck vessels. Medical control may also direct tamponade with a gloved finger.

70. b. The common signs and symptoms of cerebral hemorrhage are transient loss of consciousness, headache, drowsiness, nausea, and vomiting.

71. d. The relatively sudden onset of this condition and lack of dehydration history points to a primary dysrhythmia as the underlying cause of her presentation.

72. a. Hypoglycemia may occur in nondiabetic patients, especially in chronic alcoholics who have poor diet and the inability to properly metabolize carbohydrates. Except in cases of alcoholism and prolonged lack of food intake, nondiabetics seldom have problems with hypoglycemia. Signs and symptoms of hypoglycemia have a rapid onset. In early stages of hypoglycemia, the patient may complain of extreme hunger and thirst.

73. a. The most significant predisposing factors are old age, Type II diabetes, coexisting cardiac or renal disease, and increased insulin requirements.

74. d. More than half of all elderly patients who suffer MI do not complain of chest pain; therefore, their AMI often goes unrecognized. In the presence of chronic diseases such as diabetes, neuropathy prevents them from sensing pain as unaffected individuals would.

75. a. Oxygenated blood flows from the lungs, via the pulmonary veins, into the left atrium. From there, it passes through the mitral (bicuspid) valve into the left ventricle. It passes through the aortic valve then enters into the aorta.

76. b. Since no information is presented about the exact nature of the patient's condition, one assumes that there is a trauma mechanism involved and manual precautions must be taken. A modified jaw thrust can open an airway without disturbing the in-line alignment of the cervical spine.

77. b. Parasympathetic stimulation through the vagus nerve acts to decrease the heart rate; this paradoxically increases stroke volume because the longer time interval between contractions allows the ventricles to fill more efficiently.

78. b. Wheezing localized into one lung only minimizes the likelihood of asthma or other pulmonary disease. If a foreign body is small enough to pass through the glottic opening and carina, it will eventually lodge somewhere in either the main bronchi or the bronchioles. If the obstruction is not complete, air moving past the restricted lung passage will produce a wheeze.

79. d. The PR interval represents the conduction of the electrical impulse through the atria and AV node, up to the instant of ventricular depolarization.

80. b. Abnormally long or oddly shaped QRS complexes indicates that the impulse was formed within the ventricles and that it then traveled to the AV node. This delay in travel time is shown as a widened QRS complex on the ECG tracing.

81. d. The paramedic should always treat the patient first and use the ECG tracing as part of the total information gathered, ruling out answer choice **a.** Some cardiac medications (such as procainamide and morphine) should be administered by slow IV push, ruling out answer choice **b.** Before administering any medications, you should in fact secure the ABCs, and perform CPR or defibrillate if necessary, ruling out answer choice **c.** Answer choice **d** is correct; note that the fourth medication that is recommended for administration down the ET tube in cardiac arrest patients is Narcan.

82. b. In dysrhythmias originating in the SA node, the QRS complex is usually of normal duration because it is still conducting regularly through the AV node. Depending upon the type of dysrhythmia, the P waves may or may not be upright and similar, and the P-R interval may or may not be of normal duration.

83. b. Cardioversion is the recommended treatment for atrial fibrillation when the ventricular rate is greater than 150 and the patient is symptomatic. The other treatments listed are for nonsymptomatic patients or for when you are unclear if the rhythm is SVT or V tach.

84. c. Ventricular fibrillation and nonperfusing (pulseless) ventricular tachycardia, both life-threatening dysrhythmias, are treated alike with rapid BLS and defibrillation as the key to treatment.

85. c. The initial standard defibrillating dosage of energy is 2 joules/kg body weight.

86. d. The standard dose for fluid resuscitation is 200 ml/kg body weight.

87. a. Patients with no respiratory compromise benefit from low-flow oxygen to increase comfort and limit the size of the infarct.

Nasal cannula oxygen administration is appropriate provided the pulse oximeter reading remains high (over 95%).

88. d. Any condition that would present a significant bleeding hazard excludes a patient from receiving thrombolytic therapy.

89. b. Because the left ventricle fails to function as an effective forward pump left ventricular failure results in pulmonary edema as blood backs up into the pulmonary circulation. Left-side failure is common following an acute myocardial infarction and can also lead to cardiogenic shock.

90. a. Patients with dissecting aortic aneurysm describe their pain as extremely severe from the outset, whereas the pain of AMI tends to build slowly.

91. d. Prehospital treatment is limited to elevation and immobilization of the extremity and transportation.

92. c. Delta waves are characteristic of pre-excitation syndromes, of which Wolff-Parkinson-White is the most common.

93. b. Because the patient does not seem to be tolerating the rapid heart rate well, vagal maneuvers should be attempted first, followed by pharmacological therapy if necessary. If the heart rate increases or the patient becomes unstable, synchronized cardioversion may be indicated.

94. a. These features are characteristic of all dysrhythmias that originate in the AV node. The P wave is inverted because of retrograde conduction and is firing virtually simultaneously with the QRS, resulting in a short duration of the P-R interval (if it is present at all).

95. c. This patient is alert enough to be considered stable. However, a heart rate of 260 is difficult for any patient to manage for any period of time. Adenosine is indicated for this condition. Volume replacement is not indicated;

there is no information in regard to dehydration or other fluid loss, and a heart rate of 260 may not be able to tolerate large amounts of fluid.

96. a. A transmural infarction is also referred to as a Q-wave infarction because it is associated with Q wave changes.

97. b. Straight laryngoscope blades are preferred in children. Uncuffed tubes are needed in order to be firmly seated at the narrowing of the trachea.

98. d. All the components of the stress reaction—release of ACTH, relaxation of the bronchial tree, slowdown of digestion, release of adrenaline—prepare the body to react to the stressor as efficiently as possible.

99. a. Anxiety is a general feeling of uneasiness or apprehension that results from continued stress.

100. a. The environment she is in and the previously unseen rash, wheezing, difficulty breathing, and negative past history are keys to this being a case of possible anaphylactic shock.

101. c. You should aggressively manage the airway. It may be necessary to carefully intubate this patient, and you may get only one attempt. Once the tube contacts the larynx, the vocal chords can spasm and completely shut off the airway.

102. a. Epinephrine is a potent antihistamine and can reverse many of the effects of histamine overload. This patient is in extremis and should first be treated with epinephrine. If respiratory distress continues once the epinephrine has entered the patient's system, you may try using diphenhydramine (another antihistamine) or albuterol to bring about bronchodilation. Morphine is not indicated in this situation.

103. a. This patient is an unstable patient secondary to supraventricular tachycardia. Synchronized cardioversion is indicated to terminate the dysrhythmia. The standard dose for synchronized cardioversion is 0.5 joules/kg body weight.

104. b. This patient is experiencing a heat stroke and possible dehydration. It is important for him to receive fluid, high concentration of oxygen, and active cooling measures to reduce his body temperature.

105. c. Pronation is rotating the forearm so that the anterior surface is facing down. Supination is the opposite movement. Rotation is the type of movement required to reposition the extremity. Extension occurred when the arm was moved out from the midline of the body.

106. d. Nitronox should not be used with patients with head injury because it can increase intracranial pressure. It should not be used with patients who have pneumothorax because the drug can move by diffusion to air spaces in the body.

107. c. In a stable patient, the PASG is unnecessary. The long board will not adequately immobilize this injury because the muscles of the leg will spasm and shorten the leg. A padded board may not provide adequate traction to prevent muscle spasms either, so the traction splint is the best choice.

108. a. A burn to the highly vascularized tissue of the airway can lead to laryngeal edema and a blocked airway.

109. c. Using the rule of nines, the front of each arm equals $4\frac{1}{2}$% BSA, and the anterior chest equals 9%; the total burn covers 18% of the BSA.

110. b. The skin over a second-degree burn will most frequently appear mottled red and contain blisters. A first-degree burn will appear bright red and a third-degree burn will be charred or white.

111. c. Severe partial thickness or full thickness burns to the face, hands, feet, and perineum often warrant burn center care, even if they are not extensive.

112. d. Cover the burns with dry sterile dressings and be ready to institute aggressive fluid therapy as ordered. Wet dressings offer comfort but lower the body temperature in a severely burned patient. Gel-type dressings are being used with some success across the country in various areas, but the standard of care is still dry sterile dressing.

113. c. While the other answers are possible, based upon the fever, vomiting, and headache complaints, this is most likely meningitis.

114. b. Seizures, unlike syncope, do not usually have warning signs such as a period of lightheadedness. Some seizures are preceded by a feeling or sensation of impending seizure called an aura.

115. d. Place the patient in the lateral-recumbent position to prevent aspiration and administer supplemental oxygen as needed; provide privacy and transport.

116. c. Patients who present with altered mental status should be provided high-flow oxygen, IV access, and blood glucose levels measured. D50 should be administered when hypoglycemia is suspected.

117. d. Injected antigens are likely to cause the most severe reactions; penicillin and insect stings are the two most common causes of severe anaphylaxis.

118. a. This patient presents with symptomatic bradycardia, which would most likely be relieved by increasing the heart rate.

Atropine would indirectly increase the heart rate by blocking the parasympathetic nervous system. Epinephrine may be dangerous for this patient due to its cardiotonic side effects and the patient's age.

119. a. This patient presents in a stable, supraventricular rhythm. Because the patient's blood pressure is not low, there is time to establish intravenous access and administer adenosine to control the rate.

120. a. The patient's blood pressure is too low for safe use of nitroglycerin, furosemide, or morphine sulfate.

121. a. This finding is helpful in ruling out acute abdomen as the cause. Acute abdomen generally always has pain associated with rigidity, whereas a spider bite may be painless initially due to the neurotoxicity of the venom. Spiders rarely bite more than once, ruling out option d as a realistic clue.

122. a. Tachycardia with wide QRS complex is an important early sign of toxicity. High doses of sodium bicarbonate IV drip will help control dysrhythmias.

123. c. Although any of these individuals could suffer from heat stroke, the elderly person represents the typical profile of a victim of classic heat stroke.

124. b. This patient is experiencing early to moderate hypothermia and is likely to manifest impaired judgment, slurred speech, normal blood pressure, and tachycardia. Severe shivering generally peaks around 95° F and continues to decrease in intensity until body temperature reaches the high 80s; it then stops altogether. Respiratory depression and bradycardia occur when the temperature drops into the mid 80s.

125. d. Alcohol is a CNS depressant. People who do not frequently drink often do so before killing themselves; furthermore, alcoholics are prone to commit suicide. Suicidal patients may or may not openly discuss suicide, but you should take seriously any discussion of it by your patient. Most suicidal patients are depressed, not mentally ill. Holidays and important personal times such as anniversaries, birthdays, or death-days are high times for suicide.

126. a. Unless you know otherwise, always assume a medication bottle was full. There is nothing in this situation to indicate child abuse. Although today the quantity of pills packaged has been reduced, in order to lessen the likelihood of overdose by accidental ingestion, this child's decreasing LOC (level of consciousness) suggests there is a serious overdose situation here.

127. c. Salicylates is the correct class of drugs for aspirin.

128. b. The appropriate treatment is IV, oxygen, ECG, ipecac, and activated charcoal. Be prepared to treat dysrhythmias and to provide a fluid challenge if ordered. Sodium bicarbonate may also be ordered by medical direction, but epinephrine is not indicted for this situation. Naloxone is not indicated in this overdose situation, but could always be given if you are unsure of the substances ingested.

129. a. It is rare to treat PVCs directly; the administration of oxygen and nitrates would be used to reperfuse the myocardial tissue, which in turn may eliminate the PVCs. However, in this case, she is exhibiting more than six per minute, and they are originating from more than one site. Lidocaine may be needed to control these potentially malignant ectopic beats.

130. b. Children between one and three, who tend to put things into their mouths, are in greatest danger of aspiration of foreign objects.

131. b. The pediatric dosage is 0.1mg/kg for a child less than five and 2.0 mg for a child over five years of age.

132. c. This patient presents in pulseless ventricular tachycardia, a lethal rhythm. Immediate defibrillation is indicated to terminate this event.

133. b. The threshold for bradycardia in a newborn infant is 80 beats per minute, and the range where you would consider the need for compressions along with other treatments is between 60 and 80 BPM. Any infant with a heart rate less the 60 BPM should immediately receive compressions, but if the rate remains between 60–80 and is not rapidly increasing despite positive pressure ventilation with 100% oxygen, you should perform chest compressions for 30 seconds, reassess, and repeat as needed.

134. d. Although children are often uncoordinated and subject to frequent falls, the presence of bruises in various stages of healing would lead you to suspect that this child had been injured on more than one occasion. Carefully note the environment the child is living in and report any suspicions of abuse or neglect to the proper authorities.

135. a. The tearing feeling and the dark-colored blood are classic signs and symptoms of abruptio placenta. Placenta previa often has bleeding that is contained within the uterus due to the placenta blocking the os (opening or mouth) of the uterus.

136. d. Both lives are at stake. Oxygen is passed from the mother to the baby via the placenta. A separation greatly decreases the blood supply to the infant and the uncontrolled bleeding is dangerous to the mother.

137. a. Administering one or two large bore IVs of normal saline or Ringer's lactate is appropriate when combined with rapid transport. You should titrate the BP to 100–110 so as not to overload the circulation, causing pulmonary edema and further compromising the oxygen supply to the infant.

138. a. The most common presentation of PID is diffuse, moderate to severe lower abdominal pain, which makes ambulation difficult.

139. c. In order to preserve physical evidence of the assault, avoid cleaning wounds and do not allow the victim to bathe or change her clothing. If clothing is removed during patient care, it should be placed in a brown paper bag and handed over to police officers. Maintain chain of custody carefully to preserve the evidence.

140. b. This patient presents in unstable supraventricular tachycardia. Her condition may deteriorate quickly; therefore, immediate synchronized cardioversion is indicated.

141. b. A multipara is a woman who has delivered more than one live baby.

142. d. Signs and symptoms of ectopic pregnancy include lower abdominal pain that is often referred to the shoulder, abdominal tenderness, and rapidly developing shock. Although a ruptured appendix may be suspected, the first problem to rule out (given the pregnancy history) is an ectopic pregnancy.

143. c. Placenta previa usually presents as painless bright red bleeding that occurs in the third trimester of pregnancy. The blood may be contained within the uterus.

144. c. Because meconium staining in the amniotic fluid can indicate fetal distress, it may mean that the best thing to do is to transport the mother immediately. Choices **a**, **b**, and **d** suggest that birth is imminent and transport is not advisable. If you must deliver the infant when meconium staining is present, you should be prepared to provide immediate suctioning of the trachea and to intubate the child prior to stimulation, drying, warming, or positioning.

145. a. Suction the infant's mouth and nose immediately after the head is delivered and you can access the mouth and nose. Remember to suction the mouth first, then the nose.

146. d. Immediate defibrillation has been proven to be effective in terminating ventricular fibrillation. Even stopping for CPR in a witnessed event such as this may be more harmful than beneficial.

147. b. Stimulate a neonate by slapping the soles of the feet and rubbing the back. The infant should not be allowed to lose any body heat, and you should avoid touching the head to keep from putting any pressure on the fontanel.

148. b. Increased ICP after blunt force trauma to the head is potentially lethal and will need close monitoring and management both prehospital and within the emergency department.

149. b. As a mild anesthetic, ethanol can reduce the patient's perception of pain. It will be important to carefully and completely examine the patient for any unnoticed injuries.

150. d. The umbilical cord contains two arteries and one vein; only the umbilical vein is used for vascular access.

151. c. This is toxemia, a hypertensive disorder of pregnancy.

152. c. This patient is most likely suffering from pre-eclampsia.

153. a. Magnesium sulfate is the appropriate medication for the suppression of seizures in a preeclampsia patient. Valium may help control seizures, but magnesium suppresses them.

154. c. Seizures indicate that the patient's condition has worsened. The condition is then called eclampsia.

155. b. Evaluating the sensory, motor, and perfusion functions of an injured extremity before and after splinting will allow the paramedic to detect any loss of these functions during the process. Additionally, the documentation of the assessment will help defend the paramedic's actions in case there are long-term injuries to the patient.

156. a. Although the online medical control physician is ultimately responsible for the care the patient receives, it would be appropriate to allow the two physicians to communicate while you continue care of the patient per your online direction. You should never leave the patient unless the on-scene physician can be identified to your satisfaction and has agreed to assume care of the patient and medical direction has authorized you to discontinue care.

157. a. Medical protocols provide healthcare workers with a standardized approach to common patient problems. Online direction is provided when problems are beyond the scope of offline direction and protocols.

158. b. Falls kill more elderly Americans annually than any other trauma. It is important to carefully evaluate and manage these patients.

159. c. While it might seem unusual for an EMS provider to be a public educator, the respect of the profession by the community makes the paramedic or EMT an ideal teacher about emergency healthcare and prevention activities.

160. b. Abandonment means that a healthcare worker either terminates treatment inappropriately or turns care over to less qualified personnel.

161. a. Most states require the reporting of abuse or neglect of children, spouses, or older adults; rape and sexual assault; gunshot and stab wounds; animal bites; and certain communicable diseases.

162. b. Protective custody is used legally in cases of patients who are drunk, high on drugs, or a danger to themselves and others, when it is obvious that their condition is impairing their judgment.

163. a. Contact medical control about the specific situation before providing care; this will allow you to provide the type of care that is palliative only. Some states have specific protocols to follow with DNR patients and may even provide various levels of care in a variety of circumstances.

164. d. Although all the items mentioned in options **a**, **b**, and **c** may be part of patient packaging, the two goals of patient packaging are stabilizing injuries and appropriately preparing the patient for transport.

165. b. This incident has a hazardous materials component along with the potential for lots of patients. All the other incidents may be severe, but should not overwhelm the normal resources for the area.

166. a. Finance is responsible for the financial accounting of the incident and may not be needed in a small scale incident. In addition to tracking personnel, finance approves rental and purchase of any additional equipment needed for the incident. Logistics is responsible for acquiring resources, planning evaluates, and command sets goals and objectives.

167. b. When using the START triage system, you assess three parameters: respiration, pulse, and mental status (RPM). A patient with no respirations is considered *dead* or *dying*; if the rate is under 10 or over 30, the patient is *immediate* or *critical*. If the rate is between 10 and 30, additional assessment is needed (so you would then assess pulse, and possibly also mental status, before deciding on a category).

168. c. Scope of practice is generally defined by state statute and defines what an EMS provider can perform.

169. a. In most situations, unpermitted physical contact is a form of battery.

170. c. Childbirth can be extremely messy and involve blood, amniotic fluid, urine, and feces, so maximum precautions should be taken to include gloves, gowns, mask, and eye protection. For routine IV starts and IM drug administration, gloves alone should be appropriate BSI. All of the precautions listed are recommended by USFA (United States Fire Administration) guidelines for bleeding control with spurting bleeding but are not necessary with minimal bleeding.

171. a. Hepatitis A is enteric (or food borne) and poses the least risk for healthcare providers. Hepatitis B virus (HBV) is the major occupational bloodborne pathogen risk for paramedics. Hepatitis C occurs most frequently in IV drug abusers and paramedics are at risk of contracting this disease from accidental needle sticks. Hepatitis D occurs only in individuals who currently have or had HBV infection, and who therefore also pose a high risk to EMS providers.

172. b. Alcohol can never take the place of thorough hand washing, but when hand washing is not possible, it can offer some protection. To be most effective, you should first remove debris as alcohol cannot penetrate large protein molecules. Saturate your hands and use friction to remove particulate matter. Let your hands air dry immediately, but do not wipe them dry, as this diminishes the effectiveness of the alcohol.

173. b. Changing gloves for each new patient contact prevents cross-contamination.

174. c. Treat Mrs. Rodriguez respectfully, and give her plenty of time to respond and plenty of encouragement, before you turn to her grandson for assistance or translation. If it appears that she is nervous about her grandson being present, you may then decide to ask him to leave the room, but unless his presence is upsetting to the patient, it is OK for him to remain.

175. a. The typical abused elder is generally poor and dependent on the abuser.

176. b. This is one way to acknowledge what a patient is feeling and to encourage him or her to express those feelings without passing judgment or getting too personal.

177. a. Limit your time of exposure, stay a good distance from the source, and place shielding between you and the source. Personal and crew safety is always your first concern.

178. c. Upwind in a building helps to provide further shielding from the radioactive source. Since you will be able to communicate via radio, being able to see the scene of the emergency is not important in this situation.

179. c. Decontamination should only be performed by specially trained hazardous materials personnel.

180. c. Gamma rays are the most serious type of ionizing radiation.

CHAPTER

7 ▶ EMT Paramedic Practical Exam

CHAPTER SUMMARY

This chapter is based on the manual of the practical skills examination produced by the National Registry of EMTs. If your state uses the NREMT practical exam, this chapter states just what your practical exam will be like. If your state has its own practical exam, you'll still learn a lot by reading this chapter, since you are likely to be tested on many of the same skills.

THE EMT-PARAMEDIC practical examination assesses 12 skills by placing the candidate in life-like scenarios, complete with simulated patients and medical equipment, and requiring him or her to play the role of the EMT-Paramedic called to the scene.

The practical exam process is a formal verification of the candidate's hands-on abilities and knowledge, rather than a teaching, coaching, or remedial training session. In normal circumstances, any equipment needed to complete the exercises will be provided by the testing agency. You should, however, be sure to confirm that this is so at your site sufficiently far in advance of your test to give you time to secure the necessary equipment, if needed.

In preparing, it will be helpful to look at the NREMT Skill Evaluation Instruments. These are the scoring sheets that the examiner will use in evaluating your performance on the practical exam; there is a separate sheet for each skill assessed. Check with your EMT-Paramedic teachers and with the National Registry to secure copies of these sheets.

All candidates are urged to review all practical examination criteria in the most recent issue of the supplemental brochure *Performance Standards for Advanced Level Practical Examination Candidates* (available from the National Registry) prior to the exam.

The examiner notes the time elapsed during the candidate's performance on each section's scoring sheet. For some skills, the time it takes to perform the action is critical—for example, failing to establish a patent and properly adjusted IO line on the pediatric mannequin within a six-minute limit in Skill 11 results in automatic failure. You must familiarize yourself with such time limits as well as the steps to take for each skill and practice until carrying the procedures out in the time allowed comes easily to you.

▶ Practical Exam Content Outline

The candidate must demonstrate an acceptable level of competence in each of the following 12 skills when taking the entire practical skills exam.

1. Patient Assessment—Trauma

The candidate will be asked to make a physical assessment and voice treatment of a moulaged Simulated Patient, assuming a scenario that the testing staff will describe. (A moulaged simulated patient is one prepared with mock injuries.) This skill entails:

  a. Scene Size-Up
  b. Initial Assessment/Resuscitation
  c. Focused History and Physical Exam/Rapid Trauma Assessment
  d. Detailed Physical Exam

The scoring sheet (i.e., the skill evaluation instrument) breaks each of these sub-skills down into its parts. You should prepare yourself to know exactly what will be expected of you on a trauma call by running through this sheet over and over. In addition, the scoring sheet includes a list of possible critical mistakes at the bottom, including such things as failing to initiate or call for transport of the trauma patient within the ten-minute time limit. Be sure you know the list of possible critical mistakes, as it amounts to a statement of what the minimum standard for care of a trauma patient is.

2. Ventilatory Management—Adult

Presented with a mannequin standing in for a patient who is not breathing but who has a palpable carotid pulse, the candidate must demonstrate his or her ability to use appropriate airway maneuvers and adjuncts, bag-valve-mask device, and supplemental oxygen. The EMT-Paramedic candidate must place an endotracheal tube, demonstrate at least two methods of placement confirmation, and demonstrate the ability to suction through the endotracheal tube.

The scoring sheet lists 26 steps in the management of this situation. As the candidate works through the regimen, the examiner will provide information about how the situation is progressing. For example, after the candidate takes body substance isolation precautions, manually opens the airway, and elevates the tongue to insert a simple adjunct, the examiner will provide the information that no gag reflex is present and that the patient is accepting the adjunct device. You should know the correct procedure and practice with classmates, one playing the role of the examiner and the other the role of the test taker.

As on other skills, the scoring sheet for *Ventilatory Management—Adult* includes a list of possible critical failures at the bottom, including such things as using teeth as a fulcrum. As before, you must know this list as it amounts to a statement of what the minimum standard for care is.

3. Ventilatory Management—Dual Lumen Airway Device

This skill is similar to the preceding one except that the scenario calls for medical control to order insertion of a dual lumen airway rather than intubation. There are a total of 20 steps the candidate is expected to carry out, interspersed with information about the progress of the call provided by the examiner.

As on other skills, the scoring sheet for *Ventilatory Management—Dual Lumen Airway Device* includes a list of possible critical failures at the bottom, including such things as failing to voice and eventually supply high oxygen concentrations. As before, you must know this list as it amounts to a statement of what the minimum standard for care is.

4. Cardiac Management Skills— Dynamic Cardiology

This part and the next part of the practical exam test the candidate's ability to deal with cardiac arrhythmias and interpret ECGs. In the *Dynamic Cardiology* section, you will be expected to handle a cardiac arrest, delivering actual electrical therapy. You will be expected to verbalize everything about how you interpret the scenario you are presented with and what treatments you give. This section will resemble a "megacode."

There are 20 steps that the examiner will check you on as you proceed. In addition, the scoring sheet includes a list of possible critical failures at the bottom, including such things as failing to demonstrate acceptable shock sequence. As before, you must know this list as it amounts to a statement of what the minimum standard for care is.

5. Cardiac Management Skills— Static Cardiology

You will be presented with four prepared ECG tracings, together with patient information for each one. You must say how you interpret each rhythm and what treatments are called for.

For this section, the scoring sheet consists of four boxes, each representing one ECG strip. For each strip, the examiner will write down the diagnosis and the treatment you call for; at the end, as on the other skills, he or she will note down the time elapsed.

6. Oral Station—Case A
7. Oral Station—Case B

In both oral stations, the call is an out-of-hospital call and the candidate must manage all aspects of the situation. The sections on the scoring sheet are:

a. Scene Management
b. Patient Assessment
c. Patient Management
d. Interpersonal Relations
e. Integration (verbal report, field impression, transport decision)

The scoring sheet for the oral stations lists two possible critical failures at the bottom:

a. Failure to address anything that is considered mandatory in the given scenario
b. Performing or calling for any dangerous or harmful actions

Oral Stations in More Detail

The idea is that the oral station will allow examiners to assess the candidate's ability to think critically and manage a specific patient situation.

As noted earlier, in both oral stations, the call is an out-of-hospital call and the candidate must manage all aspects of the situation. The candidate sits across a table from the examiner, with a low barrier between them so the examiner can write out of the candidate's field of vision. The candidate is given a paper with a short description of a scenario (background and dispatch information) and is then expected to role-play with the examiner, who provides additional information as the candidate requests it. The candidate is allowed to take notes.

The candidate is told to play the role of team leader and is also told that treatments and interventions are performed only if he or she calls for them. The candidate must be as specific as possible (and as is appropriate) in the questions he or she asks and in the procedures he or she calls for. The examiner will switch roles as necessary, at one point playing the role of the person who called for help and at another playing the role of the patient, for example. The candidate will also be required to complete a radio report of the case, just as a paramedic in the field would do. Each oral station is timed and ends after 15 minutes, starting from when the examiner hands over the background and dispatch information.

The burden on the candidate is to ask for the right information and to respond to it in the appropriate way by verbalizing what his or her next move is. Be sure to follow these steps:

- Say what you will do to start.
- Get the right information by asking for it specifically.
- Establish and maintain the right order in the steps you take.
- Say explicitly what you will do at each juncture.
- Maintain a compassionate manner.
- Be thorough.
- Use good critical thinking skills throughout.

Some candidates find the experience of role-playing without props unnatural—especially with the examiner repeatedly switching roles. Be sure you practice these skills regularly before taking your practical exam so that these artifacts of the test situation don't throw you off.

NREMT strongly emphasizes the importance of Interpersonal Relations; the ability to interact compassionately and to communicate clearly with the characters in the scenario are important ingredients of success on the oral stations. The examiner will provide all the necessary information, as long as the candi-date asks for it, and will not attempt to mislead candidates in any way.

8. IV and Medication Skills— Intravenous Therapy

The examiner will describe a scenario to the candidate, who will then establish a patent IV in a mannequin arm in a way that is appropriate in that scenario. The scoring sheet for IV Therapy lists 16 steps the candidate must take in establishing the IV, and six possible critical failures, including such things as failing to establish the patent and properly adjusted IV within six minutes and failure to properly dispose of the needle.

If the candidate passed his or her NREMT Intermediate/99 practical exam within the 12 months preceding the EMT-Paramedic practical exam, he or she will have already qualified on this skill and need not take it again. (See the section of this chapter on scoring.)

9. IV and Medication Skills— Intravenous Bolus Medications

Building on the *IV Therapy* skill, the *IV Bolus Medications* skill requires the candidate to administer IV bolus medications in accordance with the given scenario once the patent IV line is established. The scoring sheet lists 13 steps the candidate must take in administering the medications, and six possible critical failures, including such things as failing to adequately dispel air, resulting in possible air embolism.

If the candidate passed his or her NREMT Intermediate/99 practical exam within the 12 months preceding the EMT-Paramedic practical exam, he or she will have already qualified on this skill and need not take it again. (See the section of this chapter on scoring.)

10. Pediatric Ventilatory Management

This skill assesses the candidate's management of a situation involving a patient under two years of age who is not breathing. The infant (presented as a mannequin) is said to have a palpable brachial pulse. The candidate must demonstrate how best to manage the situation immediately using simple airway maneuvers and adjuncts, a bag-valve-mask device, and supplemental oxygen. As on the *Ventilatory Management—Adult* skill, the EMT-Paramedic candidate must place an endotracheal tube. Also as on that skill, the examiner will provide information about how the patient is responding as the candidate carries out the appropriate steps.

The scoring sheet lists 17 steps the candidate is expected to take (15 if the candidate elects to ventilate initially with BVM attached to reservoir and oxygen), and 12 possible critical failures, including such things as failing to take or verbalize body substance isolation precautions.

11. Pediatric Intraosseous Infusion

Working with a pediatric IO mannequin, the candidate will be asked to establish an intraosseous line. The scoring sheet lists 16 steps in doing this and nine possible critical failures, including such things as failing to ensure correct needle placement before attaching the administration set.

If the candidate passed his or her NREMT Intermediate/99 practical exam within the 12 months preceding the EMT-Paramedic practical exam, he or she will have already qualified on this skill and need not take it again. (See the section of this chapter on scoring.)

12. Random Basic Skills—One of the Following:

Spinal Immobilization (Seated Patient);
Spinal Immobilization (Supine Patient);
Bleeding Control/Shock Management

In this case, the candidate is faced with a real person playing the role of the patient. It will be clear from looking at the actor which situation you are faced with and thus which EMT-Basic level skill is being tested.

The scoring sheet for *Spinal Immobilization (Seated Patient)* lists 12 steps and ten possible critical failures, including such things as failing to immobilize the head sufficiently. The scoring sheet for *Spinal Immobilization (Supine Patient)* lists 14 steps and nine possible critical failures, including such things as moving the patient excessively. The scoring sheet for *Bleeding Control/Shock Management* lists ten steps and five possible critical failures, including such things as not applying a high concentration of oxygen.

If the candidate passed his or her NREMT Intermediate/99 practical exam within the 12 months preceding the EMT-Paramedic practical exam, he or she will have already qualified on this skill and need not take it again. (See the section of this chapter on scoring,)

How Is the Practical Exam Scored and What Do You Need to Do to Pass It?

The practical exam is scored on a Pass/Fail basis, with each skill scored separately. You might pass all of the 12 skills assessed the first time, in which case you are finished with the practical exam and that much closer to becoming certified. Of course, you also might pass some skills and fail others. If you pass at least seven out of 12 the first time when taking the entire test, you are entitled to retest up to two times on just those skills you failed. If you fail again on both retests (for even one skill), you will be required to take remedial training over all 12 of the skills and then to retest on all the skills on another date. In order to sign up to take the entire practical exam again, you will have to provide documentation of remedial training, signed by the EMT-Paramedic Training Program Director or Physician Medical Director of training/operations for your program.

A note on retesting: Some facilities offer same-day retesting opportunities for candidates who fail five or fewer skills. Not all offer same-day retesting, however, and offering it is not something the NREMT requires of its testing agencies. Furthermore, the candidate is not in a position to pick and choose which skills he or she would like to retest on that or any other day: The candidate is required to schedule retesting on all the failed skills for the same day.

What does this mean for you? Suppose you passed everything but Trauma and Dynamic Cardiology the day you take the entire test for the first time. Further, suppose that you really know what to do on a trauma call, and that the only reason you failed the practical for that skill was a foolish mistake that you know you wouldn't repeat. You might be tempted to retest on Trauma the very same day. However, suppose you also know that your grasp of how to handle a Dynamic Cardiology call is not all it could be and that you failed the practical for that skill because you really weren't ready to take it. In that case, don't request an immediate retest—even though you could pass the Trauma section right away, you would also have to retest on Dynamic Cardiology right away, and you know that isn't in your best interests. Instead, put off your first retest until you have had time to study up on and practice Dynamic Cardiology calls.

Candidates for EMT-Paramedic certification who have already passed the NREMT-Intermediate/99 practical exam within the preceding 12 months do not have to take the whole EMT-Paramedic practical exam: They can apply the results of the NREMT-Intermediate/99 exam to their first full attempt of the NREMT-Paramedic exam for these four skills:

- IV and Medication Skills—Intravenous Therapy
- IV and Medication Skills—Intravenous Bolus Medications
- Pediatric Intraosseous Infusion
- Random Basic Skills

That means such candidates will be required to take the EMT-Paramedic practical exam on only these eight skills rather than the 12 listed earlier:

- Patient Assessment—Trauma
- Ventilatory Management—Adult
- Ventilatory Management—Dual Lumen Airway Device
- Cardiac Management Skills—Dynamic Cardiology
- Cardiac Management Skills—Static Cardiology
- Oral Station—Case A
- Oral Station—Case B
- Pediatric Ventilatory Management

For candidates who take this route (applying the four passed Intermediate skills to your EMT-Paramedic practical test), the rules for Pass/Fail are similar to those just outlined. However, if such a candidate fails the EMT-Paramedic practical for any skill, and fails both retests, he or she must undergo remedial training in all 12 skills. The candidate must then take the EMT-Paramedic practical exam again, but this time on all 12 skills.

No matter what the approach (testing on all 12 skills or only on the eight required of recent Intermediate EMTs), failing six or more skills means the candidate fails the entire practical exam. In that case, he or she must document remedial training on all twelve skills before retesting. The maximum number of times a candidate may take the full practical exam is three (a full practical exam being a test on all 12 skills with two opportunities for retesting on failed skills). Anyone who fails the full exam three times must again complete a state-approved EMT-Paramedic training program in order to test again.

▶ A Final Note

The NREMT-Paramedic practical exam has just one purpose—to ensure that practicing paramedics are ready to provide quality emergency medical care in a compassionate and efficient manner to patients in the field. The examiners will do everything possible to make sure that the standards of adequacy are sufficiently high. They will also make every effort to ensure that the test is clear and fair. The equipment you need will be provided and extra equipment irrelevant to the situation will not appear. No one is going to throw you a curve ball. It is your responsibility to prepare ahead of time by (i) becoming very well acquainted with the steps that you are expected to carry out on each skill, (ii) practicing both the oral stations and practical skills with other students, and (iii) knowing by heart what would count as a critical failure on any skill. If you do your part, the examiners will know it and you will pass with flying colors. Good luck!

State Certification Requirements

CHAPTER SUMMARY

This chapter outlines EMT-Paramedic certification requirements for all 50 states, the District of Columbia, Puerto Rico, and the U.S. Virgin Islands. It also lists state EMT agencies you can contact for more information about certification requirements.

THE TABLE ON pages 199–201 shows some of the minimum requirements you must meet to be certified as a paramedic in all 50 states, the District of Columbia, Puerto Rico, and the U.S. Virgin Islands. The next few paragraphs explain the entries on the table. After the table is a state-by-state list of EMT agencies, which you can contact for more specific information.

You should know that some minimum requirements are pretty standard and so are not listed on the table. For instance, you must be physically, mentally, and emotionally able to perform all the tasks of an EMT. Usually, you are required to have a high school diploma or GED before you begin training. You must have a clean criminal record. And, of course, you must successfully complete an EMT-Paramedic training program that meets the standards set by the U.S. Department of Transportation.

The first column, Time to Become Certified, means the amount of time you have between completing your training program and meeting the certification requirements. If you allow too much time to pass between taking the course and taking the exam, you could end up taking the whole course over again! In some states, the exam comes immediately at the end of training. If this is the case, you will see "Immediate" in this column.

States use their own written and practical skills exams, exams from the National Registry of EMTs, or a combination of both. The entry under **Exam** will be "State," meaning the state has its own exam, "NREMT" for National Registry, or an entry indicating a combination of both exams. Even when the state has its own exam, you'll find it's pretty similar to the National Registry exam, and therefore to the exams in this book. After all, the federal government mandates the curricula of paramedic courses nationwide. So you could expect exams based on similar curricula to be similar.

See the next column to find out if a state with its own exam also accepts the National Registry exam. Under **Accepts National Registry**, the possible entries are "no," meaning that the state requires you to go through its certification process; "yes," meaning that you can be certified in this state if you are already certified by the National Registry; or "with state," meaning that if you are certified by the National Registry, you can be certified in this state by taking that state's written and skills exam. Obviously, if the entry under **Exam** in the previous column was "NREMT," that state accepts the National Registry exam.

The same idea follows under **Accepts Out-of-State Certification**—the state does accept certification by another state, doesn't accept it, or accepts it if you take their exam. Some states require that you be certified through the National Registry if you're transferring in from out of state. For these states, you will see "With NREMT" in this column. In most cases, a state that accepts out-of-state certification will insist that your training program and your exam have met or exceeded its standards, so sometimes, it will come down to whether the state you're coming from is deemed to have done so. Some states have additional certification requirements for transferring paramedics, such as background investigations, being a state resident, being employed with an EMS agency in that state, or taking a refresher course. If you are certified in another state, you will need to show proof of certification when applying in a different state.

Some states have what is known as "legal recognition," which means they will recognize and accept your training for a limited time period, often one year. This is similar to a temporary certification. During this period of legal recognition, you apply for official certification and fulfill the necessary requirements. Once this process is complete, your certification will be good for as long as that state allows. Check with the appropriate state's EMS office for more details.

Recertification indicates the number of years from your initial certification to the time when you will have to be recertified. Recertification usually requires a given number of hours of continuing education, demonstration of your continuing ability to perform the necessary skills, or both—but you'll find out all about that once you're certified in the first place.

State	Time to Become Certified	Exam	Accepts Nat'l Registry	Accepts Out-of-State	Recertification
Alabama	2 years	NREMT	Yes	With NREMT	2 years
Alaska	1 year	NREMT	Yes	With state exam	2 years
Arizona	1 year	NREMT	Yes	With NREMT and state course	2 years
Arkansas	1 year	NREMT	Yes	With NREMT	2 years
California	1 year	NREMT	Yes	With NREMT	2 years
Colorado	6 months	State	Yes	Legal recognition	3 years
Connecticut	Immediate	NREMT	Yes	Yes	1 year
Delaware	Immediate	State or NREMT	Yes	With state exam	1 year
District of Columbia	Immediate	NREMT and state	Yes	With NREMT and state exam	2 years
Florida	1 year	NREMT or state	Yes	With state exam	2 years
Georgia	2 years	State	Yes	With NREMT	2 years
Hawaii	Immediate	NREMT and state	Yes	With NREMT	2 years
Idaho	2 years	NREMT	Yes	With NREMT	2 years
Illinois	1 year	NREMT or state	Yes	Yes	4 years
Indiana	1 year	NREMT	Yes	With NREMT and state exam	2 years
Iowa	1 year	NREMT and state	Yes	With NREMT	2 years
Kansas	1 year	NREMT or state	Yes	With NREMT	1 year
Kentucky	2 years	State practical, NR written	Yes	With NREMT and state course	$2\frac{1}{2}$ years
Louisiana	2 years	NREMT	Yes	With NREMT	2 years
Maine	3 years	State	Yes	With NREMT	3 years
Maryland	Immediate	NREMT and state	With state	With NREMT and state	2 years

State	Time to Become Certified	Exam	Accepts Nat'l Registry	Accepts Out-of-State	Recertification
Massachusetts	2 years	NREMT and state	Yes	With NREMT and state course	2 years
Michigan	1 year	State	No	With NREMT and state exam	2 years
Minnesota	2 years	NREMT	Yes	Determined case by case	2 years
Mississippi	2 years	NREMT	Yes	With NREMT	2 years
Missouri	3 years	NREMT	Yes	With NREMT	5 years
Montana	2 years	NREMT	Yes	With NREMT	2 years
Nebraska	Immediate	NREMT	Yes	With NREMT	2 years
Nevada	6 months	START certification	Yes	With NREMT and state certification and protocol exams	2 years
New Hampshire	1 year	NREMT	Yes	With NREMT	2 years
New Jersey	Immediate	NREMT	Yes	With NREMT	2 years
New York	1 year	State	No	Yes	3 years
North Carolina	1 year	State	Yes	With state exam	4 years
North Dakota	2 years	NREMT	Yes	With NREMT	2 years
Ohio	2 years	NREMT	Yes	With NREMT	3 years
Oklahoma	1 year	NREMT	Yes	With NREMT	2 years
Oregon	1 year	NREMT	Yes	Yes	2 years
Pennsylvania	1 year	State	Yes	With NREMT	None
Rhode Island	2 years	NREMT	Yes	With NREMT	2 years
South Carolina	2 years	NREMT	Yes	With NREMT or state	3 years

State	Certified	Exam	Registry	Out-of-State	Recertification
South Dakota	2 years	NREMT	Yes	With NREMT	2 years
Tennessee	6 months	State, then NREMT	Yes	Yes	2 years
Texas	Immediate	State	No	Yes, for 1 year	4 years
Utah	Immediate	State	No	With state exam	4 years
Vermont	2 years	NREMT	Yes	With NREMT	2 years
Virginia	2 years	NREMT	Yes	With NREMT	4 years
Washington	1 year	NREMT and State	Yes	With state exam	3 years
West Virginia	2 years	NREMT	Yes	With NREMT	2 or 4 years
Wisconsin	2 years	State	Yes	Determined case by case	2 years
Wyoming	None*	NREMT	Yes	Determined case by case	2 years
Puerto Rico	1 year	State	No	No	2 years
U.S. Virgin Islands	1 year	NREMT	Yes	With NREMT	2 years

* Wyoming does not have its own paramedic training program; it requires paramedics to go out of state to complete paramedic training.

▶ State EMT Agencies

The following is a list of the agencies that control EMT certification in each state, with their addresses and phone numbers. You can contact those offices for more information on their certification requirements. Visit the LearningExpress EMS website for links and more information — www.learnatest.com.

Alabama

Emergency Medical Services Division
Alabama Department of Public Health
The RSA Tower, P.O. Box 303017
Montgomery, AL 36130
Telephone: 334-206-5383
Website: www.adph.org/ems/

Alaska

Community Health and Emergency Medical Services Section
Department of Health and Human Services/ Public Health
P.O. Box 110616
Juneau, AK 99811
Telephone: 907-465-2541
Website: www.chems.alaska.gov/

Arizona

Bureau of Emergency Medical Services
Arizona Department of Health Services
1651 E. Morten, Suite 120
Phoenix, AZ 85020
Telephone: 602-861-0708
        800-200-8523
Website: www.azdhs.gov/bems/

Arkansas

Division of Emergency Medical Services and Trauma Systems
Arkansas Department of Health
4815 W. Markham Street, Slot 38
Little Rock, AR 72205
Telephone: 501-661-2262
Website: www.healthyarkansas.com/ems/

California

Emergency Medical Services Authority
1930 9th Street, Suite 100
Sacramento, CA 95814
Telephone: 916-322-4336
Website: www.emsa.cahwnet.gov/

Colorado

Colorado Department of Public Health and Environment
Emergency Medical Services Division
4300 Cherry Creek Drive South
Denver, CO 80246
Telephone: 303-692-2980
Website: www.cdphe.state.co.us/em/ emhom.html

Connecticut

Office of Emergency Medical Services
Department of Public Health
410 Capital Avenue, MS#12EMS
P.O. Box 340308
Hartford, CT 06134
Telephone: 860-509-7574
Website: www.dph.state.ct.us/ems/

Delaware
Emergency Medical Services
Blue Hen Corporate Center
655 South Bay Road, Suite 4-H
Dover, DE 19901
Telephone: 302-739-4710
Website: www.dhss.delaware.gov/dhss/
dph/ems/ems.html

District of Columbia
Emergency Health and Medical Services
825 North Capitol St NE, Room 4177
Washington, DC 20002
Telephone: 202-442-9111
Website:fema.dc.gov

Florida
Bureau of Emergency Medical Services
Florida Department of Health
mailing address:
4052 Bald Cypress Way
Mail Bin C18
Tallahassee, FL 32399
Telephone: 850-245-4440
Website: www.doh.state.fl.us/workforce/ems1

Georgia
Emergency Medical Services
The Skyland Center
2600 Skyland Dr., Lower Level
Alanta, GA 30319
Telephone: 404-679-0547
Website: health.state.ga.us/programs/
ems/index.asp

Hawaii
Dept. of Commerce and Consumer Affairs
Professional and Vocational Licensing Division
1010 Richards St.
Honolulu, HI 96813
Telephone: 808-733-9210
Website: www.hawaii.gov/health/
family-child-health/ems/index.html

Idaho
Emergency Medical Services Bureau
Department of Health and Welfare
3092 Elder Street
Boise, ID 83705
Telephone: 208-334-5994
Website: www.healthandwelfare.idaho.gov/site/
3344/default.aspx

Illinois
Division of Emergency Medical Services
Illinois Department of Public Health
525 W. Jefferson Street
Springfield, IL 62761
Telephone: 217-785-2080
Website: www.ilems.com

Indiana
Indiana Emergency Medical Services
Commission
302 W. Washington, Room E239 IGCS
Indianapolis, IN 46204
Telephone: 317-232-3908
800-666-7784
Website: www.in.gov/sema/ems/

Iowa
Emergency Medical Services
Iowa Department of Public Health
Lucas State Office Building
Des Moines, IA 50319
Telephone: 515-281-3741
Website: www.idph.state.ia.us/ems/default.asp

Kansas
Board of Emergency Medical Services
109 SW 6th Avenue
Topeka, KS 66603
Telephone: 913-296-7296
Website: www.ksbems.org

Kentucky
Emergency Medical Services Branch
Department for Health Services
275 E. Main Street
Frankfort, KY 40621
Telephone: 502-564-8963
Website: www.kbems.ky.gov

Louisiana
Bureau of Emergency Medical Services
P.O. Box 94215
Baton Rouge, LA 70804
Telephone: 225-342-4881
Website: www.oph.dhh.louisiana.gov/
emergencymedical

Maine
Maine Emergency Medical Services
16 Edison Drive
Augusta, ME 04330
Telephone: 207-287-3953
Website: www.maine.gov/dps/ems

Maryland
Maryland Department of Emergency
Medical Services
636 W. Lombard Street
Baltimore, MD 21201
Telephone: 410-706-3666
and
Maryland Institute for Emergency Medical
Services Systems (MIEMSS)
653 W. Pratt St.
Baltimore, MD 21201
Telephone: 410-706-5074
Website: www.miemss.org

Massachusetts
Office of Emergency Medical Services
Department of Public Health
56 Roland St., Ste. 100
Boston, MA 02129
Telephone: 617-284-8300
Website: www.mass.gov/dph/oems

Michigan
Division of Emergency Medical Services
Michigan Department of Public Health
P.O. Box 30195
Lansing, MI 48909
Telephone: 517-335-0918
Website: www.michigan.gov/ems

Minnesota
Minnesota Emergency Medical Services
Regulatory Board
2829 University Avenue SE, Suite 310
Minneapolis, MN 55414
Telephone: 612-627-6000
Website: www.emsrb.state.mn.us/

Mississippi

Emergency Medical Services
State Department of Health
P.O. Box 1700
Jackson, MS 39215
Telephone: 601-987-3880
Website: www.ems.doh.ms.gov

Missouri

Bureau of Emergency Medical Services
Missouri Department of Health
P.O. Box 570
Jefferson City, MO 65102
Telephone: 573-751-6356
Website: www.dhss.mo.gov/ems

Montana

Emergency Medical Services
Department of Health and Environmental
Sciences
1400 Broadway
Cogswell Building
P.O. Box 202951
Helena, MT 59620
Telephone: 406-444-3895
Website: www.dhpss.mt.gov/phsd

Nebraska

Division of Emergency Medical Services
301 Centennial Mall South, 3rd Floor
P.O. Box 95007
Lincoln, NE 68509
Telephone: 402-471-2158
Website: www.hhs.state.ne.us/ems/
          emsindex.htm

Nevada

Emergency Medical Services Office
Nevada State Health Division
1550 E. College Parkway, #158
Carson City, NV 89706
Telephone: 775-687-3065
for Las Vegas: 702-383-1381
Website: health2k.state.nv.us/ems/

New Hampshire

Bureau of Emergency Medical Services
Health and Welfare Building
6 Hazen Drive
Concord, NH 03301
Telephone: 603-271-4569
Website: www.nh.gov/safety/ems

New Jersey

New Jersey Department of Health and Senior
Services
Office of Emergency Medical Services
CN-360
Trenton, NJ 08625
Telephone: 609-633-7777
Website: www.state.nj.us/health/ems/

New Mexico

Injury Prevention and Emergency Medical
Services Bureau
Department of Health
P.O. Box 26110
Santa Fe, NM 87502
Telephone: 505-476-7701
Website: www.nmems.org

New York
Bureau of Emergency Medical Services
New York State Health Department
433 River Street
Suite 303
Troy, NY 12180
Telephone: 518-402-0996
Website: www.health.state.ny.us/nysdoh/
ems/main.htm

North Carolina
Office of Emergency Medical Services
701 Barbour Drive
P.O. Box 29530
Raleigh, NC 27626
Telephone: 919-733-2285
Website: www.ncems.org

North Dakota
Division of Emergency Health Services
North Dakota Department of Health
600 E. Boulevard Avenue
Bismarck, ND 58505
Telephone: 701-328-2388
Website: www.health.state.nd.us/ems

Ohio
Ohio Department of Public Safety
Emergency Medical Services
1970 W. Broad St.
Columbus, OH 43218
Telephone: 513-466-9447
800-233-0785
Website: www.ems.ohio.gov

Oklahoma
State Department of Health
Emergency Medical Services
1000 NE 10th Street, Room 1104
Oklahoma City, OK 73117
Telephone: 405-271-4027
Website: www.health.state.ok.us/program/ems

Oregon
Emergency Medical Services and Systems
Oregon Health Division
800 NE Oregon, Suite 607
Portland, OR 97232
Telephone: 503-731-4011
Website: www.oregon.gov/dhs/ph/
ems/index.shtml

Pennsylvania
Division of Emergency Medical Services
Systems
Health and Welfare Building
Room 103
P.O. Box 90
Harrisburg, PA 17108
Telephone: 717-787-8741
Website: www.health.pa.vs/ems

Rhode Island
Emergency Medical Services Division
Department of Health
3 Capitol Hill
Providence, RI 02908
Telephone: 401-222-2401
Website: www.health.state.ri.us/

South Carolina
South Carolina Division of Emergency
Medical Services
2600 Bull Street
Columbia, SC 29201
Telephone: 803-737-7204
Website: www.scdhec.gov/hr/ems

South Dakota
Emergency Medical Services Program
Department of Health
600 East Capitol
Pierre, SD 57501
Telephone: 605-773-4031
Website: www.state.sd.us/dps/ems

Tennessee
Division of Emergency Medical Services
Department of Health
Cordell Hull Building
425 Fifth Ave. N.
Nashville, TN 37247
Telephone: 615-741-2584
Website: www2.state.tn.us/health/ems

Texas
Bureau of Emergency Management
Texas Department of Health
1100 49th Street
Austin, TX 78756
Telephone: 512-834-6700
Website: www.tdh.state.tx.us/hcqs/
        ems/default.htm

Utah
Bureau of Emergency Medical Services
Department of Health
P.O. Box 142004
Salt Lake City, UT 84114
Telephone: 801-538-6435
Website: www.health.utah.gov/ems

Vermont
Emergency Medical Services
Box 70
Burlington, VT 05402
Telephone: 802-863-7310
Website: www.healthyvermonters.info/hp/ems/
        emshome.shtml

Virginia
Office of Emergency Medical Services
Virginia Department of Health
1538 E. Parham Road
Richmond, VA 23228
Telephone: 804-371-3500
        800-523-6019 (Virginia only)
Website: www.vdh.state.va.us/oems/index.asp

Washington
Department of Health
Office of Emergency Medical and Trauma
Prevention
P.O. Box 47853
Olympia, WA 98504
Telephone: 206-705-6745
Website: www.doh.wa.gov/hsqa/
        emtp/default.htm

West Virginia
Office of Emergency Medical Services
West Virginia Dept. of Health
1411 Virginia Street, East
2nd Floor
Charleston, WV 25301
Telephone: 304-558-3956
Website: www.wvochs.org/oems/

Wisconsin
Emergency Medical Services
Division of Health
P.O. Box 309
Madison, WI 53701
Telephone: 608-266-0473
Website: dhfs.wisconsin.gov/ems

Wyoming
Emergency Medical Services Program
Hathaway Building, 4th Floor
Cheyenne, WY 82002
Telephone: 307-777-7955
Website: wdhfs.state.wy.us/ems

Puerto Rico
Bureau of Emergency Medical Services
State Emergency Medical System
P.O. Box 2121
San Juan, PR 00922
Telephone: 809-766-1733

U.S. Virgin Islands
Emergency Medical Services
48 Sugar Estate
Charlotte Amalie, VI 00802
Telephone: 809-776-8311, ext. 2008

NOTES

NOTES

NOTES

NOTES